Wolf: Raider!

Wolf: Raider!

Three Accounts of the Imperial German
Navy Armed Commerce Raider, SMS
Wolf, During the First World War
ILLUSTRATED

The Amazing Cruise of the German Raider "Wolf"

A. Donaldson

A Captive on a German Raider

F. G. Trayes

Ten Months in a German Raider

John Stanley Cameron

LEONAUR

Wolf: Raider!
Three Accounts of the Imperial German Navy Armed Commerce Raider, SMS Wolf,
During the First World War
ILLUSTRATED
The Amazing Cruise of the German Raider "Wolf"
by A. Donaldson
A Captive on a German Raider
by F. G. Trayes
Ten Months in a German Raider
by John Stanley Cameron

FIRST EDITION

First published under the titles
The Amazing Cruise of the German Raider "Wolf"
A Captive on a German Raider

and

Ten Months in a German Raider

Leonaur is an imprintof Oakpast Ltd
Copyright in this form © 2017 Oakpast Ltd

ISBN: 978-1-78282-588-3 (hardcover)
ISBN: 978-1-78282-589-0 (softcover)

http://www.leonaur.com

Contents

S.M.S. WOLF

The Amazing Cruise of the German Raider
"Wolf"

S.S. "Matunga" as she lay in Sydney Harbour. She was a vessel of about 1,800 tons gross, and belonged to the well-known firm, Philp Line trading to the Islands. Inset is a photo. of Captain A. Donaldson, who was in command when the "Matunga" was captured by the "Wolf."

Contents

Introduction

Nothing that occurred during the Great War so closely touched Australia as the operations of the German raider *Wolf.* Though there were, during the progress of the war, particularly in the earlier stages, many rumours and alarms of enemy invasion, while many estimable citizens were able to furnish the straight tip about visitations of enemy squadrons, of battles, of the sinking of transports and capture of merchantmen, of the detection of alien enemy subjects using wireless plants in many inaccessible places, and there were those who actually saw enemy aeroplanes, yet we have no authoritive information of enemy activities in our home seas other than those of the cruiser *Emden,* the *See Adler,* and the *Wolf.* Of the two former enemy vessels little need be said here, full accounts having appeared in many sources of public information, and indeed, so far as affecting Australia was concerned, their activities were short-lived.

The *Wolf,* however, did disturb the peace of our home seas. Besides taking a considerable toll of our shipping by direct capture, evidenced by the cases of the *Matunga, Wairuna, Winslow,* and other well-known boats, she laid several nests of "eggs" (mines) around the coast of Australia and New Zealand, some of which hatched and took a further toll of our local traders. Of these, the mishap of the steamer *Cumberland* is extremely interesting. This boat was one of the Federal Houlder Shire's latest liners of nearly 9000 tons, with a dead weight capacity of 15,000 tons, her length being 474ft., breadth 60ft., by depth 36ft., and she was powerfully equipped for cargo handling, carrying four steam turbines geared to two shafts.

Leaving Sydney on her third trip on Thursday, July 6, 1917, for London *via* ports, with Captain McGibbon in charge, she got no further than Gabo Island, 288 miles from Sydney, when a violent explosion occurred in her No. 1 hold, which blew a great hole in her side.

Wireless S.O.S. signals brought help, and at 6 a.m. next morning a ship hove in sight, and passing a line to the *Cumberland*, started towing her towards shore, where the captain decided to beach her. This was successfully managed, and a good deal of her cargo salvaged.

It was then decided to endeavour to patch the vessel sufficiently to enable her to be towed to Sydney for repairs, and this being done, the journey was started. Shortly afterwards, however, very heavy weather was met, the ship started to take in more water than was safe, and it was decided to abandon her. This was not done any too soon, for just afterwards she went to the bottom. The I.W.W. organisation, (Industrial Workers of the World), in Australia were blamed for this mishap, it being currently believed that in stowing her cargo a time bomb had been secreted in her hold. It was, however, held later on at the inquest that the misadventure was due to a mine.

The Huddart Parker steamer *Wimmera* provides another instance. This time the mines were encountered in a vastly different position. The *Wimmera* left Auckland, N.Z., on June 26th, 1917, at 10 a.m., for Sydney. Proceeding up the north coast of New Zealand, she struck a mine in the vicinity of North Cape, and sunk in ten minutes. The ship's stern was shattered when the explosion occurred, and the lights failed immediately, making the work of escape exceedingly difficult. A number of the passengers and crew were lost, including the captain. Nothing was saved from this boat, all the mails she carried, including many bags for overseas ports, going to the bottom with the ship.

The big cargo carrier, *Port Kembla*, of the Dominion Line, met her fate in a different locality altogether. On the 28th June, 1917, when the *Port Kembla* was about 25 miles off Cape Farewell, the northernmost point of South Island, N.Z., she struck a mine and went down with a total loss of a most valuable cargo, estimated to be worth about £500,000. All the crew of the *Port Kembla* escaped, and they stated that during the night they heard the rattle of the machinery of the *Wolf*, which they supposed to be laying mines.

And brief mention may be made of the loss of the sailing ship *Handla Isle*, of which very meagre particulars are available.

And then, much later, we have the instance of the Sydney-owned collier, *Undola*, which never reached her home port, and of whom neither tale nor tiding has to this day been heard, it being commonly conceded that she met her fate from one of these drifting mines.

And even at this date it is by no means certain that all these mines have been located, there still exist possibilities of meeting trouble from

The ill-fated collier *Undola*, supposed to have struck one of the mines laid by the *Wolf*. She was never heard of after she left Sydney on her last voyage.

this source. Indeed, although a large number of these "eggs" have been "broken" by the trawlers sent out to search for floating mines by the Australian Naval Department, further evidence just as this book goes to press goes to show that we still have this menace with us.

The following report from Newcastle (N.S.W.), dated May 23rd, 1919, nearly two years after the cruise of the *Wolf*, is certainly convincing:—

Newcastle.—A picnic party on the beach on the northern side of Morna Point, about 20 miles from Newcastle, and fairly close to the entrance to Port Stephens, today came across an apparently unexploded floating mine, which had been washed up by the sea.

According to reports from the scene of the discovery, the mine was intact, the horns being undamaged.

Commander Fearnley, of the Newcastle Naval Station, states that, according to the information he has received, there is no doubt that the object is a mine. He will proceed to the scene tomorrow, with the intention of examining the mine and destroying it.

The amazing cruise of the *Wolf* has then an intense local interest to the people of Australia and New Zealand. Ships owned and trading with both countries were victims, officers and crews captured were men well known in every local port, with their families and relatives scattered throughout the cities and towns of the sister dominions, not to mention the cargoes, make the sum total, which accounts for this concentration of local interest. And this must be accentuated from the experiences of these men. They were, in common with people taken from boats flying other flags, cooped up in this ship for many months, a great part of the time below decks with hatches battened down, particularly at times when quick egress might have been vital to their very lives. For whenever an alarm of an enemy vessel was given, the prisoners were unceremoniously hustled below and battened down, and it might easily have happened almost at any time that an Allied cruiser dropped across the *Wolf*, which would have meant goodbye to the *Wolf* and very serious trouble for the prisoners.

These people were ultimately taken to Germany, there to experience the hardships and discomforts of the enemy's internment camps, and during all the time which elapsed, those left behind could gather no tidings of them, knowing not whether they were "safe" (*sic*) in

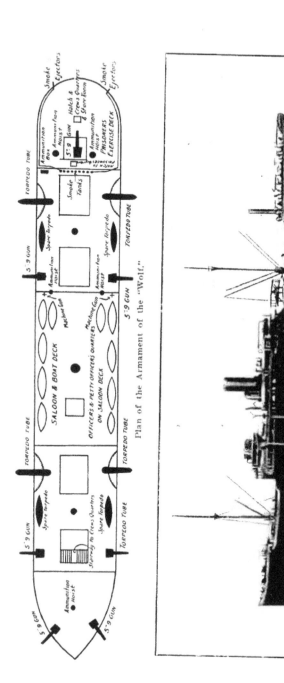

Plan of the Armament of the "Wolf."

THE *WOLF*, PREVIOUSLY A FREIGHTER, 7000 TONS GROSS BURDEN, BELONGING TO THE HANSA LINE OF BREMEN, AND WAS NAMED THE *WACHTFELS*. UPON TAKING THE MORE AGGRESSIVE AND HAZARDOUS OCCUPATION OF RAIDER THE GERMANS RENAMED HER THE *WOLF*.

Davy Jones' locker, or marooned on some lonely island in the Pacific. True it is that many rumours gained currency as to the fate of the victims of the *Wolf*. Wreckage of the *Matunga*, information of the crew being cast away on a far distant island, capture by enemy raider, all these were given on the best of authority, but no confirmation of any were forthcoming, and it was not until the *Wolf* arrived back in Germany, that the tidings came through of the safety of the crews of the vessels. It is noteworthy that the capture of the ships and the safety of those aboard was a long time public property before a cautious Defence Department bade the relatives hope "that the personnel of the *Matunga* might still be alive." Their ultimate safety is, of course, a source of extreme gratification to all, and the simple records which follow herein are from facts which Captain Donaldson was able to secure during his enforced stay aboard the raider and in the German internment camps.

And it will be readily admitted by the reader that the cruise of the *Wolf* was a most amazing voyage. To steam a distance that represents a voyage practically three times round the globe, through seas literally alive with British, French, Italian, Japanese, and American warships, for no less a period than 15 months, to capture ships flying the British, French, Spanish, Japanese, American, Norwegian, and other flags, and to arrive back with all the crews of these vessels aboard, many of whom were aboard during the greater part of the voyage, is to say the least, amazing, and can be attributed just as much to an extraordinary run of luck as anything else. The *Wolf* totally eclipsed the career of the famous *Moewe*.

Although the raider's captures were considerably less than either the *Emden* or the *Moewe*, still the damage done by her mines brought the percentage much above either. She had sailed the high seas for 15 months, with no friendly harbour wherein she could take refuge without being interned. She had captured and sunk about 48,000 tons, gross register, of Allied shipping, and 9,500 tons of neutral. (This, of course, is exclusive of the losses caused by her numerous minefields.) She had cruised unmolested through the Pacific, Atlantic and Indian Oceans, while our politicians at home were informing everyone that the German flag had ceased to fly on the high seas. She steamed a distance of over 47,000 miles, and lastly, she brought home 436 prisoners, in which were included twenty-two different nationalities.

Captain Nerger, his officers and crew deserve every praise for what they have done, and we, as Britishers, and therefore sportsmen, will

THE CREW OF THE GERMAN RAIDER WOLF. COMMANDER NERGER INSET.

not withhold the praise due them. But at the same time, I doubt if anyone would have the absolutely good luck to do the same thing again. "*Gott mit uns.*" He certainly was with the *Wolf* from start to finish. For the *Wolf* was no more than an ordinary freight steamer of about 7000 tons gross burden, with a length of 400ft. and breadth 75ft. She had in pre-war days rejoiced in the name of *Wachtfels*, and was owned by the Hansa line, of Bremen, having a speed of, at best, 13 knots per hour, and her complement of men of all ranks numbered about 350. These men were from the Imperial marine, amongst them being many skilled artisans, and had a most comprehensive tool shop and store room for spares.

Her armament consisted of seven 5.9-inch guns, two of which were mounted under the forecastle head, and by pulling a lever the plates on the ship's side were fitted to drop outwards, it then being possible to swing the guns from right ahead to the beam on either side. There was also a 5.9-inch gun mounted on both sides of the forward well-deck and the after well-deck, and the bulwarks were swung on hinges, and being controlled by levers, were dropped outwards whenever it was necessary to show a set of teeth. A gun was mounted on the poop-deck, and this was the only one that was exposed to view. It was cleverly camouflaged, however. Two dummy samson posts were erected at the forward end of the poop, and a short length of dummy derrick was fixed from the samson post to the body of the gun. The muzzle of the gun was facing aft, and on this was fitted a cap with eyebolts on it, a gin block hung from one eyebolt, and topping lifts from the dummy samson posts hooked on to the others. A small awning spread over the body of the gun completed the camouflage. It just looked like an innocent derrick.

She also carried four 22-inch torpedo tubes, two being fitted, one on either side of the fore well-deck and two in a similar position in the after well-deck, these torpedo tubes, like the guns, were hidden by the bulwarks, which dropped when required. Besides the torpedoes in the tubes there were always two others handy alongside for any emergency. These, however, were only used for practice, for never once during her cruise did the *Wolf* find it necessary to launch one of these engines of destruction at a ship. She was also fitted with numerous machine-guns, and some hundreds of sea mines, commonly called "eggs" by her crew. Besides having a well-filled ammunition magazine, she carried an ample sufficiency of small arms. Then she was provided with a seaplane, called the *Wolfchen*, or translated from the German,

CREW OF THE WACHTFELS

Little Wolf, and the use to which it was put amply demonstrates the value of these "birds" in war time. Until the Indian Ocean was reached the seaplane was stowed away below decks, and was assembled and took its maiden flight upon the day the steamer *Turritella* was captured.

According to the records the *Wolfchen* ascended to a height of 12,000ft. upon this occasion, and this enabled the pilots to scan the face of the ocean for no less than about 90 miles, observing any movements on the face of the ocean. Daily flights, usually early morning and late evening ascents, were undertaken and most of the captures, notably the *Turritella, Jumna,* and *Wordsworth,* must be credited to this auxiliary to the raider, besides which, possible risk of capture was obviated many times by reason of these "eyes."

Commander Nerger, who commanded the *Wolf,* was a man of about 45 years of age, and had, it is believed, taken part in the battle of Heligoland, being in charge of a light cruiser.

Follows then an authentic record of the *Amazing Cruise of the Wolf,* starting at Kiel (Germany), and finishing at Kiel, with the period in Germany's internment camps as the last course.

COMMANDER NERGER AND HIS OFFICERS. THIS PHOTO, WAS TAKEN ABOARD THE *WOLF* AS SHE LAY IN KIEL HARBOUR.

CHAPTER 1

From Commander Nerger's Records

Captain Nerger, the commander of the *Wolf* wrote a book on his return to Germany, and naturally used the most flamboyant adjectives in the Teuton dictionary to glorify his admittedly amazing exploit. For the purpose of describing some of the incidents of the cruise of the raider prior to the capture of the *Matunga*, the writer proposes to utilise certain portions of Nerger's narrative, and to comment on various incidents as the story proceeds. Nerger writes in the following strain:—

After endless trouble in the securing of the necessary supplies for such an enterprise as that of raider against the mighty enemy Germany was fighting, the worry to refit the ship, properly mount the armament, and stow a sufficiency of stores, ammunition, and mines, on the 10th of November, 1916, having said goodbye to relatives and friends, most of whom held very dismal hopes of ever seeing us again, we lifted anchor and set sail upon our mission.

My orders were "to operate in distant waters," particularly in the Indian Ocean, to disorganise enemy shipping and carry on maritime warfare, and to take all measures I thought advisable for this purpose, the laying of mines and minefields being mentioned as particularly desirable.

So upon the due date, we made a start, but the voyage upon which so much was hoped did not last long, for while still within the German sea patrol a fire started in one of the coal bunkers, menacing a second and assuming rather a dangerous aspect. To quench such a fire at sea was next to impossible, as a part of the ship had to be flooded and a great deal of coal would have had to be moved. So we were forced to return to port. This bad start occurred on a Friday. As a

COMMANDER KARL AUGUST NERGER

matter of course all hands said "*no luck could attend a voyage starting on a Friday,*" in accord with the still prevailing superstition. However, in harbour the fire was soon extinguished and the necessary repairs completed, and a few days later, on the 30th of November, 1916, we tried our luck a second time.

On this day a dense fog prevailed. When early in the morning we prepared to weigh anchor the mastheads were invisible in the grey veil, and at 30 paces hardly anything was visible, so we had to lay to and wait. The weather in the course of the forenoon clearing, the *Wolf* started on the second attempt to fulfil her mission, but again in vain. For the second time the *Wolf* had to return just after making a start, for the fog, which had disappeared for a short time, now reappeared with double density, making the passage through our own minefields far too hazardous to attempt.

All good things succeed at the third attempt. So we started the third time as soon as the weather cleared. For a considerable time, we had to run at reduced speed, until the evening, when the fog lifted we were able to begin our voyage in earnest. At short distances we passed our own patrols Formerly, on such occasions, greetings and good wishes were exchanged, but complete silence reigned supreme on this occasion. Of course, the patrol had been informed previously that a German ship would pass by, but who it was, where bound, and for what purpose had, of course, to be kept a profound secret. For a short time, we saw them, then gradually they disappeared in the haze—the last link which bound us to home, which probably we might not see again for a long time to come, if ever.

In fine clear weather we passed through the Cattegat, and hugged the Norwegian coast till north of Bergen, when we struck westward for Iceland, and of British warships nothing was visible, although our wireless kept us informed of their close proximity. We steamed with all speed possible. So far, all went well, although we had yet hardly entered the British lines. But the weather soon changed and we encountered a fierce storm from the north-east, so bad that we were compelled to reduce our speed to 7 miles an hour; this in the midst of the enemy lines, and the storm becoming worse and worse.

Since our voyage would probably last a long time, we had taken on board a very extensive load, and the ship's ordinary waterline was considerably submerged. We knew well that the *Wolf's* position in such heavy weather might easily become very critical. Yet this forced delay in our voyage was also very dangerous for us. It might easily happen

S.M.S. Wolf, STARBOARD VIEW

that we should have to pass between enemy sentinels at an unfavourable time. We were only too well aware that the British sea patrol was very thorough and that there were many enemy craft within easy reach. It all depended upon whether the ship had luck; for with our slow rate of progress we would be lost the moment we were sighted by the enemy, since however weak he might then be, he had ample time to bring sufficient powder on the scene before we could get away.

Even if we were running with all possible speed, the least enemy vessel could easily overhaul us, and if one of the enemy fishing boats, which also acted as watchdogs, had observed us and sent information by wireless, it would have been an easy matter for the enemy to terminate our enterprise there and then. In spite of this, I never had a moment's doubt about a favourable ending to our mission, so firmly was I convinced of my luck, which, as a matter of fact, never deserted us. None of John Bull's ships appeared, nor did we have any unpleasant experiences from the storms which raged. Indeed, we found always that the most unpleasant events ultimately turned out in our favour. After several hours the storm abated, the sea calmed, and with lighter hearts we again went ahead full steam.

But we were a little too soon with our rejoicings, as another heavy storm developed, this time from a westerly direction, which compelled us to lay to. This latter storm was worse than the previous one. The *Wolf* laboured very badly and every other minute a heavy sea swept the deck. Everything on board was moving riotously, tables and chairs careered wildly about, and meals were impossible. And there appeared no prospect of the weather mending. Incessantly the heavy seas broke over the ship, the air was filled with salt spray, and the ship shook in every fibre from the heavy pounding she was receiving. An extra heavy wave carried away a safety float provided with a calcium light, which we carried on deck, and we were not a little astonished when close to the ship a high, brilliant flame appeared, which travelled slowly with the wind.

Immediately after a second light appeared, this time on deck, and all this in a night when it was of the highest importance to our safety that we should remain invisible in our attempt to pass the enemy's lines. The calcium lights lit up the night like daylight. Of course we soon disposed of those on deck, but we were powerless to deal with the one floating on the sea. It calmly drifted further away so that for about an hour the position of the *Wolf* was distinctly visible. To complete the precariousness of our position, a heavy snow storm set in. The temperature sank rapidly. The *Wolf* was soon enveloped in snow and ice, and communication on deck was almost impossible in this ice and snow covered condition. All our guns and armour on deck was thickly covered with ice, and it would have required much time and exertion to make our weapons workable should fight have become necessary.

After a time, however, the storm abated, and we thought our troubles were over for this time. But soon we had to learn differently. Hardly had it become calm when a storm of terrible violence struck the ship from the north. We had again to lay to for 20 hours. The *Wolf* behaved very well, despite all the storms, and we encountered a good many more. And being heavily over-loaded this behaviour was all the more satisfactory, and indeed aroused considerable astonishment and envy amongst enemy and neutral captains later on, when they came to experience heavy weather with us.

Of course we did not get off altogether free of damage. Amongst other things a deal of crockery had been broken. At first I was rather perplexed on this score, as we expected later to get a good many prisoners. But I could have saved myself any worry, as captured enemy ships generously supplied us with more than we needed, besides all we required for any repairs to the *Wolf*. Sometimes in our passage through the North Sea we travelled with all lights burning to give the *Wolf* the appearance of a harmless passenger steamer quietly following her course. At others we crept along with not a light visible and our lookouts keeping a sharp lookout on all points. Without meeting any trouble, we were at last clear of the enemy lines of blockade, and could now continue our voyage. On the 10th of December we reached the free Atlantic. Immediately after passing the enemy lines, we dispensed with the use of one boiler, as economy in the use of coal, water, provisions, and other material was the first necessity of the voyage.

During the next few days nothing of interest transpired. On different routes between America and Europe steamers were sighted, which we always gave a wide berth. My officers, all of whom were in the dark in regard to my plans, shook their heads regarding my procedure. They were wholly disappointed at my avoidance of the enemy merchantmen, expecting instead that we should have taken them, but despite this and the unfavourable weather, the spirit of the men was good. The bad weather continued for the greater part of the passage through the North Atlantic. Throughout the men had been keyed up to a pitch of excitement and every day had brought its alarms. But now there was much less excitement, the risks being much less, so while enjoying a well-earned rest, we made ourselves busy with the outward part of the ship. Our problem was to avoid a conflict for the present, for even if victorious in a fight, we would very soon have lost the power to proceed with our projected war on enemy commerce.

It was about this time that we met with the wreck of a sailing ship of remarkable appearance. It was half crushed in, burnt out, and without masts. Its name was *Esberne Snare*. We looked at it from all sides, but were unable to get on board on account of a very heavy swell. There was no reason for us to trouble to get it out of the way, as it could only disturb enemy shipping. Besides I did not feel inclined to waste ammunition upon the derelict, as the British Prime Minister had declared in Parliament the war would last for 20 years, and we needed all we carried.

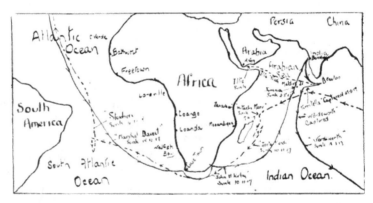

An endeavour has been made to give an indication in this small map of the activities of the *Wolf* in the South Atlantic and in the Indian Oceans.

Reference to the large map at the end will give the whole of the operations of the raider.

CHAPTER 2

Crossing the Line

On Christmas Eve we had a jollification, though the "Christmas Tree" and our presents were missing. We had none on board, on account of the nature of our expedition. Secrecy having to be kept inviolate, we had no presents or special supplies aboard for the festive season. However, every man aboard took things as they were, well knowing that now they could not be altered. From wood and cable strands, painted green, several imitations of small Christmas trees were produced; we had candles in plenty, also electric globes were made use of. Several of these trees looked very uncanny, but with a mind attuned to the occasion, everything added to the prevailing good feeling and harmony between the officers and men.

The crew were also provided with humorous newspapers and with ample good food everything went off quite well. In the officers' mess the jollification was somewhat disturbed by the Christmas tree catching fire, but no harm resulted. It only needed the necessary temperature and the snow to make our Christmas something like ordinary so far as seafaring men knew it. By this time, however, the thermometer registered about 30 degrees of heat, which was far different to snow conditions. None of us were much disturbed in our enjoyment by the milder weather, and after a short church service I briefly addressed the men, finishing with a reference to home and the dear ones left behind. And our enjoyment was not disturbed at this time by any untoward happening, though by wireless we learned that several enemy cruisers were busy in various neighbouring localities, but whether they were travelling or in harbour at Cape Verde, we were unable to ascertain.

Gradually we got nearer to the Equator. Several times I had been near it, but I had never crossed it, and to the amusement of all the men I had to submit to the ordeal of the "Neptune's Baptism." Unfortunately, there were no ladies present, who, on such occasions, play such an important role in the ceremonies, but we had a number of shirkers aboard who, by all sorts of excuses and presents tried to evade the ordeal. It was no good, however, since those who pretended to have crossed the Equator before had to verify their statement, either by showing the Baptism certificate or bringing forward the witnesses. If he failed to do so, then he was the more thoroughly baptised. The ceremony was as follows:—

One of the crew appeared as "Triton," clad in a most fantastic costume, consisting principally of bed-linen. Being announced to me, he declared he came on behalf of the god "Neptune," and stating that "H.M." would have the pleasure of visiting the ship with all his followers to perform the sacred rite of the "Baptism" on all those who had not previously crossed the "Line," and hoped to be received with corresponding honours. I replied that I considered this a great honour, and would do everything to make his stay as pleasant as possible. Then giving him some bottles of beer and some cigars, he took his departure.

The next day showed the real holiday spirit. The sea was calm; very softly the Atlantic seemed to breathe; the sun shone brightly from a cloudless deep blue sky, and soon appeared the god "Neptune" with his spouse, the noble "Thetis." The "Autocrat" of the "Oceans" looked remarkably like the ambassador of the previous evening. In his toilet, as well as that of his wife, bedclothes seemed to play the most important part. He appeared with a mighty flowing beard, which lent quite a patriarchal appearance. From the head of "Thetis," who conveyed a very masculine and muscular form, flowed locks of cable yarn right to the deck. The train of followers was both numerous and interesting. The black attendants had blackened themselves with soot from the funnel, over which they put a coat of fat, and were shining brilliantly in the sunlight.

A court fool was provided, he carried a high society hat on his head and wore a frock coat which originated from the establishment of one of the most modern tailors, and had hands and feet like a frog-, and added much to the general amusement. The court barber flourished an immense wooden razor, and the court preacher gave an address worthy of notice. Ordering the whole personnel to stand at attention, I led "H.M." and his followers along to the throne which had been erected on the main hatch, where "Neptune" seated himself and declared that he was ready to proceed with the ceremony. I thanked him for his visit, and reiterated my willingness to let the baptism both of myself and my men proceed.

The ceremony proceeded in the orthodox fashion. To the amusement of all on board, I was the first to submit to the ordeal. With two champagne bottles the men had, by artful knots and pleated strands of rope yarn, produced a wonderful though rather cumbersome double spy glass. This I was ordered to take, and look skywards to find the line. As a matter of course, the bottles had been filled with water and I got drenched from head to foot. Anything milder than this was impossible, and though the commanders also got the same treatment, all the other participants fared much worse.

Next came the baptism. Next to the main hatch a bathing sail had been rigged and filled with about 5 feet of water. Close by "H.M. Barber" had stowed his lather, which consisted of all possible and impossible smeary and disgusting material. On the other side of the bath sail was a wind sail rigged, ordinarily used to convey fresh air to the holds of the ship, but now used for the baptised to crawl through after they came out of the bath. So, after being immersed, the victims were required to crawl through this wind sail and as soon as they entered, members of "Neptune's" staff played the fire hoses upon them from both ends, thoroughly drenching the unfortunates over and over again. And if he expected that after this the ceremony was over for him and it was the turn of the next man he was grievously disappointed, for on emerging, he fell into the hands of one of "Neptune's" attendants, who now smeared his face all over with the indescribable lather, and he was then well and truly shaved by the "Barber" with the immense wooden razor. The victim was then again well doused with water and for him the actual ceremony was over.

This procedure was repeated over and over again until all had been through, and the fun was thoroughly enjoyed. Then came the conclusion of the ceremonies. "Neptune" distributed the honours. To me he presented the "Main Yard" Medal to carry round my neck, the pilots of the seaplane receiving "Flying Medals," and everybody also receiving a medal appropriate to his position. The final act was the appearance of the "Beggar Monks," who were well rewarded for their activities by an abundant harvest of presents in cigars and beer.

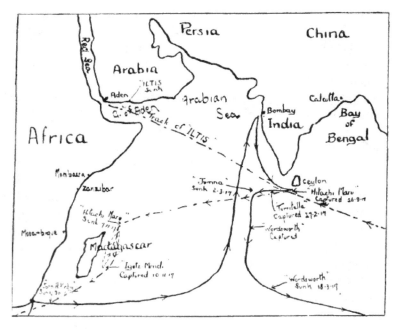

This map indicates roughly the position from which the *Turritella*, renamed the *Iltis* by the Germans, was despatched on a mine laying expedition to Aden. The larger map in the book is much more comprehensive.

CHAPTER 3

Laying Mines

On 16th of January, 1917, we reached the South African coast in perfect weather, which allowed us to see a distance of fully 30 miles. Late in the afternoon we saw smoke ascending dead ahead; shortly after we made out 7 ships, some giants with two funnels amongst them. Even had the *Wolf* been ready to spring, the appearance of an enemy armoured cruiser at their head, seemingly issuing orders for the night, rapidly disillusioned us as to our chances of working mischief. As far as we could make out it was a squadron of Australian troopships convoyed by one or more cruisers, and all thought of troubling them was quickly abandoned. We steered off very gradually, turning away like a peaceful merchantman. When they took no notice of us and were out of sight, we all breathed much more freely. A fight with one of his sort would have been disastrous to us.

That same evening, we started laying mines off the Cape of Good Hope. Very many times we had to go out of the way of steamers so as not to be discovered at our labours, for it would have been very unfortunate for us to have witnessed a ship strike one of our mines, and we contrived always to be out of sight when such occurred.

After we finished our task around South Africa we continued our voyage through the Indian Ocean, where we also continued to work on the steamer routes. Our work soon began to bear fruit. On 27th January we intercepted a wireless from Capetown as follows:

Submarines off Capetown.

We were at first rather surprised to hear of U boats having already travelled that distance, and when we learned that it was our mines that caused the impression, we were unable to understand how the usually astute seagoing Englishman should have come to that conclusion.

We certainly had all the credit of the difficulties in which the enemy's shipping found itself, and of these results we certainly had no cause for complaint. It was asserted at this time that the second largest British liner, the *Aquitania*, 46,000 tons, with Australian troops on board, had been lost in this locality.

★★★★★★

Author's Note.—Nerger's claim to having bagged the *Aquitania* is incorrect, as that fine vessel of the well-known Cunard Line is still going strong, (1918).

★★★★★★

Prisoners who came on board later on, distinctly declared that this ship had been lost at the time stated on the South African coast, thus confirming our news. The British were completely in the dark as to the cause. Then they began to suspect neutral ships of having laid mines, even going so far as to detain captains of neutral shipping for months, accusing them of laying the mines and subjecting them to prosecution for doing so. Of course, they were quite wrong. Yet through their mistake, we were not suspected, and no search followed, as far as we know. We now steamed towards Ceylon, making this neighbourhood about the middle of February. We laid mines in various localities where we judged enemy shipping would journey and of their effectiveness we very soon had reports, particularly from Bombay and Ceylon. Off Colombo we had some very unpleasant moments.

In our occupation of mine laying we were compelled to run close in shore, and while operating off Colombo, we came within the glare of the port searchlights. We were close to the entrance of the harbour laying mines. The night was dark and well suited for our purpose, when suddenly two searchlights appeared, searching the darkness. Moment by moment they came nearer, converging upon each end of the *Wolf*. Every moment we expected the lights to play on the ship, but they just stopped short of us, and then went further afield. It was a most thrilling period. Would they discover us to be an enemy mine-layer? The hearts of all the crew beat much faster, and all experienced a sense of great relief when the searchlights passed on. For all the excitement, however, we did not discontinue laying mines for a moment.

During the next day we intercepted a wireless message stating that the *Worstershire*, a 7000 ton steamer, had sunk from an internal enemy explosion. We knew well that this was no internal explosion, but that the *Worstershire* had run upon one of our recently laid mines. The ship went down twelve miles out from Colombo, and again the enemy was puzzled. Indians and neutrals were accused of secreting infernal machines on board or of having laid mines. A few days later another ship, the *Perseus*, of about equal tonnage to the *Worstershire*, ran upon a mine near the same spot, and from reports, which we received later, it was clearly shown that about Colombo a great amount of shipping: was lost. It was also stated later that the P. and O. Liner *Mongolia* (well known in the Australian trade) ran upon a mine months later, in June, and was not by any means the only ship that had been lost by striking a drifting mine.

In Bombay it was soon known that all these mishaps were due to mines. Intercepting a wireless, we found that the enemy had discovered the secret and had informed general shipping of the existence and exact locality of a minefield, adding "port is closed."

THE R.M.S. *MONGOLIA*, SO WELL-KNOWN IN AUSTRALIAN PORTS, WAS SUNK BY A MINE OFF BOMBAY. SHE WAS A LINER OF ABOUT 11,000 TONS.

CHAPTER 4

Capture of the "Turritella"

Our mission in this part having been fulfilled we now prepared for a cruise much further afield in the endeavour to still further disorganise the enemy's commercial shipping, by the sinking of enemy merchantmen.

On 27th February we found ourselves between Aden and Colombo, and early in the morning espied a steamer. We had learned from our wireless that no neutral shipping travelled on this route, so surmised that it must be an enemy ship. At 8 o'clock in the morning we put a shot across her bows and had her safe and sound. It turned out to be a one-time German vessel named the *Gutenfels*, captured by the enemy and renamed the *Turritella*.

Having recaptured her we decided that she should be added to the German fleet as a mine-layer, changing her name to the *Iltis*. To this end, a big gang of my crew were soon on board, minelaying doors were cut in the counters of the tanker, rails laid on her decks for mines, and wireless was fitted up. About 50 mines were placed aboard, and the Chinese crew were left to assist the prize crew, which consisted of Lieutenant-Captain Brandes and 27 men. Towards evening we took leave from our new consort, ordering her to lay mines in the Gulf of Aden, and appointed a place for a future meeting.

Captain T. G. Meadows, of the *Turritella*, was a New Zealander—a big, hefty fellow, full of a rough good-humour, and whose main argument was that the war would last for at least another ten years. As a matter of fact, he once bet Lieut. Von Oswald, the prison officer (nicknamed by the prisoners "Little Willie") £500 that the war would not be over until 1927. He had the distinction of being the only shipmaster to put in a full year on board the *Wolf*, although Captain W. S. Wiekman ran him close, being just one day short of the year when we

THE *TURRITELLA*, AS SHE LAY ALONGSIDE THE *WOLF*.

landed at Kiel. Along with his officers, nine in number, he soon made himself at home, and having a decidedly humorous vein was able to keep up the spirits of the other prisoners. One of his jokes is worth relating. He had just completed one year aboard the *Wolf*, and early in the morning he accosted the flying master or pilot, with a very earnest mien, and the following conversation resulted:—

"Good morning, flying master."

"Good morning, captain."

"Do you know I am just one year aboard today, a whole year at sea, a prisoner on board a German man o' war?"

"I am pleased to hear it," said the flying master, "you shall have something special to celebrate the occasion with."

"Well, flying master," said Meadows, "will you do me a favour?"

"Yes," agreed the officer, "if it is possible."

"Well," said the captain, "will you ask Captain Nerger if he will present me with the Iron Cross of the first class, if possible, or if not possible, then of the second class?"

It was a long time before the flying master could be induced to see the joke.

One day, at which time the *Wolf* was approaching Germany, he was discovered holding portion of a trousers leg tied at both ends. Questioned, he said it contained all his belongings gathered over the past 30 years, and he was ready should they have to swim for their lives, so that he would not land as a vagrant.

Two days later, in the early morning, we discovered the steamer *Jumna*, bound from Torre Veijo to Calcutta with a cargo of salt. Captain Wiekman, of the *Jumna*, had been running in the war zone since the commencement of the hostilities, and anticipated a quiet spell after leaving Suez. His gun had been taken off at Port Said, it being supposed that there was nothing in the Indian Ocean to molest Allied shipping, so about seven o'clock in the morning we found ourselves about two miles distant, the enemy running much slower than we.

★★★★★★

I (the author) will interrupt Nerger's story here to describe what subsequently occurred, as the prisoners saw it. When the *Wolf* got a little closer her sides were dropped and the gun swung out. A shot was fired across her bows, but failed to frighten her, however, and she came on heading straight for the *Wolf*.

The Germans, as usual, got very excited; they put a shell hurriedly into the breech of the port after-gun before it was swung out, and

S.S. *JUMNA*, ABOUT 5,000 TONS, AND CARRIED A CARGO OF SALT WHEN CAPTURED.

the breech was closed, but meeting an obstruction, caused the shell to explode. This did great damage, destroying the after bulwarks, and main rigging, damaging the tackling on the mainmast, and killing four men and wounding twenty-four seriously. An oil tank caught fire and blazed furiously, while some ammunition on deck exploded with great noise. From the other end of the vessel. However, a shot was thrown across the bows of the enemy, and stopping, they soon had a prize crew in charge. They took the prisoners on board, and after two days' work to get all the coal on board (for coal was their very life blood), they sunk the ship). Captain Wickman was a quiet, studious man, never to be seen without a book, hardly giving himself time for meals before returning to his beloved studies.

I am afraid that Nerger, who seldom, if ever, saw the prisoners, is mistaken in Captain Wickman, of the *Junna*. I naturally came to know him well, and I would certainly never dream of describing him as a bookworm. He was a very cheerful little chap from South Shields, with the Tynesider's bump of argument developed in a remarkable degree, as we soon learned. In this respect I might also add that his cousin. Captain J S. Shields, of the *Wordsworth*, ran him very closely. The last-named was also a South Shields man, and he kept us alive. He would spend his time provoking arguments, and then, when most of us were at the point of losing our tempers, he would calmly stroll off with a quiet smile on his face to start another row elsewhere.

A fine stamp of Scotchman was Mr. Stephens, second officer of the s.s. *Junna*. He was seventy-three years of age, and could get around as "spry" as most of us. He came through his captivity without a day's sickness, and was held in high respect by the Huns, although they never offered to release him.

A wireless was intercepted shortly after describing every detail of the *Wolf*, which was rather unpleasant news for them, and could only be traced to the *Iltis*, which they surmised had been captured either during or after the performance of her task. It was thought that the Chinese crew had given a good description of the *Wolf*, and the Indian Ocean would now become far too warm for her, since, although she could effect an excellent disguise with her telescopic masts and funnel, she would be sure to be stopped for examination on sight. This inference was correct, as was found later.

I have been able to gather something concerning the end of the *Iltis*, and will set it forth at this stage. It appears that after parting from the *Wolf* the *Iltis* steamed straight for Aden, and there laid her mines

THE SINKING OF THE *JUMNA*. FROM A PHOTO, TAKEN ABOARD THE *WOLF*.

without being seen. She was returning to the rendezvous previously arranged upon when she was sighted by a small British gunboat. The commander of the gunboat signalled the *Iltis*, and inquired her name, where from, and where bound. The *Iltis* gave a fictitious name, and replied that she was bound from Aden to Bombay. The British commander, not being satisfied, turned and followed her, and at the same time wirelessed Aden to find out if a ship of that name and class had left there. The reply came back that no vessel of that name or class had left the port. He thereupon promptly ordered the *Iltis* to stop, and fired a shot across her bows. The Huns stopped, fixed two bombs on the *Iltis*, got into the boats, and pulled away.

A few minutes later the bombs exploded, and the *Iltis* ex-*Turritella*, went to the bottom. The Germans and the Chinese crew were taken on board the gunboat, and there the Chinese gave a full description of the *Wolf* to the commander. This description was at once wirelessed to Colombo, and was, of course, intercepted by the *Wolf*. Nerger therefore soon knew that nis consort was no more, and that it was advisable for him to leave that locality immediately, before the British bull pups got on his trail.

S.s. *WORDSWORTH*, A STEAMER OF ABOUT 5,000 TONS, CAPT. J. S. SHIELDS IN COMMAND.
SHE WAS CARRYING A FULL CARGO OF RICE FOR ENGLAND WHEN CAPTURED BY THE *WOLF*.

CHAPTER 5

Nerger Bags the First Sailer

On the afternoon of March 11th another vessel was sighted, and the *Wolf* gave chase, coming up with her victim in about two hours. She proved to be the steamer *Wordsworth*, of London, out from Bassien to London, with over 5000 tons of rice aboard valued at over £300,000. She had very poor coal on board, and was steaming very badly, making about 6 knots, consequently the *Wolf* had no trouble in coming up to her. The *Wolf* wanted both coal and rice from the *Wordsworth*, and as the sea was too rough for the vessels to lie alongside each other, the *Wordsworth* had to be taken along with the *Wolf*. For seven days the *Wordsworth* was in company, and many were the attempts to get alongside, but the *Wordsworth* persistently refused to stop her graceful rolling exhibitions for a single minute. Finally, the Germans lost patience, and on the 18th March, thinking probably that the enemy cruisers would be looking out for him, Nerger ordered a boatload of rice and all the stores to be transferred, and the *Wordsworth* was sunk with bombs.

Captain J. W. Shields, of the *Wordsworth*, was surprised on boarding the *Wolf* to find his cousin. Captain Wickman, already installed as a prisoner. They had not met for many years previously.

Through the Indian Ocean the *Wolf* steamed in a south-easterly direction round Australia, and very soon ran across a sailing vessel in ballast. It turned out to be the *Dee*, Captain Rugg, from Mauritius to Westralia. They obtained some necessary provisions, and sunk the ship. Captain John B. Rugg and his mate were the only white men on board the *Dee*, the rest of the crew being Mauritius niggers.

Captain J. B. Rugg, of the barque *Dee*, was a Londoner, but many old-time Sydney shipping folk will remember him when he traded to Port Jackson in such well-known sailing craft as the *Neatsfield* and

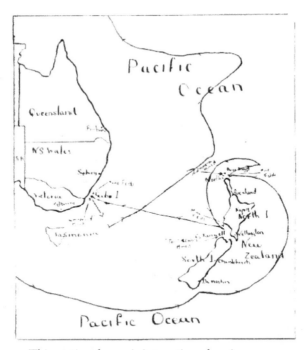

This sectional map is interesting, showing
particularly just how close the raider got to
Australia and New Zealand.

the *Gladstone*. He was a typical sailor of the old school, and had stuck
faithfully to his early love, the "wind-jammer,'" and he regarded us
poor mortals who had changed to "steam" as persons quite inferior
in every way.

Continuing the translation of Nerger:—

We now travelled around Australia and stayed several days in the
southern part of the Tasman Sea, south of New Zealand, to intercept
grain and coal ships, so that we might replenish our vanishing stock of
coals. Unfortunately, our hoping was in vain, as coal transport to South
America from Australia seemed to have completely ceased. Several
weeks we were waiting here without seeing a ship, and then steamed
further north. Here also no ships came our way, so we then made our
way around the Antipode Isles, north of the Bounty Isles, towards
Cook Straits. All communication seemed to have ceased; even the
occasional intercepted wireless messages brought nothing new, except
that on 7th of April, 1917, America had declared war on Germany.

Barque Dee, of Mauritius, in command of Capt. J. B. Rugg, captured by the *Wolf*, 30.3.17. She was bound for Bunbury, W.A., to load timber, when captured.

The *Dee* went down with all sails set.

On 14th of May an intercepted wireless, directed to a firm in Australia, informed us that the captain of the American schooner *Winslow*, was prepared, in pursuance of his contract, to take lading from Sydney. We stood north of New Zealand, and as we sighted nothing either from deck nor by using the seaplane, which we utilised on every occasion fox spying, I thought it wise to repair, and so steamed for Sunday Island (Kermaedoc Group) to overhaul the machinery.

EXIT THE *WORDSWORTH.*
BOMBS WERE, AS USUAL, PLACED ABOARD.

CHAPTER 6

Capture of the S.S. "Wairuna" (N.Z.)

I will again interrupt, and state what occurred here. In a snug anchorage, with no likelihood of being disturbed, they commenced to give a good overhaul to both engines and boilers. The *Wolf's* officers spent a great deal of their time on shore exploring the island. On several occasions some of the prisoners were given one of the boats, and allowed to go fishing. Of course, they had to give their parole not to escape, but the Germans took no chances, and always had a boat full of armed sailors cruising about handy. The fish were plentiful, and made a much-needed change in the menu of the prisoners.

On the 2nd June the Germans started to rig gear for shifting coal from No. 4 hatch into the bunkers, and during the afternoon the ship's band discoursed vile music on the poop, to the annoyance of some and amusement of others among the prisoners. Suddenly a change came over the band; first one man dropped his instrument and fled off the poop, to be followed in quick succession by the others, until only the poor chap at the big drum was left, and he was banging away for all he was worth. On looking to see what had caused this uncalled for and most un-naval like behaviour, the prisoners saw a large steamer just clearing the point quite close inshore. Immediately all was confusion on the *Wolf.* The prisoners, as usual, were hustled below and battened down. The *Wolf* only had steam on one boiler, but she had her trusty "buzzfly," the seaplane, ready to drop in the water.

Meanwhile, on board the other vessel, which was the *Wairuna*, Captain Saunders was wondering what the mischief this vessel was doing anchored at Sunday Island, and was studying her closely through his glasses when suddenly he heard a buzzing noise overhead, and lo! there was a seaplane flying the German ensign. A few minutes later the seaplane swept low across the bows of the *Wairuna*, and dropped

WAIRUNA, AS SHE LAY AFTER BEING CAPTURED BY THE *WOLF*.

something on her forecastle head. The crew naturally thought it was a bomb and ran aft, but nothing happened. One of them was persuaded to see what it was. It proved to be a small canvas bag, weighted, and contained the following message:—

> Steer towards German cruiser, and do not use your wireless; if you do not obey this order your bridge will be bombed and your ship shelled by German cruiser.

To emphasise this message a bomb was dropped just ahead of the *Wairuna*, which exploded on touching the water. The *Wairuna* was stopped and shortly after a motor launch, with Lieut. Rosa and a prize crew, took charge of her. In the meantime, the *Wolf* had got under weigh and was steaming out, but on seeing that her assistance was not required she returned to her anchorage. The *Wairuna* was brought in and anchored. The *Wairuna* belonged to the Union Steamship Company of New Zealand, and was bound from Auckland to San Francisco. Her general cargo was, I believe, valued at over a million pounds. Captain Saunders received no information from the naval authorities at Auckland of the presence of an enemy raider in the Pacific.

Captain Saunders, of the *Wairuna*, was a Londoner, and was the only one of us privileged to receive a note by aerial post from Commander Nerger. He is well known by those that travel by the Union S.S. Co.'s trans-Pacific services, and will return to the route shortly in charge of a new *Wairuna*.

Next morning the *Wairuna* was brought alongside the *Wolf*, and work commenced taking over coal and cargo. The *Wolf* scored 1100 tons of coal from the *Wairuna*, besides 350 tons of fresh water, milk, meat, cheese, and other provisions, also 40 sheep, which were very welcome. On the evening of the 6th June two of the prisoners decided to make an attempt to escape. They reckoned that if they could swim ashore they were alright, as the Germans would have a hard job to find them in the thick bush with which the island was covered. Just before sundown they managed to slip unobserved over the stern. They intended to hang on to the propeller until dark, and then swim for the beach. The nearest point of land was at least a mile away, and rather a nasty surf on the beach.

What happened to them no one knows, but the general opinion is that the poor fellows perished in their attempt to swim for liberty. They were a couple of fine young men; Mr. Clelland was chief officer and Mr. Steers was second engineer, both of the s.s. *Turritella*. The cu-

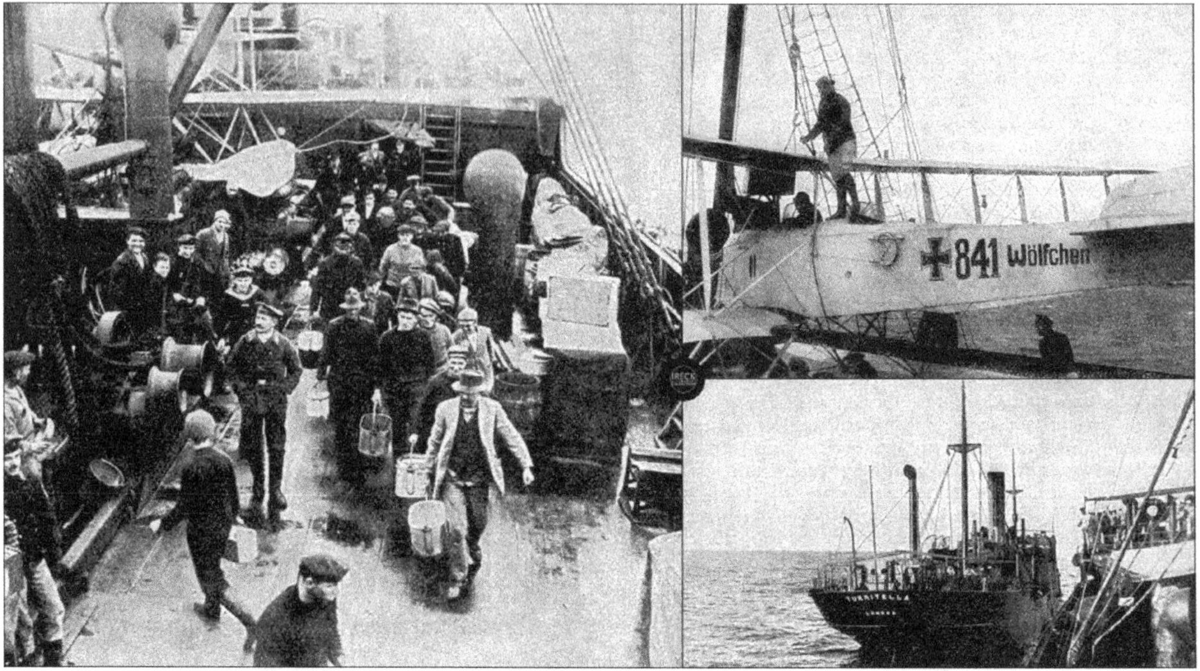

THE WOLF IN ACTION

rious part was that they were not missed by the Germans until three weeks later, as they neglected to have a roll-call of prisoners during that time.

When, on having a roll-call of the prisoners, it was discovered that two were missing, the prison officer Lieutenant Von Oswald (better known to the prisoners as "Little Willie," on account of his typical Prussian arrogance, and likeness to the German crown prince), fairly excelled himself. He told the prisoners that it was not a gentlemanly action to escape, and that up till then they had been treated as guests of the *Kaiser*, but in future they would be treated as prisoners of war. This was received with the greatest amusement by the prisoners, and "Little Willie," being a German, could not see the funny side of it.

When Commander Nerger heard that two prisoners were gone, he immediately ordered all prisoners to be kept below for 21 days, only to be allowed on deck for one hour per day for exercise. "Little Willie" was confined to his room for seven days for neglect of duty in not having a daily roll-call of the prisoners.

After taking over all the coal and filling up all available space with cargo, Nerger decided to sink the *Wairuna*. Accordingly, one morning both ships proceeded to sea for this purpose, but a sail was sighted to the eastward, so the *Wairuna* was sent back to the anchorage, and the *Wolf* gave chase. The vessel was quickly overtaken, and a prize crew put on board. She proved to be the American four-masted schooner *Winslow*, from Newcastle, N.S.W., to Apia in Samoa, of which we had already been advised by wireless. Her cargo consisted of benzine, fire-bricks and 300 tons of coal, the two latter items being very acceptable to the *Wolf*. Fire-bricks were badly wanted for her furnaces. The *Winslow* was therefore taken into the anchorage.

The following day the *Wairuna* was taken out to meet her fate. Two bombs were exploded under her bottom, but she refused to sink, so the *Wolf* opened fire on her with her 5.9-inch guns. The shooting was very poor, and it took 36 shots before the *Wairuna* took her final plunge, and Davy Jones cut another notch on his stick.

Now came the *Winslow's* turn. She was brought alongside, and all the coal and a quantity of fire-bricks were taken aboard the *Wolf*. She was then taken to sea to share the same fate as was meted out to her British sisters. First two bombs were tried, but the *Winslow* only smiled at them. Being a wooden ship, she was a tough problem to sink. Two more bombs were fixed, one aft and one forward. These almost blew the entire ends of the ship out, but still she floated serenely.

THE WOLF'S 15CM GUN

The guns were now brought to play on her, in order to shoot away her masts. Thirty-eight shots were fired without a single hit, but the thirty-ninth shot hit the bowsprit and brought down all four masts, but the hull still floated complacently on the surface. The *Wolf* gave her best, and steamed off in disgust.

Captain Trudgett, of the schooner *Winslow*, which, by the way, was the first American vessel captured by the *Wolf*, was born and bred in London, having in early manhood gone to the States. The ill-fated voyage on the *Winslow* was intended to be his last before settling on shore to that occupation beloved by sailors until they try it—chicken farming.

The *Wolf* was now ready to go on with her visiting list, and leave her cards on Newealand and Australia. Of course, she would make sure that no one was at home before doing so. From Sunday Island she steamed straight to the north end of New Zealand, and laid her "hell machines" somewhere between the Three Kings and the North Cape.

From there she dodged down the west coast and into Cook Straits. Here she laid two fields, about 25 mines in each field, and then set her course for the Australian coast. Somewhere in the vicinity of Gabo Island she laid a field of 19 mines, and commenced to lay a second field, when something gave her a holy fright, for she suddenly went off at full speed to the east-south-east, and never again approached the Australian Coast. On the following day she hauled up to the north-ward, and continued going north midway between Australia and New Zealand, then north-eastward towards Norfolk Island.

THE WOLF'S GUNS

CHAPTER 7

The "Beluga" Captured

Continuing from the translation of Nerger's records:—

On the 6th of July an intercepted wireless informed us that the *Cumberland* had run upon a mine about 10 miles from Cape Gabo, and was calling for assistance. The answer, which we took to be from a Japanese cruiser, was the query? "Whereabout is Cape Gabo?" Sydney also replied to the S.O.S., saying that assistance had been dispatched from Jervis Bay, then followed another wireless from the Jap saying "he had been informed that an internal explosion and not a mine was the cause of the trouble, and begged for further advice." For several hours nothing transpired, then someone wirelessed:

Cumberland continuing her voyage under own steam.

This was not exactly pleasant news to us, but soon after the Jap Wirelessed:

Arrived alongside *Cumberland* 11 o'clock this evening and sent several officers on board. Ship lies with a list of 21 degrees to starboard. The position is most critical. The ship is deserted. I will stand by until daylight to see if help is possible.

The captain reported that the misfortune occurred at 8.40 in the morning, as the ship was a few miles off Gabo Island. Two distinct explosions occurred and the ship had to be anchored After a vain attempt to stop the leak, the ship began to sink by the nose, seeking her resting place on the bottom of the ocean. Following the experience of the *Cumberland* we read in newspapers taken on a captured vessel later, of numerous "internal explosions" which had taken place in various localities to vessels trading around the Australian coast. These were credited to I.W.W. organisations. Of course, we knew better, having

BARQUE BELUGA, ABOUT 500 TONS GROSS. SHE WAS AN OLD WHALER, AND WAS COMMANDED BY CAPT. CAMERON, WHO WAS ACCOMPANIED BY HIS WIFE AND LITTLE DAUGHTER.

no doubt that the ships had ran into the mine fields sown by us.

The *Wolf* now steered, without seeing a single vessel, on a north-easterly course, out of the Tasman Sea towards the Fiji Isles. After several days they sighted a small barque named the *Beluga*. This vessel had formerly been an American whaler, and was laden with benzine and gasoline, which was very welcome, as the *Wolf* was very short of both. Lieut. Zelaske, with a prize crew, took charge of her, and before anything could be done with her another vessel hove in sight, and the *Wolf* cleared off after it.

This steamer, which it was believed was the *Fiona*, belonging to the Colonial Sugar Refining Company, got away, however, and the *Wolf* was cheated of her prey. After a couple of days' absence, she returned to the *Beluga*, and after transferring what cargo and stores were needed, together with the personnel of the *Beluga*, the *Wolf* opened fire upon the sailer, and she soon began to burn. Explosion after explosion followed from the oil which had been left on the ship, and this, scattered on the surface of the ocean, soon had a vast area of fire, a burning waste, huge tongues of flame darting in all directions. It was an awe-inspiring sight, but as darkness was setting in the *Wolf* judged it safer to leave the locality, since the glare might attract something in the way of a warship, although they seemed to be a scarce commodity just in that neighbourhood.

Captain Cameron, of the *Beluga*, had his wife and little daughter Anita with him, a charming little girl, who, in course of time, on account of her merry pranks, received the name of "*Board Plague*" (ship's plague) or "Sunbeam." Anita, who was about 6 years of age, was an everlasting source of pleasure to all on board. She was very soon on the best of terms with all on board, particularly with Paul, a petty officer. She had her nose into every corner of the ship, and so when the ship got into the tropics and the heat increased so that when the men were off duty they would lay about on deck sleeping, Anita would creep up armed with a piece of cotton and tickle them on the nose until they would sneeze violently. In this way she became known as "Board Plague." Her favourite amusement when the ship's band was playing, was to get her "darling Paul" to lift her up and put her head in the bell of the big bass instrument. Certainly the little girl plagued everyone on board and made life at the same time much more endurable.

Speaking of Captain Cameron, of the *Beluga*, as he had his wife and child with him when the vessel was captured, I may say that the party was at once taken to another part of the ship. They were kept

Anita Cameron, daughter of Captain Cameron of the *Beluga* and "Darling Paul." The Germans called the little girl "*Bordplage*", meaning "Ship's Plague."

apart from us, and I, therefore, never once had an opportunity to speak to him.

The latitude of Hunter Island was the scene of the next capture, the fine American Schooner *Encore* being the next lamb to fall into the clutches of this ever-ravenous *wolf* in sheep's clothing. The *Encore* was timber laden from Puget Sound for Sydney, and was in command of Captain Oleson. Bad weather delayed the transferring of stores from the *Encore*, but at the first opportunity this was done. Also, of course, the crew came over, and helped to increase the number of guests at the *Hotel Kaiserhof*, as the prisoners facetiously called the raider. After this the American was well drenched with oil and set alight, and soon burnt out. The *Wolf* now made her way out around Fiji, and hoped to pick up a suitable fast collier. Of course, it was necessary that the collier should be fully loaded. The *Wolf* could take her along and bunker whenever the opportunity offered.

On 27th of July we found ourselves (says Nerger) still in the neighbourhood of Fiji. The next day we intercepted a wireless to Rabaul, reading:

Burns, Philp, Rabaul, Donaldson, left Sydney on 27th, *via* Newcastle, Brisbane, 340 tons general cargo, 500 tons Westport coal Rabaul, 236 tons general cargo Mandang, signed Burns.

Who was Donaldson? We puzzled over the matter until we intercepted another wireless:

29th July, 8 p.m., steamer *Matunga* to Brisbane. Arrive Cape Moreton noon Monday.

Now we had the solution of our puzzle, as Donaldson could only be the captain of the *Matunga*. Calculating the probable speed of the steamer we concluded that about the 5th of August would bring him in sight.

Every day the seaplane was put in commission to inform us of the approach of any ship, but with no result. On the 5th of August, just as the seaplane reached deck a wireless came through:

Captain Donaldson to Burns, Philp, Rabaul. Arrive 2 a.m. Tuesday. Arrange Burrows coal direct.

Burrows! Who was that Burrows? We knew only one Burrows, an American destroyer being named that way, and we made sure it was this boat that was referred to.

Our position required some consideration. The *Matunga* was close by, and would be in our hands next morning. We turned round and steamed slowly towards her. Sure enough, late at night her lights came clearly in sight. We were exactly where we should be to intercept her, and on the approach of daylight she was in our hands. It turned out ultimately that Burrows was the captain of the former German yacht *Komet*, now stationed at Rabaul, and renamed by the English *Una*.

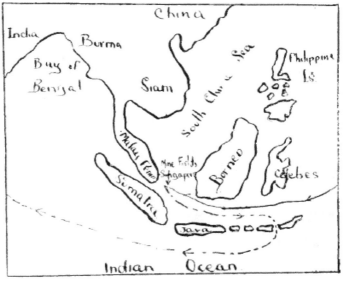

This sectional map indicates the approximate position of the capture and also the sinking of the *Matunga*, the continuance of the outward voyage to Singapore, where mines were laid, and the start of the return journey. The large map in the book is, of course, much more comprehensive.

CHAPTER 8

The "Matunga" now Comes on the Scene

On the afternoon of July 27th, 1917, when I said goodbye to my wife, little did I think that it would be many long weary months before I should see her again, much less anticipate the pleasure of a seven months' cruise on His Germanic Majesty's raider and mine-layer *Wolf*, and subsequent imprisonment in various *Gefangenenlagers* in Germany.

I was due to sail that evening for Rabaul, the capital of German New Guinea (now held by Australian forces), via Newcastle and Brisbane, and was due back in Sydney again in less than a month. My ship, the s.s. *Matunga*, of the well-known Burns, Philp line, was a most comfortable and seaworthy craft, and the naval authorities at Sydney had informed me that morning that all was clear in the Pacific. So there appeared little for me to worry about other than the comfort of my passengers.

In this respect, however, the Naval Intelligence Department was a long way out in their knowledge which will be evident presently. I called at the office of the company on my way to the wharf, in case there was any change in my itinerary, but nothing fresh having cropped up, I went down to the ship. As usual, on sailing day, several firemen were missing, they were up having a parting drink with their pals before closing time at 6 p.m. The second engineer was buzzing round the various hotels in Sussex Street, Sydney, mustering them up, and at 7 p.m., all being aboard, we cast off, negotiated Pyrmont Bridge safely, and steaming down the harbour, cleared the Heads at 8 p.m.

We entered Newcastle at daylight the following morning, and after completing bunkers, we proceeded up the coast to Brisbane. On the evening of 29th July I sent a wireless message to Brisbane informing

CAPT. MACINTOSH. CAPT. LAYCOCK, CAPT. DONALDSON. CAPT.
CAINES—CAPTURED WITH THE *MATUNGA*. THE MILITARY
OFFICERS WERE RETURNING TO RABAUL AFTER SPENDING
FURLOUGH IN AUSTRALIA.

my company's office that I would be off Cape Moreton at noon next day, never for a moment thinking that a German raider was picking up that message. We duly arrived at Pinkenba on the evening of the 30th, and after embarking mails and passengers sailed again at 10 p.m for Rabaul. The passengers were mostly military officers and men of the Rabaul Garrison returning. They were Colonel Strangman, Major and Mrs. Flood, Captains Cain, MacIntosh and Laycock, together with Warrant-Officer W. O. Kennedy, and fourteen soldiers.

Among the civilians aboard were Messrs. McNally, Noble, and Green, who were interested in large cocoanut plantations on Bougainville, and were on their way up for an inspection of their property. We had a fine trip during the next few days and nothing worthy of note occurred. The passengers amused themselves with shuffle-board tournaments and other deck games during the day, and at night Messrs. McNally, Noble, and Green kept us lively with music and singing.

On the evening of Sunday, August 5th, just before dinner I sent a wireless message to my company, Messrs. Burns, Philp, Ltd., Rabaul, as follows:—

Arrive 2 a.m. Tuesday, arrange Burrows coal direct, Donaldson.

Amongst my cargo was 500 tons of best Westport coal for H.M.A.S. *Una*, and in order to avoid delays I wanted to arrange for Commander Burrows to bring the *Una* alongside on my arrival so that I could proceed to work both coal and general cargo.

About 8 p.m. that evening the passengers commenced singing hymns, and I told them it was most unlucky to sing hymns aboard ship, because something was sure to happen. Of course I was only joking with them, but in the light of after events they began to think there might be something in what I had said. At 11 p.m. that same night we picked up a war warning wireless, sent from Woodlark Island, advising all clear in the Pacific—rather funny when the *Wolf* was lying within sixty miles, having already operated to some purpose in Australian waters. However, we knew nothing of that, and believed what Woodlark advised, turning into bunks without a thought of German raiders, floating mines, enemy seaplanes, or other menace of Hun ingenuity.

The morning of August 6th dawned, a date which all aboard the *Matunga* will remember for many a year to come. The weather did not look very promising, since there were numerous rain squalls about. Shortly after daylight my chief officer, Mr. McBride, observed the

THE SEAPLANE WOLFCHEN MEANING LITTLE WOLF. THE PICTURE SHOWS HOW SHE WAS
HOISTED OVERBOARD INTO THE SEA FROM THE DECK OF THE WOLF

smoke of a steamer away broad on the port beam, that was to the westward of us. He thought she was the s.s. *Morinda*, one of our own vessels, also running to Rabaul, *via* British New Guinea ports, and naturally did not trouble to report to me. At 6.45 my steward brought up my morning tea, after which I turned out for my bath. Mr. Mc-Bride then told me that the *Morinda* was in sight to the westward. I doubted this, because according to her roster the *Morinda* should have been sailing from Rabaul that day, on her return voyage.

I went up on the bridge, and had a look through my glasses at the stranger, and soon saw it was not the *Morinda*, as McBride thought. Although at this time her hull was not quite above the horizon, still the placing of the stranger's masts and funnel were sufficient for me. I had brought the *Morinda* out on her maiden voyage from Home, and knew every peculiarity about her. I put the stranger down as a Japanese merchantman, because we had on previous trips passed Japanese steamers on this route from Australia to Japan, and we were well aware of the frequency with which they were trading to our country during these war times.

I went down and had my bath, and on my way back met several of my passengers, who were discussing the vessel in sight, and who asked what I thought it was. I told them it was probably a Jap, but remarked jokingly that it might be an enemy raider. On getting to the bridge I could see that the other ship was steering about three points more to the northward than we, and was closing in on as gradually, just the course to take her well clear of the south end of New Ireland, so I went on with my morning toilet.

I had just finished shaving when the chief officer reported that the vessel was keeping away from us. This seemed queer to me, because if she had any speed at all she could easily have crossed our bows. However, about five minutes later she straightened up on her previous course, and I had another look at her through the glasses, and fancied she had the appearance of a Japanese auxiliary cruiser which had been in Rabaul about eighteen months before. So I ordered my chief of-ficer to hoist our ensign and get the other fellow to show his colours, but as she closed in on us again I began to have my doubts, her build altering ray opinion as to her being owned by the Japanese.

Closer observation soon convinced me that she was undoubtedly a German built vessel, but whether one of the interned Germans I could not say. However, we were not left long in doubt, because, hav-ing closed in upon us, the stranger now hoisted two signals. The chief

LIEUT. STEIN AND PILOT FUBEK. WHO MADE THE
MANY FLIGHTS IN THE *WOLFCHEN*, WHICH WERE OF
SUCH MATERIAL ASSISTANCE IN FILLING THE "BAG" OF
THE *WOLF*.

officer went to the chartroom to read the signals from the signal-book as I made them out with the glass. The first was, "Telegraphic communication stopped." I knew then we were up against a German raider. The second signal was, "Stop instantly." The chief officer immediately jumped to the telegraph and put it over to stop, but I put it full-ahead again, remarking' that we would make them waste a shot at least. I told the chief to call all hands and clear away the boats, but he had hardly left the bridge before the German naval ensign floated to the stranger's mainmast head and bang came a shot across our bows. As I had nothing to reply with and, moreover, had women aboard, I deemed it advisable to stop. I went to the wireless room and asked the operator if he could send an S.O.S. out, but there was no current on, and this was, therefore, impossible, so I gave him all my codes and wireless instructions to take down and have burnt in the furnaces.

Had we been able to get a wireless message out it would have been jammed, because, as we found out afterwards, the *Wolf*, for such was the stranger, had a very powerful wireless set, which would have been able to render our messages useless, and anyhow, there was no effective help nearer than Sydney. The *Una*, which was at Rabaul, was only a slim built yacht, with very light guns, and the *Wolf* would have blown her out of the water in a few minutes. Hearing a buzzing overhead I looked up and there was a seaplane, the *Wolfchen*. Although she had been in the air since 6 o'clock that morning, and had, according to information which we received later, located the *Matunga* hours before, this was the first time we had seen her. A pretty sight she made flying overhead as peaceful as a bird, but it would have been prettier to me had she been painted with our rings of red, white, and blue, instead of the black cross of the Germans.

The Matunga

CHAPTER 9

"Good Morning, Captain Donaldson"

I did not anticipate that the raider, being so far from his base, would take any prisoners aboard, and so expected him to sink the *Matunga* and let us make the best of our way to land in our boats. Therefore, I gave orders for the boats to be provisioned, and our motor launch to be put over the side with a good stock of benzine aboard, so that she could tow the boats. The nearest land, New Britain, was then only about 70 miles distant.

The *Wolf* now lay about a mile away from us, so there was no chance of us ramming her. The seaplane meanwhile circled over the *Matunga* until the raider's launch, with the prize crew, were on their way towards us. She then landed gracefully on the water close to the *Wolf*, and was taken aboard.

The prize crew, fully armed, now boarded us, and the officer in charge. Lieutenant Rosa, came on the bridge, saluted, and said "Good morning. Captain Donaldson." Ye gods! To be addressed by name was a bit of a shock to my nervous system, but I managed to return his salute. Before I could make any reply, he went on telling me I was late, that they had expected me the previous day. I was getting more and more bewildered, and when he asked where the 500 tons of Westport coal was stowed, and hoped the general cargo was mostly eatables, I exploded, and asked him "what the devil he knew about the Westport coal."

He told me they had picked up a wireless message sent from Sydney to Rabaul giving date of my departure, and full particulars of my cargo, and that they had been waiting for me for three days. He then ordered me and the officers to be ready to go aboard his vessel in twenty minutes. He did not say "to go aboard the *Wolf*," he refused to give the name of his ship.

I got some of my clothes together, and Lieutenant Rosa said I could get the rest of my gear in a couple of days when the *Matunga* would be alongside his ship. So about 9 a.m. a boat was ready to take us across, but before going I asked Lieutenant Rosa to take care of my passengers and see that they were well treated, which he readily promised. From what I heard later on, when the passengers were brought aboard the *Wolf*, he certainly carried out my request most handsomely. All the crew and passengers of the *Matunga*, with the exception of myself, my three officers, wireless operator, military officers and men, who were put aboard the *Wolf*, were left aboard our ship, Colonel Strangman and Major Flood, of the A.M.C., were also left on the *Matunga*. On approaching the *Wolf* we could see the poop deck was crowded with prisoners who had, we found later on, been taken off sundry prizes before our advent.

On boarding the *Wolf*, I was taken aside by one of the officers, and questioned on all sorts of things, what garrison there was at Rabaul? Was the port fortified? etc., etc. Naturally he did not get the truth. He seemed extremely anxious to find out who or what Burrows was, this man I had mentioned in my wireless the previous night. He suggested that Burrows was the name of the man to whom my coal was consigned, and of course I remarked it was quite possible it was. About an hour later the same officer came along to me and he seemed quite upset. He said I had told him a lie. I remarked that I had probably told him more than one. He said that the *Burrows* was an American destroyer, and asked if our coal was for her. Naturally I said "sure thing, it was," but he didn't seem at all satisfied even then. He then told me he knew New Guinea waters well, having been an officer on the German survey ship *Cormoran*, and had assisted in the survey of these waters. He asked after several German residents in Rabaul, and knew them all well.

Meantime Captains Caines, Laycock, and McIntosh had arrived on board the *Wolf*, and were being interrogated by some of the other officers. We were then taken aft and had to strip and undergo medical examination by the two doctors, then Lieutenant Wolffe and two other officers of the *Wolf* came along and tried to get some more information from us. Wolffe was a German merchant service officer, and spoke English splendidly, he very kindly relieved me of my binoculars, which I had brought over in my pocket. We were then taken down below and introduced to the prisoners' quarters.

The quarters were in the No. 4 'tween decks, and looked anything but comfortable, the decks both overhead and under foot were bare steel, and the ship's sides were bare, except for the usual wooden stringers. It had never been properly washed down since the coal and mines with which the *Wolf* had been loaded when she left Germany, had been removed. However, Lieutenant Von Oswald, who informed me that he was the prison officer, said it was all to be washed out and painted white. Dinner came along just then, and the previous victims of the *Wolf* came down below to join us at the meal.

We found that there were nearly 200 prisoners, some had been on board the *Wolf* for 5 months, so an early release for us did not seem at all probable. The dinner consisted of a plate of pea soup, and what looked like brown bread, which on closer inspection proved to be dough, the outside was burnt black, but the inside was quite raw, and moreover, it had dubious greenish streaks through it.

However, prisoners could not be choosers, and the pea soup was excellent and reminded me of my old sailing ship days. The afternoon was spent in an examination of our kit by the Germans, they took away all navigation books and instruments, also cameras and binoculars. Our clothes were put into an iron drum and steam blown through them, they evidently thought we Britishers needed disinfecting, at any rate they were not taking any risks.

CHAPTER 10

Introducing "Little Willie"

In the meantime, both ships had got under weigh, the *Matunga* being ahead, and were steering to the northeastward, giving the coast of New Ireland a wide berth. The afternoon was scorchingly hot, with not a breath of air stirring, the sea being like the proverbial mill pond. The poop deck, which was our only place for exercise and air, was covered for about a third of its none too great length, by an old tarpaulin, taken from the s.s. *Wainuna*; this served as an awning, but permission to spread it had to be sought from the bridge, and when we secured the commander's permission, we had to be ready to furl it at a moment's notice if anything was sighted.

Tea came along at 5 p.m., and this sumptuous meal consisted of some more of the dough with the emerald hue in it, and tea, of course no milk, and I forget now whether there was sugar that night, probably there was. On this fare I could see myself fast becoming fat and bloated, with nothing to do and no possible means of getting sufficient exercise. When all the prisoners were on deck, there was barely moving room on the small poop deck, hampered as it was, with the dummy hatchway, wheel box and other enemy deceiving gear, and it was certainly very uncomfortable. We found the Germans taking life very seriously, also, indeed, they seemed absolutely devoid of humour, as the following incident will show.

While we were taking the air on the poop deck the German officer in charge of the prisoners was always ready to enter into conversation with the prisoners. This man's name was Lieutenant Von Oswald, and early he was nicknamed "Little Willie," on account of his somewhat distant resemblance to the German crown prince. On our first night aboard "Little Willie" was conversing with the military officers and myself when I asked him to give my compliments to Commander

Nerger and request that he send a wireless message to Sydney informing them that we were all safe aboard the *Wolf*.

Poor "Little Willie" took me quite seriously, and entered into no end of explanations to show that such a message would give the *Wolf's* position away. He could not see that we were pulling his leg, poor youngster. He had never been away from the North Sea before, and had just got his commission, so imagined he was quite a man of experience. We were permitted to remain on deck that night until 10 o'clock, and never shall I forget my first night on board the *Wolf*. The heat was bad enough up on deck, but down in the 'tween decks it was Hades.

Hammocks were slung, two tiers of them, one over the other, and the atmosphere was as thick as a London fog with tobacco smoke, the perspiration simply running off the mostly naked bodies of the prisoners and making pools on the deck. This was a very great contrast from my own nice airy cabin on the bridge of the old *Matunga*, and I certainly knew which was preferable. It was war, however, and we had to make the best of it. We might yet get the best of the *Wolf*, for I knew that numerous messages would be dropped over from the *Matunga* during the night, and in all probability would be picked up by any vessel sent out from Rabaul when we failed to arrive there in time.

In connection with the matter of throwing messages overboard to let the world at large know of our whereabouts, a number of exciting incidents occurred. When the *Matunga* was following the *Wolf* after the capture, so soon as night fell the Germans on board commenced a grand carousal on the liquor supplies that we had left behind. With the usual Teutonic thoroughness they soon became intoxicated, and, in fact, many of them were speedily in a state of helplessness. Those of the passengers left behind seized the opportunity to throw numerous messages overboard in tins and bottles, and the boatswain scratched a message on a lifebuoy and heaved it overboard.

From what I subsequently learned, it is now evident to me that if any of those of our people left on board had known anything of navigation, they could have overpowered the prize crew easily, and made off with the ship to safety. Had they done this, or had any of their messages been picked up, there may have been a different tale to tell; but the Fates decreed otherwise.

Later on, during the months that followed, messages were sent overboard by us, but I have never heard of any of them being picked up. The Germans were particularly active in preventing us consigning

THE *MATUNGA* AS SHE LAY IN PIRATE COVE (NEW GUINEA).
IT WAS HERE THE GERMANS PLUNDERED HER OF ALL THEY
VALUED PRIOR TO TAKING HER OUTSIDE TO BE SUNK.

these notes to the sea, and tins, bottles and boxes, or in fact anything that floated, was broken and destroyed by them before we could get hold of them. On one occasion we came near to outwitting their vigilance, but the upsetting of our plans cost Capt. Meadows, of the *Turritella*, three days in the lock-up.

Someone had, by what extraordinary means I know not, discovered a football among the prisoners' effects, and when off Singapore we formulated a plan to attach a message to it and throw it overboard. The leather cover of the ball was painted with black and white stripes to make it conspicuous bobbing about on top of the waves, and a message describing the *Wolf*, her armament, and the position of the minefields she had laid was enclosed in a bottle to be attached to it. Several of us had smuggled the ball on to the after-end of the poop just at nightfall one warm evening, and were ready to blow it up when Capt. Meadows, who had the bottle and the message, came up from below.

The captain emerged from our quarters with his pyjamas and a towel in his hands, announcing to all and sundry that he intended to take a bath before turning in. He stood on the deck smoking for a few moments, but when he started to walk towards us two sentries sprang at him, having evidently got wind of the affair. Capt. Meadows, being as strong as an ox, simply carried the two Germans to the side, and with a mighty heave he threw the bottle, message, pyjamas and towel overboard. There was great consternation among the Huns after this, but they did not know what had been hurled over, and could never find out. The captain, however, they argued, had committed an offence, and he accordingly was sentenced to three days' detention.

CHAPTER 11

A Spell in "Pirate Cove"

At noon on the 7th August the *Matunga* had almost dropped out of sight astern, so the *Wolf* stopped and waited for her to come along. On hearing that the *Matunga* could not make better speed unless her tubes were cleaned Nerger ordered them to clean the tubes right away. Both vessels lay stopped until just before sunset, then everything being satisfactorily fixed, we proceeded to the W.N.W., doing about eight knots.

That night we were given permission to sleep on deck, as a start had been made cleaning up our palatial quarters in No. 4 hold. This beautiful spot rejoiced in many names, such as "The Hell Hole," "The Hotel de Luxe," and later the "Occidental and Oriental Hydro."

From the 8th to 13th August, both vessels steered nearly due west, almost right on the equator. During the forenoon of the 13th both ships stopped about eight miles off the land. Our position then being somewhere off the north-west extremity of Dutch New Guinea. The seaplane was launched and made a flight right over the land and up and down the coast. When she returned the *Wolf* steamed straight in for the land with the gunnery lieutenant at the mast-head conning her in.

A narrow passage between two bold headlands was safely negotiated and we found ourselves in a beautiful landlocked bay surrounded by high hills, thickly covered with dense tropical growths of all kinds. The *Wolf* anchored in the middle of the bay, which was about three to four miles long and a good mile in width at its narrowest point.

About half an hour later the *Matunga* was brought alongside, and work commenced taking cargo and coal aboard the *Wolf*.

A guard was landed ashore to keep a lookout on the hills overlooking the sea, and every night the motor boat patrolled the narrow entrance to "Pirate Cove," as we named the harbour. When we were on deck we were not permitted to go within six feet of the rail, sentries armed with rifles parading round us all the time. This was to keep us from having any communication with the natives, who used to come off in their canoes.

That night the *Matunga's* crew were brought aboard; also my three civilian passengers. All prisoners were chased below at sunset to spend the night in an atmosphere reeking with the smell of new paint, made thick with tobacco smoke and a temperature bordering on Hades.

Next afternoon some of the junior officers, seeing that a particular sentry, whom we named "Sherlock Holmes," was hovering round trying to hear what was being said, began whispering and pointing to the nearest shore as a good place to swim for. Sherlock Holmes evidently reported to headquarters that the prisoners were going to try to escape. Just before we were sent below for the night, we noticed that the searchlights were being rigged up on the after end of the boat deck, and also two machine guns were being fixed in position to command our end of the ship. About 11 p.m. we were awakened by a shot fired on our deck and heard the sentry clambering up on deck shouting at the top of his voice.

We jumped out of our hammocks to find out what was wrong, when suddenly we heard rifle shots on deck, and on looking up through the solitary hatch that was off, we could see beams of the searchlight sweeping our end of the ship and star rockets going up by the dozen. Next minute the machine-guns opened fire, and for five minutes things were pretty lively. Then the German officers came running along fully armed and looking as scared as bandicoots, cursed and raved and ordered us to muster for roll-call. On completing the roll-call and finding no prisoners missing, they looked very sheepish and ordered us back to our hammocks.

It transpired later, that on the report of "Sherlock Holmes," they expected us to break out, and the alarm was to be a shot. The sentry down among the prisoners got nervous, and seeing someone crawling under the hammocks (you had to crawl to get anywhere, after the hammocks were slung) immediately "got the wind up" and fired his revolver.

Luckily no one was hurt, but the after ropes between the two ships, were cut to shreds by the machine-gun fire.

The gods were very good to us during our thirteen days' stay at Pirate Cove. Regularly every afternoon we had a glorious downpour of rain, and so could catch water to bathe and wash our clothes with.

The bay seemed to be well inhabited with crocodiles, as we saw several swimming around, so it was not an ideal spot for trying to escape by swimming ashore.

The work of discharging the *Matunga* went on slowly. Every bit of cargo, except the benzine and kerosene, was taken on board the *Wolf*, also all the coal, both cargo and bunkers. The divers were also busy. All the time during our stay here, they were down scraping and cleaning the *Wolf's* bottom.

On the morning of Sunday, the 26th August, we were permitted to remain on deck to see the torpedo practice. They made very good shooting, being considerably more expert with the torpedoes than they were with the 5.9 inch guns.

At 10 a.m. the *Matunga* proceeded to sea, closely followed by the *Wolf.* About twelve miles off land both ships stopped, and Lieutenant Dietrich, the mining officer, and his crew went on board to fix their bombs. At 1.30 p.m. the first bomb exploded in the port side of the engine-room bilge, and the ship settled quickly by the stern with a heavy list to port. At 1.32 p.m. the second bomb went; it was placed under the water at the after end of No. 2 hatch. The ship gradually straightened up with the after deck awash, and at 1.37 p.m. she went down stern first, her bow cocked well in the air. My feelings were anything but cheerful, for I was very fond of the old *Matunga.*

Shortly before we left Pirate Cove the three horses we had on board the *Matunga* were slaughtered to provide fresh meat. This, of course, did not appeal to the British, indeed a good deal of sentiment attached to the animals, but this had to give way to the need of those aboard for fresh meat. Some of the Germans who were familiar with horse flesh as a food were jubilant at the thought of this change of diet, but those unacquainted with it were highly indignant. The subsequent happenings in connection with this item in the menu were humorously told by Nerger himself in his record of the voyage:—

> The ship's officers' mess was directly underneath my cabin, and the appearance of the meat course was followed by a violent stamping and galloping by those present. This was meant to be a reflection upon the horseflesh. To get even with these recalcitrant officers, I gave orders to the cooks and stewards that no mention of horseflesh was to be made to the officers and no indication given as to the days upon which it was served.
>
> Upon one day the cooks served mock hare, whereon the

stamping and galloping again occurred, ending in a wild tumult, officers shouting 'Horse-flesh we do not eat.' None of the mock hare was eaten by any of them. Two days later the cooks produced a favourite German dish, *sauer braten* (savoury roast with an acid taste) from the horse-flesh, and I ordered that it be served as roast beef. '*Sauer braten*,' exclaimed the officers, 'is certainly not horseflesh,' and they enjoyed it hugely, not an atom being left after the meal. Afterwards they were told that it was horse-flesh, and it was a very hard job to convince them of the fact.

THE *MATUNGA* AS SHE APPEARED BEFORE THE FILIAL PLUNGE ON 26.8.'17. THE GERMANS PUT TWO BOMBS IN THE HOLDS OF THE SHIP, AND SEVEN MINUTES AFTER THE FIRST EXPLOSION SHE WENT DOWN.

Chapter 12

A Minefield for Singapore

The *Wolf* now steamed away to the south-west, and the Germans told us that they were now going to carry out the most ticklish part of the whole cruise. We at once jumped to the conclusion that Singapore was now to receive attention. She still had fully one-hundred mines left. These systematically laid around the entrance to Singapore, would do considerable damage to shipping in the East.

The seaplane was dismantled, and stowed away down in No. 3 'tween decks, so that there was nothing about the *Wolf* to cause any suspicion to passing vessels. She proceeded at her usual cruising speed of eight knots, through the numerous islands of the Celebes.

On August 30th, about 1.30 p.m., we passed about four miles south of the lighthouse on the Braile Bank, and so into the Java Sea. Here the speed was increased, and I think she was doing her best, possibly 10½ or 11 knots. For although the divers had spent a lot of time cleaning her bottom at Pirate Cove, still they never got right under her; she was only cleaned to the round of the bilge. So that there was still a large patch of grass and shell-covered surface to push through the water, also one boiler was in a very dicky condition.

During the night on September 3rd, a beautiful moonlight night, the *Wolf* was steaming up Karimatta Straits, no lights showing from anywhere, and all eyes alert for anything in the way of hostile cruisers. Suddenly a suspicious-looking craft was sighted. Immediately the alarm bells went, and we could hear all hands tumbling out hurriedly to battle stations. Everyone was pitched to the highest key of excitement, for the approaching vessel was made out to be a cruiser. The Germans said she was one of our *Juno* class. Everything was ready. Should the cruiser see the *Wolf* and signal for any particulars from her, at once two torpedoes would have been launched at her. However,

Nerger's luck held good, for either the cruiser did not see her at all, or else considered it not worthwhile to take any notice of her. She passed the *Wolf* within three miles, and went her way, little suspecting that a German raider and mine-layer had slipped by on such a fine clear night.

The following night 4th September, "Mines," as we called Lieutenant Dietrich, and his crew had a busy time. At 7 p.m. they commenced getting the mines up from No. 3 hold. They were run along the deck, on rails properly fixed for them, and run into sidings under the poop. Here the rails ran out to the ship's side, where the mine dropping doors were. Each mine rumbled right over our heads and we could hear the splash as they dropped.

The *Wolf* kept at full speed all the time while laying the minefield. At 11 p.m. the first mine was dropped, and from then they went merrily at about 2½ minute intervals. The number of mines laid that night was a source of great argument among the prisoners. Some said they counted 106, others 99, and so on, but I think somewhere about 100 would not be far wrong.

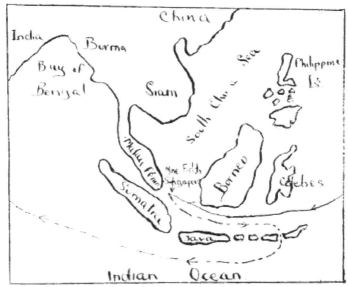

This small sectional map shows the route pursued by the *Wolf* after she sunk the *Matunga* Singapore marks the end of the outward voyage. From thence the *Wolf* proceeded to hit the return trail. The large map in the book includes this section.

Personally, I did not argue, as after counting five, I fell asleep and did not waken until I heard the subdued cheer, given by the mining crew when the last mine had been dropped.

As soon as the last mine was gone, the *Wolf* turned on her tracks and made back for the Java Sea. The Germans had "the wind up" properly, for several times next morning, the alarm bells went and they tumbled out hurriedly to battle stations. Once while we were on deck the alarms went, and we were hustled unceremoniously below. They thought they saw an aeroplane coming out over the land, but it proved to be a bird.

That day the topmasts were lowered and the funnel raised, this completely altering her outward appearance. From a vessel with long topmasts and a moderate funnel, she was now a stumpy masted tramp with a fairly high funnel.

She continued back in about the same track that she had come, right along the Java Sea, passing steamers every day, but taking no notice of them. It was much too risky to molest shipping in these enclosed waters.

On Sunday evening, 9th September, she entered the Atlas Straits, between the islands of Lombok and Sumbawa, and passed through during the night into the Indian Ocean. She continued due south until 9 a.m. the following morning, and then hauled to the westward, in about latitude 10 S. Now followed a long spell of inactivity, and here I propose to give my readers some idea of our life on board the *Wolf*.

CHAPTER 13

Conditions in the "Hotel De Luxe"

As I have already mentioned, our quarters were situated in the No. 4 'tween decks, the only means of entrance and exit being through a small hatchway under the poop, and by means of a wooden ladder, with only room for one to pass at a time. The quarters were roughly 65 feet long and 45 feet wide, and the sides, deck and ceiling were all steel. It was partitioned off by the erection of a double tier of empty store eases, these empty cases being our wardrobe, as we had nowhere else to keep our things. In the port after corner dwelt the captains, chief officers, and chief engineers, in a space measuring 25 feet by 18 feet. Forward of this were the junior officers, engineers, and apprentices. Amidships, at the forward end, was the "neutrals" territory, and the remaining space was occupied by the crew.

We had portable mess tables and benches. These, of course, had to come down at night time, to make room for the hammocks. The hammocks were slung in double tiers, one over the other, and so close together that one usually had to get in at the end and crawl down. The hatchway overhead measured about 20 feet by 14 feet, but during the night we were never permitted to have more than one hatch open, this gave us a five by two air space, but should anything heave in sight, then everything was covered and the hatch battened down.

There was always at least one armed sentry down below, and three or four more at the top of the ladder. When capturing a vessel or laying mines, a steel plate was dropped over the exit, the guard doubled, and a nice little box of hand grenades ready, in case we tried to get out.

Our position, previous to getting rid of the mines, was sort of between the devil and the deep sea, had she gone into action. Just forward to our quarters were the mines, while just abaft us was the after magazine full of ammunition. A shot striking the *Wolf* anywhere abaft

PHOTO OF SOME OF THE PRISONERS ON THE *WOLF*, SHOWING THE
VARIED NATIONALITIES. MANY OF THESE MEN WERE ABOARD THE
WOLF UPWARDS OF TWELVE MONTHS. A NUMBER OF THE *MATUNGA*
COMPLEMENT ARE SHOWN IN THIS GROUP.

her engine-room meant that the majority of us went west "one time."

At 6 o'clock every morning we each received about two inches of fresh water in the bottom of a bucket, with this we had to bath ourselves and wash our clothes. I tell you it took some doing, especially when there was a fresh wind blowing. We had to get right up on the poop to bathe, and it was so crowded up there that half the time you did not know whether you were soaping yourself or the fellow next to you. When you finished this feat and started to get below to dress you were sure to get smothered in dirty water and soapsuds, squeezing your way through this naked mass to the ladder. The only deck we were allowed to use was the poop, and this was so hampered with hatchways, ventilators, a dummy wheel box, and a 5.9-inch gun, that when any more than half of us were on deck at once, there was no room to take exercise of any kind.

When on deck there were always three armed sentries with us, and another always had the telephone apparatus to the bridge, on his head. There were telephones from each gun, and each torpedo tube to the bridge.

A masthead lookout was always kept, and immediately anything was sighted the cry of "*Alle gefangenen unter deck*" (all prisoners under deck) was given, and down below we were hustled, hoping each time that it was a British cruiser coming along.

They were continually practicing torpedo and gun drill, and every day the guns and torpedoes were cleaned. During all these little diversions we were kept down below. A fan was fixed up down below, which would perhaps work for two nights, and then be off duty for repairs, until the poor overworked electrician had a minute to spare to fix it. But even when the fan did work the temperature in the tropics down below was pretty moist.

How we all managed to keep so fit was marvellous. The food was at times pretty bad and at other times quite good. Our menu depended on the class of ship captured, if it was a well found vessel, then we all fared well and *vice versa*.

Perhaps one of the things most greatly missed by a number of us was the regular exercise to which we had always been accustomed. On the overcrowded deck space allotted to us it was almost impossible to carry out our usual practices in this direction, but towards nightfall, when there was less congestion, a few of us would manage a brisk walk round and about, with some difficulty and often amusing consequences. Captain Saunders, who fortunately had a good knowledge

87

of the "physical jerks" that military recruits go through in camp, took classes in hand, and when opportunity offered we went through the lessons in good order. This, I think, helped us a good deal in keeping healthy and well.

Our other amusements were limited indeed. There were fortunately numerous packs of cards on board, and we played every game we knew night after night in our quarters. For the most of the time we had the electric light, but on occasions when there was a scare among the Germans, or when they thought it wise to take precautions against being sighted, the globes were shaded, and playing became impossible.

It was a comforting thing to those of us that smoked to have a reasonable supply of tobacco. We were given an allowance of half a pound per month, and sometimes could secure a little more. The tobacco came from the captured prizes, and there was always plenty until near the end of the voyage. Then the shortage was acute, and up among the icefields we were on short commons, and often would have paid anything for a plug of the fragrant weed.

We now spent a very monotonous sixteen days, cruising slowly to the westward. It was evident that the Germans did not want to get back to the vicinity of Ceylon, until the southwest monsoon had finished, and fine weather again prevailed there. Many were the conjectures of the prisoners during those hot sleepy days. Some of us thought that now he had finished his mines, he would send us off at the first suitable opportunity. Christmas Island, we thought would be a suitable place to land us on, as we knew the communications between there and Singapore were very irregular. However, we passed the longitude of that island, and were still in a quandary as to what was to be done with us.

The German officers said that we would not be long before we would be sent in, but I don't think Commander Nerger ever took anyone into his confidence in these matters, and he personally changed his mind about things so often, that one never knew what to expect next.

CHAPTER 14

Capture of the "Hitachi Maru"

On the morning of September 26th we were somewhere near the One and a Half Degree Channel, through the Maldive Islands.

The seaplane was again brought up on deck and assembled. This operation usually occupied about 24 hours. About 11 a.m., just a few minutes after they had got the engine of the seaplane working, smoke was sighted to the eastward. The *Wolf* immediately stopped, put the seaplane into the water, and a few minutes later the latter buzzed into the air and disappeared in the direction of the smoke. She returned about noon, and all was hustle to get her on board. The commander himself came on the after end of the boat deck, and yelled, cursed, and danced like a madman until the seaplane was on board.

The *Wolf* then went off full speed to west-south-west. We were shaking hands with ourselves and were sure the long-looked-for cruiser was now on the *Wolf's* heels. However, at 1.30 p.m. our hopes were again dashed to pieces, for the *Wolf* again stopped, sent the seaplane up, and turned round and steamed back towards the smoke, which could now be plainly seen from the deck.

The *Wolf* approached the other steamer on a parallel course. When within about 1½ miles of her she signalled "stop immediately, telegraphic communication stopped," and a warning shell was fired across her bows. The other vessel hoisted his answering pennant, signifying that he understood, and also blew three short blasts on his whistle, indicating that he was coming full-speed astern. Nevertheless, he swung round on the starboard helm, without reducing his speed, and turned his stern towards the *Wolf*. The *Wolf* could now see that he carried a gun aft; it was previously hidden from them by the awning over the after deck, and the gun's crew were starting to clear away the gun. The *Wolf* dropped all her bulwarks and showed her set of teeth, at the same

S.S. *HITACHI MARU*, A JAP MAIL STEAMER WELL-KNOWN IN AUSTRALIAN PORTS. A VESSEL OF ABOUT 7,000 TONS, SHE CARRIED, WHEN CAPTURED, A CARGO VALUED AT CONSIDERABLY OVER £1,000,000.

time sent another shot across the bows of the Jap For by this time they had seen that she was the Japanese steamer *Hitachi Maru*.

As the Jap still refused to stop, the *Wolf* shelled the after deck, and one shell burst among the gun's crew of the Jap, but still she kept on going, and a fresh crew rushed to man the gun. The *Wolf* kept up a steady fire with her 5.9 inch guns, and at that close range it certainly reflected no credit on the gunners that so little damage was done to the Jap When the shells started to burst around the decks, several of the Japs, jumped overboard. The seaplane now took a hand in the game, and dropped a bomb into the water ahead of the *Hitachi Maru* and she stopped. Boats were hurriedly lowered from the Jap with the latter's passengers aboard. One of the boats dropped into the water end-on, and it was a marvel to everyone that so few were drowned.

While the prize crew were on the way across, the Jap, commenced using his wireless, and at once the *Wolf* put a shell right through her wireless room. This shell went clean through both sides of the wireless house, and the operator, seated in his chair, was unhurt. The shell exploded against one of the engine-room ventilators, killing one of the engineers, who happened to be standing there, and also burst up the funnel.

Boats were lowered from the *Wolf*, and picked up several people who were swimming in the water. Among those picked up in the water was a young Britisher, a passenger on the *Hitachi Maru*, who happened to have been on the R.M.S. *Mongolia* when that fine vessel struck one of the *Wolf's* mines off Bombay, so he evidently was not born to be drowned.

The passengers and crew of the *Hitachi Maru* now came on board the *Wolf*. Some of the former had been injured in the process of lowering their boats. There were several British women passengers, who certainly must have had some nasty shocks to their nervous systems, but next morning they showed no signs of the terrible ordeal through which they had passed. Most of them spent the night in deck chairs on the after well-deck of the *Wolf*.

The steering gear of the Jap had been damaged by the gunfire, and a gang of men were sent over from the *Wolf* to repair it. At 8 p.m., the damaged steering gear having been repaired, both ships proceeded south at slow speed.

Next morning both vessels steamed in among the Maldive Islands. The *Hitachi Maru* anchored, and the *Wolf* went alongside her and made fast. All the *Hitachi Maru* passengers were now sent aboard,

The Hitachi Maru

likewise the Jap stewards and cooks. Work was immediately started, taking over cargo and coal from the Jap She had a very valuable cargo aboard, and was bound from Japan to Liverpool, *via* Singapore, Colombo and Delagoa Bay. This vessel at least had reached Singapore from the north without striking the *Wolf's* minefield. This puzzled the Germans somewhat.

We were able to see some of the effects of the gunfire on the Jap The after-deck round the gun and the deck under it were covered with blood. One shell had burst just under the boat-deck, upon which the gun was mounted, and had burst up the deck around the gun, but the gun was absolutely undamaged. Another shell had holed her just above the waterline at No. 4 hatch; another caught her under the port counter, exploded in the second-class bath rooms; and the one, already mentioned, which went through the wireless room. Altogether the *Wolf* fired fifteen shots, and these at practically point blank range, so the gunnery was far from good. The Jap had not fired a single shot. The gun she carried was a fine 1.7 inch gun, and while part of the crew were busy with cargo, another crowd dismantled the Jap's gun and took it aboard the *Wolf*.

We were not allowed to communicate in any way with the Japs, who were accommodated in No. 3 'tween decks. Captain Tominagu, of the *Hitachi Maru*, and his officers were also housed in No. 3.

Captain Tominagu kept very much to himself, and was not quartered amongst us. He felt the loss of his ship keenly, more especially on account of the fact that so many of his crew had been killed. Eventually up amongst the ice-floes of the Arctic he slipped over the side, and was not missed until it was too late to return and search for him.

Altogether there were thirteen deaths over this capture, eleven by gunfire and two by drowning. Had the *Hitachi Maru* realised in time what manner of ship the *Wolf* was, she could have given the *Wolf* a bad time, as she was capable of getting up a speed of 15 knots. However, the captain had been informed in Colombo that there was nothing to fear until he got into the U-boat area, and naturally he had no suspicion that the vessel approaching him was anything but a peaceful merchantman.

The Jap's cargo was of great variety. Rubber, copper, tin, hides, tea, and silk were the main things the *Wolf* devoured, but I must not forget the canned crab. Ye gods, I never want to see a beastly crab in my life again, much less eat one. After the Jap's capture I think we had canned crab for every blessed meal; in fact, I quite anticipated that if we ever did get ashore again we should all be walking sideways.

Amongst the Jap's passengers were a number of young Britishers, going home to join up. In the second-class there was a Chinese woman and child, a Hindu woman, five Portuguese soldiers, and several Indians going to the Cape. Luckily the women in the saloon all had their husbands with them.

The women passengers on the *Hitachi Maru* must have had some exciting experiences. They were kept on the ship during the period she was in attendance on the *Wolf*, and were afterwards transferred to the *Igotz Mendi* after her capture. On this ship they continued their unpleasant voyage, and were still aboard when the vessel reached the Danish coast. How they fared or what became of them I have never learned.

Only 200 tons of coal were taken from the *Hitachi Maru*, as Nerger intended to take this fine ship home to Germany with him, but in case of accidents he took as much of her cargo on board the *Wolf* as she could hold. Also the holes in the Jap's hull were repaired, and the holes in the funnel plated over.

Both ships lay in this anchorage for five days, within 600 miles of Colombo, where there were two British cruisers lying when the *Hitachi Maru* left.

Numerous native boats came off. Some came alongside the *Wolf* and sold fruit, but others kept their distance, and seemed very dubious of her, especially when they saw the seaplane.

All the womenfolk were put on board the *Hitachi Maru*, also all prisoners over sixty years of age and under sixteen.

At daylight on the 3rd October the *Wolf* cast off from the Jap, and proceeded to sea, leaving a prize crew of fifteen men under command of Lieut. Rosa, and a number of neutrals, who volunteered to work the ship for the Germans.

CHAPTER 5

The Sinking of the "Hitachi Maru"

The hunt was now for coal, as without this commodity there was no hope of taking the Jap along with them. The ground chosen was somewhere just east of the Equatorial Channel, and under easy steam the *Wolf* cruised slowly east and west, north and south, across the usual shipping tracks.

During the night of 5th October a vessel was sighted, with all her lights burning brightly. This vessel the *Wolf* found out by judicious use of her Morse light to be a Dane; I think she was the *Zealandia*. So intent were they in watching the Dane that they failed to notice the approach of another vessel, without any lights showing, which came up on the starboard quarter of the *Wolf*. When this second vessel was suddenly seen great commotion was caused on the *Wolf*. "Prepare for action" alarms went and torpedo doors were dropped with a thunderous bang. They thought she was a British auxiliary cruiser, and when the vessel suddenly hauled sharp across the *Wolf's* stern they made sure the game was up. However, even then they funked opening an action. Their torpedo might miss its mark, and then they would have to fight. This was a thing the *Wolf* did not intend to do, unless of course it was an unarmed merchantman, or one with the usual one gun mounted aft.

However, their fears were soon allayed, for the vessel quickly crossed astern of the *Wolf*, and hauled back on her old course again. But the sudden fright had so upset the German equilibrium that she was some miles ahead of them before they realised she would be a valuable prize. Being dark, they did not care to tackle her, as she might have a gun. So the *Wolf* set after her, trying to keep within range until daylight. The other vessel proved to be too fast for this; at daylight she was well outside the range of the *Wolf's* guns. From what we could see of her when allowed on deck for our bath, she seemed to be a vessel

WOLF LAUNCHING A TORPEDO

of from 10,000 to 12,000 tons, one funnel and two masts, and was evidently bound for Colombo.

The *Wolf*, seeing the chase was useless, eased up her speed, and, as soon as the other ship was out of sight, she turned round and went full speed in the opposite direction, namely, to westward. They evidently thought that the other steamer might have seen the seaplane on deck, and would report her as a suspicious craft to Colombo.

About 5 p.m. we closed in with the Maldive Islands again, and stopped, put the seaplane over, and sent her in with a message to the *Hitachi Maru*. On the return of the *Wolfchen* she was whipped on board lively, and the *Wolf* ploughed off again full speed to the west.

For six days we steamed west-south-west, but nothing came within the vision of the hungry *Wolf*. On the afternoon of the 12th October the course was altered to about south-south-east, and at 10 a.m. the following morning we met the *Hitachi Maru*. Both ships steered slowly to the southward, and on the evening of the 14th the *Hitachi Maru* left us, steaming even more south.

For the next six days the *Wolf* hunted vainly for a prize. She steamed north, then east, then south, and then west, back and forward, across what she considered the steamer tracks, never more than eight hours on the same course, but no sign of shipping could be seen, and the Germans congratulated themselves that, between the "U" boats and the *Wolf* they had quite plainly wiped the British mercantile marine from the seas.

It was quite evident now that the Jap could not be taken home in triumph. All the coal would be required for the *Wolf* herself, and then it would require strict economy in coal consumption if she was to reach Germany.

On the morning of the 20th we again met the *Hitachi Maru*, and both vessels steamed in under the lee of the Cargados reefs. The *Hitachi Maru* anchored, and the *Wolf* moored alongside her.

These reefs are about three hundred miles north-north-east of Mauritius, and afforded an excellent anchorage from the fresh south-east trade winds. They are in about 15 degrees south latitude, and roughly about 60 degrees east longitude. Here we had some good sport fishing from the poop. Some days we had a good haul, other days not a single fish could be caught. Anything that could be used for a line was there, and some of the prisoners manufactured excellent hooks from ordinary nails. The fresh fish was greatly appreciated by prisoners and crew. The German officers offered to buy fish caught by the prisoners, but in most cases prisoners gave them without payment.

Having now decided that the *Hitachi Maru* must be sunk, as it was impossible to take her along without plenty of coal, the crew was started shifting coal from the *Wolf's* No. 3 hold into the bunkers, so as to make room for storage of as much of the *Hitachi Maru's* cargo as possible. While one gang was shifting coal, others were hard at work at the other end of the ship taking over cargo from the Jap

For the next week we had a very cheerful time. The ships were naturally swung head to wind, and this gave us the benefit of all the coal dust that was going. And there was a scarcity of water to wash in. "Little Willie" was approached on the subject of getting an allowance of water in the evening as well as in the morning, for we did not care to turn in covered in coal dust. "Willie," however, would not listen to our request. Later the request was put before Lieutenant Deitrich, the mining officer, and he went at once to the engineers and got us an allowance of water morning and evening while the coaling went on.

The *Wolf* had now filled up all available space with the Jap's valuable cargo, copper was put in the bunkers under the coal, and some of it in the magazines. The storerooms were well stocked, especially with flour and that confounded canned crab. I should imagine that the Japs, had been collecting crabs for centuries, and sent them all along on the unfortunate *Hitachi Maru*.

When supplies were being transferred from captured vessels to the *Wolf*, there was always plenty of bustle and hurry. At first we expected that the Germans would compel us to assist, but they did not; the work, for the most part, was always done by their own crew. Some of the neutrals, however, worked, but they were volunteers, and the Germans offered to pay them at the rate of nine shillings a day. Whether they were eventually paid up I could never ascertain.

To accommodate the single men passengers, a room had been made in No. 3 'tween docks, the married couples and the army officers were again housed in the rooms on the saloon deck. Another member was added to the members of the officers' mess, a Japanese lieut.-engineer of the Japanese Navy, who was travelling as a passenger.

Having now gorged herself to repletion, the *Wolf* took her victim out to the open sea to destroy her. The *Hitachi Maru* was sunk by bombs on the 7th November about thirty miles north-west of the Cargados reefs. She sank head first, and turned right up on end as she went down. Great quantities of wreckage came to the surface, amongst which the most prominent was the round-topped ammunition house, which was swept off the after boat-deck by the rush of water as the ship went down.

SNAP OF THE *HITACHI MARU* AS SHE LEFT
FOR HER LAST RESTING PLACE.

CHAPTER 16.

A Consignment of Coal

During our stay at Cargados, the chief officer told us that we would all either be at home for Christmas or be free to send news home at that time. We surmised this to mean that the *Wolf* had only sufficient coal to reach the Canary Islands, and if unable to replenish her stock before reaching there, would go in and intern. But we knew her luck, and had our doubts.

The course was again set to the south-west. Mauritius was passed without incident. At daylight on the 10th November we were awakened by the usual commotion caused by the alarm of "Stations," and immediately guessed that the *Wolf's* marvellous luck had not yet deserted her.

The vessel was captured without a shot having to be fired. When permitted to go on deck, we found the new prize steaming along quietly behind us. She was painted a light grey outside, and had a yellow funnel with the letters A.S. on it. At once some of the prisoners recognised this mark, and said she was one of the "Ally Sloper" line of Bilboa. This she proved to be, although to this day I have been unable to find out what the A.S. really stood for.

The prize, and she was a prize indeed to the *Wolf* (for without her she had no hope of ever reaching Germany again), was the Spanish steamer *Igotz Mendi*, with a cargo of 6800 tons of coal, consigned to the British authorities at Colombo. She had loaded her coal at Delagoa Bay. The crew, being Spaniards, and therefore neutral, were left on board to carry on the working of the ship, and only a small prize crew was placed on board. Both ships turned round and steamed back towards the Cargados Reefs.

The *Wolf* had now got what she had been hunting for so many long months. With this quantity of coal she could take the Spaniard

S.s. *Igotz Mendi*, a Spanish vessel, which was captured by the *Wolf*. She carried a fine cargo of coal, which was a great prize for the German.

along with her, and replenish her bunkers whenever necessary. Coaling was started immediately the *Wolf* was fast alongside the Spaniard, and continued without stoppage night and day until the bunkers could hold no more.

As soon as the *Wolf's* appetite for coal was satisfied, she cast off from the Spaniard and anchored. All hands were then engaged in painting. A gang was sent over to the *Igotz Mendi*, and the gay Spaniard's bright colours were hidden under a complete covering of war grey. The *Wolf* was also treated to a coat of paint, but her colour was made much nearer black than grey.

The womenfolk and their husbands were once again shifted. This time they were housed in the rooms of the Spanish officers and engineers, who kindly gave up their quarters, and had some rough accommodation put up for themselves under the poop. A couple of sick prisoners were also put on board the Spaniard, but owing to lack of accommodation those over sixty and under sixteen years of ago had to be left on the *Wolf*.

One night during our stay at Cargados the wireless of a cruiser was picked up not far off. At daybreak the *Wolfchen* was sent up, and returned with the news that a Japanese cruiser was passing about 40 miles to the northward of us, bound west. Everything was got ready for a quick move away, if she should happen to cruise down our way. Axes were placed handy fore and aft to cut away the mooring ropes between the two ships, and a full head of steam was raised on the *Wolf*. But nothing happened. The *Wolfchen* made two more flights that day and one the following morning, but nothing more was seen of the cruiser.

At noon on the 17th November both ships left the anchorage and proceeded to the south-west. At 7 p.m. the *Wolf* turned round and steamed away to the eastward. However, after it was dark and the Spaniard well out of sight, she turned again to about west-south-west.

We now had a very acceptable change of prison officers. Lieut. Dietrich, the chief mining officer, having successfully laid all the "eggs" under his charge, and therefore having nothing particular to do, was appointed to look after us in place of "Little Willie."

We all liked "Mines," as we called him. He was about the only German on board with a sense of humour, and always had a cheery smile for us. No complaint was too trivial for his attention, and our comfort was well looked after when he took charge. We used to look forward to 8 p.m. in the evening, as at this time "Mines" made his

PRIZE COMMANDER ROSE, WITH THE CAPTAIN AND SECOND OFFICER OF
THE SPANISH SHIP *IGOTZ MENDI.*

It was from this boat that the Germans secured 1000 tons of coal, which
enabled them to get back to Germany. The prize was also intended for
Germany, but ran ashore on the coast of Denmark.

pilgrimage into "Hades," and always stayed to have a yarn with us, and see if we had sufficient ventilation for the night. There were now nearly 400 prisoners on board, and although there was a fan for drawing down the cooler air from on deck, and distributing it throughout the quarters by narrow metal channels, still, unless one had the luck to have his hammock slung right under the exit of one of those channels, there was no air stirring. "Mines" would always give orders to have some more hatches taken off, if we asked him—a thing his predecessor would never have done.

CHAPTER 17

Ford's for Everybody

As the African coast was approached the course was gradually altered to the southward, keeping about 100 miles off shore.

On the morning of the 30th November, blowing a moderate south-east gale, a barque was sighted, head reaching to the southward, under lower topsails and foresail. She was ordered to heave to. With difficulty, and a good drenching, a prize crew boarded her. She was the American barque *John H. Kirby*, of New York, bound from that port to Port Elizabeth and Durban. She had a mixed cargo, the principal items being 270 Ford motorcars and a large quantity of canned goods.

Commander Nerger makes the statement that the *John H. Kirby* carried armoured cars for the troops in East Africa, and imagines, I think, that he has saved East Africa by sinking a few Ford Cars, which, by the way, were not armoured, but simply common or garden Fords.

Luck still held, for within an hour of the capture the wind dropped and the sea went down, so that work was commenced boating the stores over to the *Wolf*, and this was kept going until sunset. The methods which the Germans adopted to secure the most necessary portions of the cargo or stores of vessels captured show how thoroughly planned was every detail of the cruise. From the ship's papers printed requisition forms were secured by the purser, who filled them in with lists of what he required from the captured vessel. Everything was set out fully, and when the document was completed it was presented formally to the commander, who appended with a graceful flourish the bold signature of "C. Nerger."

After that the despoilers would commence their ravages. While the stores were being boated from the *John H. Kirby*, a deputation of his own officers requested that Captain Nerger would present them all with one of the Ford motorcars each rather than send them to the bottom. Nerger, entering into the joke, granted the request, providing, however, that each man should bring his own car aboard. Needless to relate, Neptune and his satellites are the only ones to enjoy the pleasures of motoring with that shipment of cars. The crew of the *John H. Kirby* were brought on board, and proved to be mostly neutrals. I think there was only one true American on board her.

Captain Blom, a Finn, was in command. He said that he was uncertain of his position, as he had only one chronometer on board, and that was broken, and did not know that he was so far past his first port of call until the *Wolf* collared him. At daylight the work of boating cargo over was again commenced, and went on gaily until about 11.30 a.m. Then some disturbing wireless must have been picked up, for the work was stopped suddenly and "Mines" was sent aboard her in a hurry to sink her.

Before the unfortunate barque had gone to her rest below the *Wolf* was off full speed to the westward. We rounded the Cape on the 3rd December, in ideal weather, smooth seas and brilliant sunshine, and so, after a long spell, the *Wolf* again entered the Atlantic, steering about west-north-west.

THE *JOHN H. KIRBY*, SNAPPED AS SHE SUNK
BENEATH THE WAVES. BOMBS AGAIN WERE
EMPLOYED FOR THE DESPATCH OF THIS VESSEL,
AND NO DIFFICULTY WAS MET IN SENDING HER DOWN.

We at once came to the conclusion, which eventually proved correct, that he was making for the Island of Trinidad—not the West Indian island of that name—about 600 miles off the east coast of Brazil, there to have a general overhaul of engines and boilers, replenish bunkers, and be ready for the run through the British blockade area. We knew that, previous to the outbreak of the war, this island was uninhabited, and would suit the *Wolf's* requirements admirably.

The *Igotz Mendi* was met on the 6th December, and a few boatloads of stores were sent over to her. She kept in company until the following day, and then went off, steering more to the westward than the *Wolf.*

The *Wolfchen* was now undergoing repairs, as they had had a bit of an accident with her when landing from the last flight. The sea was choppy at the time, and she struck the water at the wrong angle, and broke one of her floats. This immediately filled with water, and tipped her nose under. Boats were sent to her, and several men had to climb out on the tail while she was towed back alongside. The covering material was by this time quite rotten, and she had to be completely recovered, and the engine given a thorough overhaul after its immersion in the salt water. Japanese silk from the *Hitachi Maru* was used for covering the wings, and it proved to be excellently adapted to the purpose.

There was also a slight outbreak of typhoid fever among the Japs, and everyone on board was inoculated against the disease. Luckily it did not spread.

We continued in a straight line for Trinidad at a speed of nine knots. This was about the extreme limit of speed which the *Wolf* could now attain: her bottom was covered with shells, and long grass streamed along her waterline.

Just before sundown on the 14th December a barque was sighted steering to the north-east. The *Wolf* was unable to get up to her before dark, so she dodged after her all night, and by 6 a.m. next morning a prize crew was in charge of the barque. This vessel brought along some of our allies, who were not yet represented among the prisoners. She was the French barque *Marshall Davout*, bound from Geelong, Victoria, to Dakar, with a full cargo of grain. She was armed with two 8in. guns for submarines, and was also fitted with wireless. Captain Brett, like a sensible man, did not attempt to use his pop-guns, but surrendered quietly.

The crew and stores, including a live pig, were brought over to the

THE FRENCH SAILER MARECHAL DAVOUT,
CAPTURED ON HER HOMEWARD VOYAGE FROM
GEELONG, VICTORIA. SHE HAD 3,500 TONS OF
WHEAT ABOARD, WHICH WAS SENT TO THE BOTTOM
WITH THE SHIP.

Wolf, and at 1 p.m. the *Marshall Davout*, with her 3500 tons of grain, disappeared below, the usual two bombs being sufficient to give her her knockout.

Captain Brett was rather despondent over the loss of his ship, but was quite confident that the *Wolf* would never reach Germany. Most of us were of the same opinion. Our confidence in the navy was very strong. Captain Brett was a native of Brittany, where France's best sailors hail from. He was so firmly convinced that the raider would meet her fate before reaching home that he was the most disgusted man on board when we eventually steamed into Kiel.

The following day the *Wolfchen* was again brought on deck, and being assembled, made a flight just before sunset, but evidently saw nothing to report.

We had now twenty different nationalities represented among the prisoners, and considering the manner in which we were all packed together, it reflects great credit on the men that there were so few disputes and quarrels. Of course, there was occasionally a stand-up fight between some couple who could not settle it otherwise, but taken on the whole they behaved splendidly.

CHAPTER 18

Capture of the "Storobrore"

Commander Nerger, in his records, makes several caustic remarks about the enmity between the Britishers and the Japs, and goes so far from the truth as to say that on several occasions his crew had to separate us. These are absolute lies. In the first place, the Japs, lived in a separate hold, and used a different deck for exercise; in fact, there was very little chance of talking to the Japs, much less fighting with them. It was only during the last few days of the cruise that we were thrown any way into close contact with them, and I am certain there never was any fighting done, not even a quarrel, excepting perhaps a few heated arguments over "fishing rights" during our stay at Cargados.

Of the few fights that took place I would like to say that they were never provoked by discussions on questions of nationality or the war. For the most part they were between British sailors, and arose from arguments about some ship or port they had visited, or from a dispute concerning their own comfort.

The 19th of December brought the Spaniard back to us. We were then about sixty miles east of Trinidad, and both ships proceeded towards it. It was Merger's intention to send the *Wolfchen* up at daylight to see if anything was about, and also to ascertain if the island was still uninhabited. During the night, however, all doubts on the latter question were settled. A wireless message was picked up. It was from Vice-Admiral Martinz, of the Brazilian Navy, to the Military Commander of Trinidad. So Brazil had evidently fortified Trinidad, in order to keep raiders from using it as a base.

On receipt of this message both steamers at once turned round and steamed to the eastward, away from the island. The Germans had not anticipated this, and it came rather as a shock to them. However, by 10 a.m. the day following they had recovered, and their plan was now to go south again clear of the limit of the south-east trade winds, and there do the coaling and necessary overhaul. Both ships hauled to the southward at a speed of seven knots.

For three days we continued to the southward, and on the 23rd December both ships stopped. The captain of the *Wolf* was waiting a chance to get alongside the collier, but at present the swell was much too high, and even in the smoothest of water the *Igotz Mendi* could beat anything I have ever seen for rolling; she was an absolute marvel at it.

Next day there was no steam on the *Wolf's* boilers. The swell, though subsiding gradually, was still enough to keep the Spaniard going like the pendulum of a clock. This was Christmas Eve, the second which the *Wolf* had spent at sea, but to us the first, and we most devoutly hoped, the last.

Scurvy was now beginning to take hold of some of the prisoners, principally among those who had been the longest on board. The doctors, of course, said it was rheumatism, but most of us had seen too much scurvy in our early days at sea in old sailing ships not to know the disease when we saw it.

In these days of sickness among the captives, who were mostly the men from the *Jumna* and the *Wordsworth*, the two German doctors that were on the strength of the raider provided the medical attention. Our own two doctors, Majors Strangman and Flood, who were captured with the *Matunga*, were never permitted to visit the hospital, nor were their medical services ever utilised. In fact, these officers were confined to a separate part of the ship, and I was only once permitted to come into contact with them during the whole voyage.

Christmas Day spent on board a German raider in the South Atlantic is not exactly the manner in which most of us had intended to spend it. But nevertheless the Germans did the best they could under the circumstances. We had plenty to eat, and in our mess Commander Nerger sent us along some wine, which, by the way, was loot from the *Marshall Davout*," and a cigar each, both being fully appreciated.

During Christmas Day part of the crew were employed taking fresh water in the boats to the *Igotz Mendi* for her boilers, another gang were busy scraping and painting the ship's side along the waterline.

On Boxing Day there was still a lump of a swell coming along at times, but coal had to be got somehow, so at 4 p.m. the *Wolf* steamed alongside the Spaniard and made fast. Numerous heavy rope fenders were hung between the two ships, but these had to be continually replaced. The *Wolf* lay with hardly a movement perceptible, but the collier did all the antics that she knew, and pounded the *Wolf* so heavil.y that at times it knocked you off your feet, unless you grabbed something or someone hurriedly. Work was immediately started coaling, working both ends of the ships, and continued without stoppage throughout the night and all the next day. But towards late afternoon things began to get serious for the *Wolf*. Her plates were all started just at the waterline in the bunkers, and water was coming in at the rate of eight tons per hour, so at 6 p.m. the *Wolf* cast off, and she was listed to port, so as to keep the damaged plates as much above water as possible.

The Spaniard's side in places was like a piece of corrugated iron. It was certainly a lively bout while it lasted. We all pitied those poor women on the *Igotz Mendi*" I managed to have about ten minutes' conversation with Major Flood and his wife whilst we lay alongside. Mrs. Flood had always been a very poor sailor, but the *Igotz Mendi* had quite cured her. She could now stand on deck like an old sailor, and bent to the roll in true nautical style.

Both ships now shut down steam again and went on with necessary overhauls to boilers and engines. Stages were slung over the sides of the *Wolf*, and she was painted all over outside. Engineers were also at work trying to stop the leaks.

"Mines" told us that if we cared to write a letter he would get it sent over to the *Igotz Mendi*, just in case anything happened to the *Wolf* before she reached home.

On the evening of the 30th December, at 6.45 p.m., both ships had got under weigh again, steaming about 5½ knots, as the *Wolf* still had at least one boiler under repairs. The course was set about north by east. The *Wolf* was kept with a list to port, as the damage to the plates on the starboard side had not yet been repaired. Nothing of note happened during the next few days, the ships jogged on in the same direction and the same 5½ knots speed.

The outbreak of scurvy was now increasing; over 20 of the prisoners were suffering from it, and every day was adding more to the list. The stock of medicine was now pretty well exhausted, although the medicine chest of every ship captured was always emptied and brought over to the *Wolf*. However, the main thing for the scurvy patients was fresh vegetables, and of these there was a scant stock.

At 10 a.m. on the 4th January a four-masted sailing ship was sighted, but as she was in ballast and had the Norwegian colours painted on her sides, the *Wolf* let her go without boarding her. However, about 1.30 p.m. he changed his mind, and turned round and went full speed after her. I expect he was afraid that she had noticed the seaplane on his deck, and might shortly fall in with a cruiser and report the *Wolf*.

The breeze had freshened up in the meantime, and the *Wolf* had a long chase. I think that if the breeze had held good the *Wolf* would never have caught her, but as usual luck favoured her, and at about 3.30 the wind fell away light, giving the *Wolf* a chance to get up to its prey. At 5 p.m. a prize crew was sent on board the sailing ship, which proved to be the *Storobrore*, bound to Monte Video in ballast from Beira. The crew of the Norwegian were brought on board just after dark, and work went on boating stores over until 11.30 p.m., when she was sunk in the usual way, by bombs.

That morning the *Wolf* had flown the red ensign of the British mercantile marine, but in the evening she flew her own naval ensign and pennant. The reason given for sinking this neutral was because she had been purchased from British owners since the outbreak of hostilities.

The position of the *Wolf* at this time was latitude 17 deg. 17 min. south and 26 deg. 27 min. west longitude. Our calculations were only about 15 miles out in the longitude. Our accurate knowledge of the *Wolf's* position was a source of wonder to the Germans, as they had taken all our instruments, books, and charts from us. But they could not hide the sun and the stars, and those were quite good enough for us to tell, within a few degrees, how the *Wolf* was heading. Also, Mr. McKenzie, chief officer of the *Wairuna*, had smuggled through a small chart of the world, and on this we pricked off our positions daily. This was the *Wolf's* last piece of maritime destruction, the *Storobrore* being the fourteenth and last ship captured by the now famous raider.

The captain of the Norwegian was berthed with the passengers amidships, and his crew in No. 3 hold with the Japanese. On the evening of the 6th January another attempt was made to get alongside the Spaniard for more bunkers. It was his last chance, as the prospects of being able to lay alongside each other in the North Atlantic at this time of the year were not at all promising. Hence he took the risk before crossing the line. The weather was not at all ideal for the undertaking. There was a heavy swell and rather a bumpy sea on. But it had to be now or never, and we turned in that night praying that the collier would bump in the whole side of our prison.

Coaling was started immediately, and the coal was dumped anywhere; so long as it was on board the *Wolf*, that was all they cared about. In the morning the starboard after gun was nearly buried in coal. The ships pounded and punched each other all night and up till 4 p.m. on the 11th. The old leaks were opened afresh, and numerous new ones started, but she now had sufficient coal to take her to Germany, and that was the main thing for them. As soon as the vessels cast off, stages were slung over the starboard side, and all outward traces of damage covered with paint. At 8.30 p.m. both ships proceeded to the north-north-east.

At 9 a.m. the following morning the *Wolf* stopped, presumably more trouble in the engine-room, but at 4 p.m. she went off full speed to the northwest, with the quite evident intention of running across the steamer tracks at right angles during the night. The *Wolfchen* was dismantled and put down below, and never flew again as long as we were on board.

On the 22nd January, the *Wolf*, again under the British red ensign, stopped a four-masted Danish ship in ballast, but allowed her to proceed. The Spaniard was again met on 23rd January, and communicated with. She then left us, going more to the eastward.

During the passage home from Cargados the engine-room staff had been busy, welding, bending and joining copper pipes, which had been looted from the various steamers captured. These were now being fitted throughout the prisoners' quarters, and connected with the deck steam pipes. This was to be our system of steam heating, and it proved a Godsend through the cold icy regions of the North. Steam pipes were also fitted under each torpedo tube, so as to have them ready for use, whatever the temperature might be.

We made our way slowly up the North Atlantic, keeping pretty well in mid-ocean all the way. Only four steamers were sighted between the Equator and Iceland. We met with north-westerly gales, hail and snow.

CHAPTER 19

On the Road Back

On 27th January, the *Kaiser's* birthday, was to have been celebrated with great ceremony, but the weather fortunately upset their plans. The gale, which started on the previous day, increased to hurricane force on his Germanic Majesty's birthday, with a very high cross sea running. This was the only time I had ever known the *Wolf* to roll, but she certainly made up for the lost time that day. Just as we were about to sit down to breakfast a heavy lurch sent everything crashing off the tables, and our much looked forward to breakfast was no more. Everything was tightly battened down, and this made the atmosphere anything but pleasant for us below.

Forward in the bunkers things were still more unpleasant. The heavy straining of the ship had opened up the damaged plates on the ship's side, and the cold Atlantic waters were doing their utmost to get into the bowels of the ship. At one time I believe it was coming in at the rate of 40 tons per hour, but I cannot vouch for the truth of this statement. Anyhow, judging by the faces of the Germans, things must have looked pretty serious for them for a time.

Commander Nerger says that during this gale he saw many strained and anxious faces among the prisoners. This is rather funny, as, firstly, he never saw the face of a single prisoner during the hurricane, and secondly, most of us were old sailing ship men, with far and a long way more experience of gales and hurricanes than ever Commander Nerger knew about.

We continued to keep the bad weather with us. As we drew further north, hail and thick, blinding snow accompanied the biting cold wind, and in spite of our steam pipes below it was bitterly cold and damp. The bare steel deck which we had to stand on kept our feet like blocks of ice. The scurvy patients had increased by this time to fifty, and a fresh hospital was screened off down in the 'tween decks. This hospital was in charge of Sergeant Webb, of the A.A.M.C., and no words can express the care and attention which he showed towards his numerous patients. He was assisted in his work by Corporal Grady, of the same corps, and they were both highly complimented by the German doctors on arrival at Kiel.

In about 60 deg. north and 30 deg. west on the 5th February the *Igotz Mendi* was again with us, but communication between the ships was confined to signalling. Various reports circulated round the *Wolf* after this last meeting with the Spaniard. Some of the Germans said that the *Igotz Mendi* had passed two British cruisers, and anticipating being held up, had got two bombs ready to blow the ship up with, and that the chief officer of the Spaniard had watched his chance and thrown the bombs overboard. Others said that it was a large transport full of American troops, that she had passed close to. Whether there was any truth in either rumour I am not in a position to say, but I notice that Nerger mentions in his book about two cruisers, so I guess it was all fairy tale. It was now evident, in spite of the fact that the Germans said the British blockade only existed on paper, that the *Wolf* was attempting to get through the Denmark Straits, between Iceland and Greenland.

On the morning of the 7th of February we were awakened by the noise of crunching ice along the ship's side. Our deck being just at the waterline, we could hear it very plainly. At 8 a.m., when we went on deck, a thick haze was hanging over the water, and nothing could be seen more than a quarter of a mile off, but that was quite sufficient for most of us; it was so bitterly cold that five minutes on deck was enough.

Within the range of a quarter of a mile there were a few patches of clear water, but for the most part it was nothing but loose ice, some of it from about 12 to 15 feet above the water. I am a "tropical bird," and have no use for ice, except to keep things cool in warm weather, so the beauty of it did not appeal to me in the least, and I made a hasty retreat below to a slightly warmer atmosphere, which, though much denser with tobacco smoke than on deck, was certainly more congenial to me.

The *Wolf* was steaming dead slow, zigzagging in and out among the ice, and continued on all that day and night. But early the following morning the attempt to penetrate the Straits had to be abandoned.

The previous evening the captain of the *Hitachi Maru* was missed.

The Germans searched everywhere, but no signs of him could be found. Next morning it was known that he had committed suicide by jumping overboard. A letter which he had given to his chief officer, to be opened if anything should happen to him, proved that he had intended to do so. Death must have been instantaneous, I should think, in that ice-cold water. On the 9th February we turned to the eastward along the south of Iceland, and the Germans were put on war watches. For the next few days we continued to the eastward. The weather was fine and clear, but not a sign of British patrol vessels was seen.

The 14th February, daylight showed up the coast of Norway, and the *Wolf* was steering straight for it. After being allowed on deck for one hour, we were ordered below, and this was our last time on deck for over three days. All the prisoners who had been housed amidships were now brought aft, some were lucky enough to get berthed in the two warrant-officers' rooms under the poop, but the others were brought down into our quarters, so that there was now not room to swing a mouse, let alone a cat, in.

The stewards who went along for our tea that night said that we were passing a lighthouse about a mile off. On giving a description of the light, the Norwegian captain said it was the Marstenen Light, so the *Wolf* was well within the three-mile limit. The weather continued fine all along the Norwegian coast, and throughout the rest of the cruise ideal weather prevailed. But that British cruiser which we all prayed so hard for never showed up.

At 1 p.m. on the 17th February we were allowed on deck for one hour. It was a beautiful day, with bright sunshine, but bitterly cold. We were cruising along the Danish coast, just about three miles off. At about 5.30 p.m. that evening the *Wolf* met the first of the German patrol vessels, and signalled her name. The patrol was doubtful of her, believing that the *Wolf* had been lost months before, but on finding that it really was the *Wolf* safely back again, great cheering took place. At 6.30 p.m. the *Wolf's* anchor rattled down on German bottom for the first time in fifteen months, and I guess all hands breathed a tremendous sigh of relief.

The *Wolf* had completed a marvellous cruise, having been 15 months on the high seas, and this would long remain in the minds of the German people.

CHAPTER 20

Back to Kiel

We were rather puzzled on the morning after our safe arrival to find all the officers and crew with scowling, discontented faces. We expected to see them all one huge smile. However, it was not long before our "Intelligence Department" found out what was wrong. Orders had been issued that no one was allowed to communicate with their relatives or friends, and no communication was allowed with the shore. This was pretty bad considering that they were all supposed to have been lost long before this.

The *Wolf* was anchored, as nearly as we could make out, somewhere just inside the Little Belt, and was a long way from land. The only vessel at hand was a cruiser, acting as guardship. Shortly after breakfast a submarine came along close past the *Wolf* and gave her "three cheers." Later on the guardship picked up her anchor and steamed round the *Wolf*, her crew cheering the returned heroes. Some fresh vegetables were procured from the guardship in exchange for tea and canned crab. The vegetables were given to the scurvy patients. All the rest of the prisoners were stripped and examined for signs of scurvy by the doctors.

On the morning of the 20th February, a torpedo boat from Kiel came alongside. She brought the naval *attaché* from Berlin, who had been in command of the raider *Meteor*, which was sunk in the North Sea by a British cruiser. He came down to our quarters, and on leaving made the remark that we would find things in Germany different to what wo had been told. This put us in rather a quandary, as we did not know whether things would be better or worse than we had anticipated.

Meantime, on deck a brisk trade was going on. The crew of the destroyer were eagerly exchanging cigarettes and tobacco with the pris-

PRISONERS ON BOARD THE *WOLF*.

THIS PICTURE WAS TAKEN WHEN THE SHIP LAY IN KIEL HARBOUR.

oners for soap, and the prisoners thought they made fine bargains until they attempted to smoke the so-called tobacco. The smell reminded one of a bushfire. On examination it was found to be made out of ordinary dry leaves from any tree except the tobacco plant. They had evidently harvested the leaves in the autumn, and manufactured them into a tobacco substitute.

On Sunday morning, the 24th of February, just a week after entering German waters, the *Wolf* picked up her anchor and proceeded towards Kiel Harbour. It was now quite evident that she had been waiting for the *Igotz Mendi* to come in, before she made the grand entry into port. However, rumour had it that the Spaniard was ashore somewhere, so the *Wolf* had to make her entry alone.

On nearing Kiel Harbour we were all sent below in order that we should not see the channels in through the mine fields. But as soon as we entered the harbour the sentries absolutely chased us up on deck. We were exhibit number one for that day.

There were fifteen beautiful battleships and battle cruisers besides numerous other fighting craft in Kiel that day, and as the *Wolf* steamed slowly up the line the crews cheered loudly, and the bands played on each ship as we passed.

At 3 p.m. the *Wolf* anchored in the middle of the stream, and a few hundred yards away lay the previous raider *Moewe*. All afternoon the *Wolf* was surrounded by all manner of craft, steam launches, motor boats, and rowing boats, in which were the naval and military officials, with their wives and families. We poor prisoners seemed to cause them quite a lot of amusement, especially the Japanese and niggers. Several of the German crew who were given liberty that evening came back the following morning very disgusted with the state of things ashore. They said that they had to come on board to get a decent meal, as there was very little to be had on shore.

Every man Jack on the *Wolf* was decorated with the Iron Cross. Captain Nerger was given the "*Poure le Merite*," all the officers the Iron Cross of the First Order, and the crew of the Second Order. We naturally asked if they did not have a Third Order for prisoners of war.

There was one kind of souvenir that I did not secure when in Germany, and that was the "Iron Cross." Many of these were offered to me for twenty *marks*, but I declined to do business at the price. Many of the stewards of the *Matunga* bought one or two, but I considered them to be dear even at five *marks*.

It was amusing, too, when these Iron Crosses were being handed

GREETING THE CREW OF S.M.S. WOLF, BERLIN, 1918

out to the crew of the *Wolf.* The men simply filed past an officer and the bauble was handed to them in the same way as a tot of rum. When the officers received theirs, however, there was a sort of celebration, and the admiral came aboard and handed the honour to Nerger and his officers.

During our stay on board the *Wolf* at Kiel numerous young submarine officers came down to our quarters. A great many of them were ex-merchant service men, and they were all very confident that the war would be finished in two months from then. They said nothing could stop the Germans from getting through to Paris now. One day there was a reception on board, and cinematograph pictures were taken of the afterdeck, with the band playing and the prisoners walking about. All the neutrals except the Finns were landed two days after our arrival at Kiel. The Huns said the Finns would be sent to Finland to fight for their country against Russia.

CHAPTER 21

All Prisoner's Ashore

On the 28th February we were informed that we would leave the *Wolf* at four o'clock the following morning for Karlsruhe Camp. This party was to include army officers, shipmasters, officers and engineers.

The morning of the first of March will long remain in our memories. It was blowing a blizzard, and the decks covered with snow, getting thicker every minute. We first had to carry all our baggage along the deck and put it on board the tender. We were then mustered and counted over the rail like a mob of cattle.

On landing from the tender we had to drag or carry all our trunks and luggage nearly a quarter of a mile through snow and slush to the railway. This meant making six or seven trips to and from the tender in the thick, blinding snow. The route was lined on both sides of the street by soldiers. At 5.30 a.m. we steamed out of Kiel station, wet and cold, but not by any means miserable, as we were all jolly glad to get ashore again, even if we were prisoners.

I was lucky enough to get into a second-class compartment, so had a fairly comfortable seat. There were six prisoners in each compartment with an armed soldier. We were not permitted out of the compartment during the whole journey, which occupied 40 hours. We were given a good hot stew at Altona about 11 a.m., and again that evening we had coffee and sandwiches at Gottingen. It had snowed unceasingly all day, and it was only occasionally that any heat was switched on in our compartment.

At 10 p.m. on the 2nd of March we arrived at Karlsruhe, and were marched under a strong guard to what appeared to be an hotel. Here we were put four in each room, and were quite comfortable, only for the fact that we were locked in and unable to see out of the windows, as they were all painted over on the outside.

This hotel was used as a fumigating base. All officers, before going into the prison camp, had to come here, have all their effects fumigated, and have a bath. This latter part was rather amusing, as we were all anticipating a nice bath in this hotel after our long train journey. But we were told that we could not have one until our turn came, and it was said in such a manner as to imply that a bath was a terrible ordeal to go through. For four days we were kept in that room, and then they took all our clothes away and gave us a sort of shirt combination to wear. We were then taken to the bathroom, fitted with four showers, hot and cold, so there we had the time of our lives, and did not in the least want to come out when ordered to do so. We were taken back into the room we had previously occupied, and found that they had not even changed the bedclothes, so had we been covered with vermin on arrival the fumigation and bath would have been wasted, for the vermin would still have waited for us in the bedding.

After six days in this palatial hotel we were marched to the camp. There we were thoroughly searched, person and baggage, all money taken away, and also anything that they considered might help us to escape. My scissors were confiscated, and when I protested the Hun officer said that I might cut the wire with them. A few days later I was in the canteen, and to my astonishment noticed that the scissors were there for sale. On inquiring the price, I was informed that I might have them for five *marks*. We were also charged eighteen *marks* for our food and baggage on the journey from Kiel.

The camp at Karlsruhe is situated almost in the centre of the town; in pre-war days I should think it had been a playground of some kind. It was surrounded in the first place by a high barbed wire fence, then a wooden fence about ten feet high surmounted by more barbed wire, and six feet inside the wooden fence there was yet another barbed wire fence. Inside were nine wooden huts, or barracks, as the Germans called them. One of these was used by the *kommandant* and various camp officials, one for a dining-room for the prisoners, and off this were two small rooms for reading and writing. Another barrack was for amusements. The remaining huts were living quarters, and were divided off into rooms, the largest accommodating eight prisoners. Each room had a stove in it, and there was an unlimited supply of coal at this camp. There was plenty of ground for exercise, a thing we appreciated very much after the confined space of the *Wolf*.

The food supplied by the Germans to officer prisoners of war was anything but plentiful, and badly cooked. It consisted of a jug of coffee

Officers' internment camp at Karlsruhe. It was here that the officer prisoners from the *Wolf* were first sent after arrival in Germany.

substitute for breakfast at 8 a.m., nothing to eat with it, and of course no sugar or milk in it. At noon dinner varied slightly, and consisted of a plate of vegetable soup, and a piece of rye bread. The variation was that twice a week, if you were lucky, you managed to find a small piece of meat in the soup. Tea at 6 p.m. was either the soup left over from dinner or a few potatoes in their jackets. Of course, we might have lived on this, but it certainly did not appease one's hunger. Had it not been for the generosity and kindness of the naval and military officers who were in receipt of parcels from home, we should have fared pretty badly.

We had two muster rolls per day, one at 9.45 a.m. and the other at 8.45 p.m. All lights were out at 9 p.m., but we could walk about till 11 p.m.

During our stay at Karlsruhe several alarms for air-raids were sounded, and immediately all traffic in the streets was stopped until later the "all clear" whistle was sounded. Unfortunately, nothing came over Karlsruhe. Our air squadrons were paying marked attention to Mannheim at that time. German flying machines were continually flying over our camp, doing all sorts of stunts. Some days after our arrival a few more prisoners from the *Wolf* arrived. Sixty of them had been lauded on arrival at Kiel, and taken to hospital suffering from scurvy, but a few weeks of fresh food had put them all right again.

CHAPTER 22

On to Heidelberg

On the 19th of March a batch of 30 officers was sent from Karlsruhe to Heidelberg, and I was one of them. We travelled to Heidelberg in a first-class compartment, and on arrival there marched out to the camp, which was situated about two miles from the station, and well outside the town limits. Here we were again thoroughly searched, and all our civilian clothes taken from us.

Heidelberg Camp had, besides the usual wooden barracks, two large stone buildings. The larger of the two was for prisoners' accommodation, and very comfortable quarters they were. The other contained on the ground floor a dining hall and kitchen, also the wet and dry canteens. The first floor had another kitchen, and a large billiard-room with two English and two French billiard tables, and numerous card tables. I had not the luck to get berthed in the main building, but was quite comfortable in the huts, being lucky to get into a small room with a very quiet, studious army officer. Here, again, the British officers were exceedingly good to us; food and tobacco were given to us liberally, and I made many good friends whilst in this *lager*, and was quite content to remain in this camp for the remainder of my captivity.

The evening after my arrival at Heidelberg the British officers gave a pantomime production of *Sinbad the Sailor*. It was without a doubt an excellent production. The whole thing, music included, had been written by officers in the camp. It went with a swing from start to finish, most of the airs being very catchy, and the "girls" were splendidly got up and very fetching, especially the three Bagdad beauties. This was one of many excellent plays I had the pleasure of seeing here. The French officers vied with the British, and the competition was very close.

OFFICERS' HUTS AT HEIDELBERG *LAGER*. ABOUT 700 OFFICERS OF VARIED NATIONALITIES WERE INTERNED HERE, AND IT WAS HERE THE BEST CONDITIONS WERE MET WITH.

There was a splendid orchestra composed of the officers. It consisted of nine violins, two 'cellos, cornet, trombone, piano and drum. Their rendering of some very difficult pieces was excellent, and would have taken the shine out of many London orchestras.

At Heidelberg the roll-call hours were 10.30 a.m. and 4.30 p.m. All prisoners had to be in their own rooms at 9.30 p.m., and lights out at 10 p.m. the guards made two rounds, one at 10 p.m. to see that everyone was in bed, and again at 5 a.m. to see that no one had escaped during the night.

The usual routine here was as follows: Rise at 7.30 a.m., and go over to the bathroom for a shower; then shave and dress; go to the cookhouse, and endeavour to get a vacant hole on the stove to cook breakfast on.

There were some amusing happenings in the cookhouse, and language at times was not fit for the drawing-room. A man would be diligently kneeling down toasting bread at the front of the stove, and someone's pot of either porridge, coffee or cocoa would suddenly boil over. The owner of the pot would hurriedly grab his pot, and generally manage to spill a good portion of the contents down the neck of the unfortunate toaster. There were generally twice as many men in the cookhouse as there were holes in the stoves, and a pot was no sooner lifted off than a dozen were trying to get the vacant place.

Numerous nationalities were represented; English, Scotch, Irish, Welsh, Australians, Canadians, French, Belgian, and a few Servians. To hear a Scot with a broad accent trying, in a mixture of broad Scotch and French, to make a French orderly understand what he wanted was indeed very funny.

After breakfast came the "*appell*," or roll-call. Then if you were lucky enough to have a court, you had a game of tennis, or a game of billiards: if neither of these were available, an hour's walk around the camp was the usual thing. Then lunch, which was usually composed partly of Boche food and partly of your own.

A smoke and a yarn brought it up to time to boil water for afternoon tea, provided you had any. After this you strolled over to the billiard-room to read the latest war news, which was posted on the board about this time.

It was then time again, if you were "Peggy" for the mess, to squeeze into the cookhouse and try to grab a hole on the stove to cook dinner on. After dinner a stroll, billiards, or bridge was the order until 9.30 p.m. We were allowed to go out for a walk on parole twice a week,

Heidelberg Offizier, Gefangenenlager. This picture shows the main building. In pre-war days it was a training camp for non-commissioned officers for the German Army.

forty officers being allowed out at a time. Some of the walks around Heidelberg were very pretty, but very hard going, as they always took us up on the hills. The view from one of the hills overlooking the old town of Heidelberg was really very fine, and well worth the tramp.

Here also Hun flying machines were always flitting about. One day a machine, which had been showing what he could do over the camp, came a cropper into a field adjoining the camp. This was greeted by loud cheers from the prisoners.

Commander Whitfield was senior officer of the camp while I was there. He had commanded the destroyer *Nomad* in the Jutland fight. The *Nomad* was sunk, and Whitfield was picked up by the Germans badly wounded in several places. He was a fine stamp of naval officer, a cheery word and a smile for everyone. He replenished my tobacco pouch on several occasions.

On the 20th April all merchant service men were notified to be ready to leave the camp at 4 p.m. We were going to Fuchberg. None of the officers had ever heard of it, and no one seemed to know exactly where it was. Anyhow we marched out of camp at 4.20 p.m., very sorry to leave such comfortable quarters.

We entrained at 5 p.m., and left for Fuchberg. As usual, we had an armed soldier in each compartment. These soldiers were men who had been wounded at the front, and who were not yet fit to return.

Everyone I met was disgusted with the war, and did not care which way it ended so long as it ended soon. The soldier in our compartment, who was a mere lad, said he was nineteen years of age, and had been on the Roumanian front, in Servia, the Italian front, and lastly on the Western front. The latter front was the one they all dreaded having to return to.

At 9.30 p.m. we arrived at Frankfurt, and were marched out of the station to a Red Cross hut, which had been erected in the street opposite the Carlton Hotel. Here we were served with a jolly good supper, Hamburg steak, potatoes and macaroni. The waiter in full evening dress attended to our wants, and spoke English fluently.

We were then marched back to the station, and left Frankfurt at 12.45 a.m. At 7.30 next morning we arrived at Cassel, and were taken into the station restaurant for breakfast. This consisted of coffee substitute, cheese substitute, meat paste and bread. Here we were served by three waitresses, who were not averse to a little flirtation with the British "*gefangeners*." We also topped off our breakfast with a cigar. Of course, we had to pay for all these meals ourselves. Although all money was taken from us when travelling from camp to camp, still the German officer in charge, who paid for everything, kept account of what we had, and it was deducted from our accounts at the new camp.

Some of the younger members were quite appreciative of the "glad-eye" of Gretchen, and loudly deplored their lack of the gift of tongues so that they could have declared their feelings. But, then, they could never have arranged an appointment. This puts me in mind of a little picture that was flashed on our astonished gaze when we were travelling back from the Uchter camp to Clausthal. The train was wheezing along slowly, and we were gazing disconsolately out of the windows, when lo! and behold—there, reclining under a hedge was an English Tommy, with each arm around the waist of two young German girls. He appeared so happy in his captivity on that wayside farm that we could not refrain from giving him a hearty cheer.

CHAPTER 23

On the Track Again

About 10 a.m. we arrived at Warburg, and here we were side-tracked until 3 p.m. During that time numerous Red Cross trains came in, chockful of wounded German soldiers, and many of them had their wounds very sparsely bandaged. They all had a very drawn and nervous look in their faces, and had evidently just been back from the front, being unwashed, unshaven, and, like most German soldiers that I have seen here, generally untidy.

Those wounded Germans were in a pitiable plight. Down and out hardly describes their appearance. We had expected that they would have shown some interest in us, but we received scarcely a glance. They were the personification of hopeless misery and blank despair.

After a lot of shunting we were finally attached to the tail end of a freight train with a carriage full of wounded Germans, and off we went on to a typical country line. Six p.m. brought us to Paderborn, where the Germans got off for the hospital. Here, again, we were side-tracked. After the officer had cursed everyone at the station, he went to the telephone, and finally we were converted into a prisoners' special, and buzzed off with an engine all to ourselves.

At Soest about 9.30 p.m. the officer marched us all into the station restaurant, much to the amusement of some and indignation of other good Germans, who, with their wives and families, were enjoying their evening beer. They were ordered out of one end of the room to make way for us prisoners.

This little scene was a striking demonstration of the power of the militaristic classes in Germany. When the diners were ordered out they went with great promptitude. A few there were that muttered sullen guttural curses at our unfortunate band, and glared malevolently at us, but the majority hurried forth with astonishing celerity. I

CLAUSTHAL OFFIIER GEFANGENENLAGER. IT WAS SITUATED 3000 FEET ABOVE SEA-LEVEL, ON TOP OF THE HARTZ MOUNTAINS. THE FAMOUS HAUPTMANN NIEMEYER WAS IN COMMAND HERE. NIEMEYER, IT WILL BE REMEMBERED, EARNED A REPUTATION FOR HIS BULLYING AND OVERBEARING TREATMENT.

have often wondered whether the grumblers had paid for their meal and had been moved off before they finished it.

Here we had supper, having had nothing since breakfast. It consisted of potato salad, meat paste, sandwiches, coffee and beer. It was found that we had come the wrong way, and would have to go back a considerable distance before we could get on the track for Minden. However, after travelling all night again we finally reached Minden at 7 a.m. Here we got out and marched up a couple of streets to where a steam tram was waiting. We boarded this, and buzzed away once again into rural Germany. At 8.30 a.m. we detrained at Uchter, and found our heavy luggage, which had not left Heidelberg until long after we did, but had evidently gone the right way. After making a bargain with a carter to bring our luggage out to camp for three marks a head, we set off on the march to our new abode. It was a good four miles' walk, and a great disappointment at the end of it.

The camp was situated right in the centre of a black, desolate moor, full of bogs, and covered for the most part with heather. It had the most dreary outlook I have ever seen, and probably seemed more so to us, coming from the beautiful country around Heidelberg. It was composed of about 10 wooden huts, each one fenced off from the other by wire-netting and barbed wire, and the whole camp was surrounded by a 12ft. fence of the same materials, not even a wooden fence to shut out the miserable view.

Here we were handed over to the care of non-commissioned officers, there being neither *kommandant* nor officers in the camp. The only other prisoners were a few British and French Tommies. We found out that this had been a "*straf*" camp for Tommies, but was about to be made into an officers' camp. This news was not at all comforting. We were informed that if we attempted to approach any of the wire fences we would be promptly shot.

There were only three or four Tommies here, and we were in a different compound to them. Once or twice we tried to get into conversation with them through the wires to learn something of their experiences, but the sentries were very wary, and chased us off whenever we approached the barriers. Thus we learned nothing of them or the French and Russians cooped up with them.

After being counted and found to correspond to bills of lading, we were taken into one of the huts, and here the head N.C.O., on looking at the list bearing our names, nationalities, etc., saw Australians on the list, and at once ordered all Australians to step forward. He was greatly surprised when my officers and self moved out, as he had quite made up his mind that the Japanese officers were the Australians, and it took some few minutes to impress into him that the Australians were not a coloured race.

"What!" he exclaimed in guttural tones, "these Australians? There must be something wrong here. All the Australians are black." Probably he was from some far-off province, for I found later that many Germans knew as much of our country as we do ourselves. But anyhow his surprise was genuine.

The hut had no division in it, just a bare shed with wooden bunks, roughly built up in the centre, all together, one on top of the other. You had to crawl in at the end of your bunk between two other people. The beds and pillows were thin bagging filled with heather, roots and all, and made anything but a comfortable mattress.

The food at this camp was slow starvation, as our food parcels had not yet succeeded in catching up to us. Owing to shifting round so much, we were entirely dependent on the Hun catering. Coffee substitute for breakfast, nothing to eat with it, a dirty-looking mess that they called soup for dinner, and a similar mess for tea, accompanied by a loaf of rye bread, one loaf between every eight men. We existed on this menu for eight days. There were no bathrooms, the only water we had to drink was from a pump, situated alongside the latrines, the latter being in a filthy state, and most unsanitary. The water had a peculiar taste, and turned everything brown even the short spell we had there it turned most of our teeth brown; what it did to our "Little Marys" I cannot imagine. We all thanked heaven that we had been inoculated against typhoid whilst at Heidelberg, for the stench in this place was vile.

I still have unpleasant memories of that synthetic tea that the Germans gave us. I do not think that there is anything else in the world that tastes like it, for it was the vilest decoction I have ever come across. I strongly suspect to this day that it was made of desiccated boot leather, flavoured with street sweepings. The coffee also was a mystery mixture, of which the secret is known only to German science, and they are welcome to retain it. I must say that it was not so bad as the tea, for at a pinch we could drink it. Of the substitute cheese I prefer to remain silent. Men with more forceful and extensive vocabularies than I have described and anathematised it millions of times.

On the following evening two German officers arrived, and when they saw our quarters they shook their heads. We asked when the *kom-*

mandant was coming, as we wished to protest against the conditions of the camp. They told us to write to the *kommandant*. This we did, and a few days later the *kommandant* put in his first appearance, and after barking at several of the prisoners because they had no caps to wear, he informed us that the water from the pump was quite good, but not to drink too much of it. If it was good, why was all the water used by the German officials carted up to them from the village of Uchter?

CHAPTER 24

"Now for Clausthal Lager"

On the afternoon of 29th April, we were told to pack up and be ready to walk to the station at 7 a.m. the following morning, as we were being shifted to Clausthal Lager. We were quite bucked up on hearing this, even though we knew that Clausthal was under the same notorious 10th Division as Uchetmoor, still it could not be much worse, and on the other hand it might be a good deal better.

We had a wet tramp to the station and once more boarded the train. During all our travelling through Germany none of the civil population ever showed the slightest sign of enmity towards us. Work girls at the stations would smile at us and give us a friendly wave of the hands.

The thing that we noticed most all over the country was the scarcity of men. The railway porters were all women and boys, the stokers on the engines were girls, also the guards on the freight trains, and on some of the passenger trains. The latter looked quite smart dressed in knickers and tunic, and always had a smile for the *gefangeners*.

After a cold journey, during which we managed to procure a hot meal (vegetable stew) at Hanover station, we reached the foot of the Hartz Mountains, and were side-tracked there for three hours. Our progress up the mountains was extremely slow, as the gradients at times were fairly steep. The locomotive also was badly in want of repairs; when in motion it was hidden in a cloud of steam, which seemed to escape from every conceivable portion of its anatomy. At 10 p.m. we arrived at Clausthal station and detrained. Then started a most unpleasant tramp to the camp. It was blowing hard and sleeting harder, as we trudged through the mud and slush for forty minutes to the camp, and we anticipated going to bed wet and hungry.

On arrival at the camp, however, we were taken right into the dining hall, where an excellent meal was served, including wine. This was given us by the prisoners already in camp, and although they were not permitted to welcome us in person, they had certainly done so by the spread set before us. During the meal, which, by the way, was our first civilised feed since leaving Heidelberg, we were taken into the music-room in batches of six and thoroughly searched.

Having replenished bunkers to our satisfaction, we were taken over the huts, and were soon fast asleep. The main building was, in pre-war time, known as the Peacock Kurhans and Hotel, and had a most beautiful situation. It was 3000 feet above sea level, and on one side were two lakes, about one hundred yards outside the wire fence. These lakes were backed by a thick pine forest, and made a very pretty picture.

The sight which greeted our eye on turning out next morning was anything but pleasant. May Day, and everything was under a six-inch coating of snow. Some said it was beautiful, but it did not appeal to me, as I detest snow and cold generally. During the morning we made the acquaintance of our fellow-prisoners; two hundred in this camp, all British, and a healthy looking lot, up to all sorts of devilment. They heaped tobacco on us, a luxury we had not enjoyed for some days, and wanted to hear all about the *Wolf*.

The *kommandant* here was one of the famous "Niemeyer Twins," his brother being in charge of the Holzminden camp, which like Clausthal was under the control of the 10th Army Corps, the head of which, Von Hanish, was noted for the brutal indignities he forced on the Britishers under his charge.

Hauptmann Niemeyer, better known as "Old Harry," was a tyrant of the worst kind. Nothing was too petty for him to use as an excuse to vent his spleen on us. To look at him was generally quite sufficient to earn you three days in the cells, and it was quite a common thing to see from eight to ten officers at a time being marched off to the "jug." Almost everything one did was, according to "Old Harry," "Against the German war law, you know." This expression became quite a stock phrase in the camp.

Niemeyer was a man of peculiar temperment, but he was probably a typical Hun. He had been a commercial traveller in the United States, and could speak English well, but he was overbearing and unreasonable. At one time, as a great concession, he permitted a number of us to buy foils and boxing gloves for purposes of exercise, he receiving his usual commission on the sales. Then he suddenly seized these articles and removed them from the camp, alleging that the foils were weapons of offence, and that the boxing gloves could be used to enable us to easily scale the barbed wire fences. One habit of his was to stop in front of a prisoner and roar out at him: "Don't you do it."

The prisoner would mildly inquire: "Do what?"

"Escape!" he would bawl. "You were going to try; the sentries have orders to shoot you, so don't do it!"

This was the first camp I had been in where dogs were used. Here every night, at least four of the sentries had a vicious looking brute of a dog attached to the belt by a short lead. No prisoner from Clausthal ever managed to reach the Dutch frontier. The escapes were numerous, but all failed. Some would be out for twelve days, only to be brought back and do a spell in "jug" for their trouble. Tunnelling was tried on two occasions. The first tunnel was started from under one of the huts, and after months of weary labour it was completed. Everything was ready for a general escape, but an Irish orderly gave the show away to "Old Harry," with the result that thirty officers were placed under arrest and tried. One of the prisoners implicated was put in the cells for seven months, three months of which were spent in a cell alongside the pig-sty, only a thin wooden partition between the two.

The second tunnel was started from under the music room, in the main building, and the main foundations of the building had to be cut through in different places. Another three weeks' work would have completed it, but luck was out. "Old Harry's" brother rang up one morning from Holzminden Camp, telling him that 29 British officers had escaped from there the previous night by a tunnel. This, of course, roused "Old Harry's" suspicions, and he immediately had a search made, and found the tunnel. Numerous articles of wearing apparel were found in the tunnel, and these were taken and locked up by the Germans, as evidence against the owners. However, during that night, some smart work on the part of the tunnelling committee retrieved all the evidence. So the Huns are still at a loss to find the diligent burrowers.

One of the most amusing escapes from this camp occurred shortly before my arrival. Two prisoners rigged themselves up to represent "Old Harry" and one of his *Lager* officers. Where they got the clothes from is still a mystery, but I believe their make-up was splendid. One evening, just at dusk, they walked boldly up to the gate and the sentry let them out without question. Sometime later "Harry" himself came along, and the sentry was a bit puzzled and told him. that he had just let him out, or someone very much like him. "Harry" smiled and said,

"Oh, that will be my brother from Holzminden," and off he went to his house, expecting to see his brother there. However, as no brother was found, the *lager officer* was sent for. He also had seen no signs of the brother from Holzminden, so then the hue and cry was raised.

Another good attempt was made one very wet afternoon. Most days were wet at Clausthal. However, this particular day was worse than most; also it was blowing strong. The escapee, a young flying officer, watched his chance, and when the sentry turned his back to the blast, he skipped across the plot, crawled through the barbed wire into the neutral zone, and clambered up and over the twelve-foot high fence, topped with barbed wire, and was gone before the sentry had turned round.

HAUPTMANN NIEMEYER.

CHAPTER 25

"Old Harry" "Strafes" the Camp

On the morning of June 22, on parading for roll call, we were surprised to find the whole of the camp guard, with their rifles, lined up on the *Appel* ground. "Old Harry" came along, and mounting the steps, informed us that the camp was to be "*strafed*," as a reprisal against some camp in England. We were not allowed to play any games, no music or concerts, no walks, and, lastly, we were to have four roll-calls a day, instead of the usual two. He also told us that we had permission to write one extra letter that month, to tell the people in England that we were being "*strafed*." We unanimously agreed not to send a single line about the "*strafe*," and this worried "Old Harry."

Every day he would ask someone why we did not write to England and tell them. The "*strafe*" lasted a month, and during that time we never had a dry day; it rained and blew continually. Spanish Grippe paid a visit to the camp at this time, and nearly half the prisoners were down with it. This suited the Huns nicely, and gave them a good excuse for keeping us standing on *appel*, while they sent the guard, one at a time, round to each room to see if the sick men were in their respective rooms.

At this time, we of the mercantile marine were ordered to give up all our clothes to the Huns. We were only allowed to retain one uniform suit. "Old Harry" accused us of supplying civilian clothes to the military officers for escape purposes. He also said, much to our amusement, that he had found a ship's compass on one of the escapees. A ship's compass would be such a handy thing to carry round, especially when it came to climbing barbed wire fences. He evidently thought it was a sort of first cousin to a pocket compass. All our civilian clothes had been taken from us at Heidelberg camp, and we had not seen them since, so it was impossible for us to have anything suitable for escape purposes.

He also ordered that all new boots arriving in parcels were to have the soles pulled off in order to see that they contained no maps or compasses. Tennis racquets were either split right down the handle or had holes bored through them. All our food was cut and hacked to pieces. If you drew a tin of sausages from the tin room, each sausage would be cut into at least four pieces.

One of "Harry's" worst cases was his treatment of a young R.N.A.S. officer. This officer was caught while attempting to escape, and was taken before "Harry," who ordered him to be stripped. This was carried out by the Hun guard in no gentle fashion, and he was then ordered to kneel before "Harry." Of course he refused, and the guards were ordered to force him to his knees. However, at this point, his fellow escapee, a Cameronian Highlander, took a part in the game, and "Harry" backed down.

There was a system of paper money at the various prison camps, and notes were issued to us in exchange for our own good coin. Each camp had distinct and separate notes of various denominations that could only be used to purchase goods within the confines of the barbed-wire. The crew of the *Matunga* and the other captured vessels fared worse than we did in their own camp. They changed their English money for the German paper currency, a shilling for a *mark*, and when they were at work in the country, and were earning three and a half *marks* per day for navvying on the railway, they had no opportunity to spend it. One of my boys told me that the cigarettes on sale were made of dried grass, an egg cost a *mark* and a half, and a wild hare six *marks*. I understand that these men had a better time than most of the other prisoners through being in the country. The Japanese were not of these labouring parties, but were sent to work in factories at Hamburg.

The sentries at Clausthal Camp were always fully armed, and some moved about among the prisoners, as well as others being stationed outside. The N.C.Os. were a source of the greatest annoyance to us, however, for they were continually poking their noses into our business, and we never knew the moment one of them would suddenly enter our huts.

One day the interpreter came to me and asked for my diary as he had been ordered to censor it. I don't know who had told him about my diary, but I knew that if I refused to give it up, they would search my room and find it, so I handed it over. Next morning on

Appel "Old Harry" called me out and mustered all the guard around me, and told them I had called them Huns. I was then taken into the *kommandatur.* where "Harry" and his satellite, the long *lager* officer, shouted and yelled at me in German for calling them Huns, alluding to me as "*Swinehund.*" This was too much for me, so I used some rather unparliamentary language, and was marched down to the cells under an armed guard. I got three days for "undue behaviour to the *kommandant.*" A few days after my release I was sent back to the cells for eight days for calling the Germans Huns. However, I managed to get my paints and sketch book smuggled down to me, so passed the time away nicely.

About four days after my second release, the *lager* officer stopped me and informed me that I must wear blue pants. I had been wearing a pair of grey flannel pants, with the regulation stripe, for at least a month, having bought them from an army officer, for playing tennis in. And now I must wear them no more. Next morning, I donned my blue pants for *Appel.* After *Appel* I was ordered to my room, where I found a *lager* officer, interpreter, and two sentries. They had ordered the other occupants out of the room. I was told to strip, and they searched all my belongings, even hauling my bed to pieces. As nothing was found to incriminate me, they asked for the grey pants and took them away. Next morning, I was sent to the cells for three days for being the proud possessor of two pairs of pants.

In regard to my diary, I was always in fear and trepidation that I would be detected writing it up. I employed many devices to outwit the inquisitiveness of the Germans, and finally hit upon an original and quite satisfactory scheme. I had several rolls of toilet paper, and on this I scribbled my notes, always carefully re-rolling the parcel when I had finished. When I was searched so thoroughly in my hut on the occasion previously referred to, I was in dread lest my plan should be detected. Several times did the searchers handle the rolls, but they never suspected anything, and putting them down departed in disappointment. All the same it was an anxious moment for me, as had it been discovered Niemeyer would certainly have given me six months.

But I could not keep my notes for the whole of the period of my internment, and I cast about to find some means to smuggle them to England. The first opportunity presented itself when a batch of officers were being sent to Holland to be exchanged. To one I entrusted the first instalment of my precious manuscript, and it reached London safely. At a later date I repeated the same practice and gave a second

The first three German notes issued during the war. The top note for 50 *pfg.* was before the war valued at 5*d.* in English money. The one showing 5 *pfg.* would represent about one-half penny in English money. These were solely for prisoners use, and were of no value outside the camp.

The note at the bottom is for one *mark*, equal to about ten pence in English money (before the war). Prisoners who desired to exchange English money had to pay as high as one and six for this note, but made no difference in its purchase power.

instalment, and some very valuable photographs to a young Victorian who was in the exchange party. Unfortunately for both of us, he and his friends had just reached Aachen when the arrangements for exchanging prisoners were suddenly declared off. Only three men of that lot managed to get through, but of my friend or my papers and photographs I have never heard since. Whether he is alive I am unable to say, for my inquiries have not discovered any trace of him. This loss meant that I had to rewrite much from memory on my return.

CHAPTER 26

Camp Amusements

A few days later news came into the camp that a representative of the Netherlands Embassy was on his way to Clausthal. We had been waiting for him for months, having written numerous letters requesting his presence here. The day before he arrived two prisoners were sent off in haste to Holland. One was a young naval doctor, captured in the Jutland fight, who had been kept a prisoner for over two years. The other was the *padre*.

After investigating thoroughly all the complaints made to him, the Dutch representative said that Clausthal was undoubtedly the worst officers' camp in Germany. After his departure "Old Harry" was a different man. From then onwards no one was sent to the cells unless he attempted to escape. This was a change, as the record for the previous month had been fifty-five cases of officers sent to the "jug."

To pass away the time and make life behind barbed wire bearable, the prisoners had to create their own forms of amusements and invent their own forms of exercise. Permission for all kinds of games had to be obtained from the *kommandant*, and as we had to buy all materials and implements for sale from the Huns, and incidentally pay exceedingly stiff prices, "Old Harry" seldom withheld his sanction. He saw to it that he received a fairly good commission from those privileged to supply our wants. We had two excellent tennis-courts, made by ourselves, and members of the Tennis Club could always manage to get a court at least once a week. But as the same four players usually kept together, that meant four courts a week, of one hour's play each. The Tennis Club fee was 30 *marks* a season, and for this sum balls were supplied. The players who had the first court for the day were expected to roll and mark the courts.

A nice miniature golf links was laid out at Clausthal under the supervision of that well-known crack player, Captain C. K. Hutchison. The longest hole was only about 50 yards; the greens small, with plenty of bunkers to try one's temper. But in spite of this I think that golf was our principal form of outdoor exercise, and many keenly contested competitions, both singles and foursomes, were fought out, and betting at times ran high. Golf was also the bane of the Hun sentries' life, for the balls were continually being knocked into the "neutral zone," where no prisoners were permitted to go. The sentries, who lived in dread of "Old Harry's" wrath, were afraid to kick the balls back to us, in case he might see them. On the other hand, they did not like to lose the chance of perhaps a tin of dripping or jam, which might be given them from the prisoners for returning the balls. In the end, however, their "Little Marys" generally prevailed over their fear of Kommandant Niemeyer, and the rubber spheres came back to us.

We had an Amusement Committee, which, for the small sum of 3 *marks* per head per month, gave us an excellent return for our money.

Firstly, we had a full brass band of forty instruments, and although most of the prisoners had never played an instrument in their lives before, after a few months, during which we non-musical prisoners had to suffer fearful and awful agonies from their noises in the music room, they blossomed forth into a really fine band, and gave us some excellent concerts. Besides the brass band, we had an orchestra of over twenty instruments, which would put many London orchestras in the shade. No piece was too difficult for them to tackle, and the results were always extremely satisfactory.

To our Dramatic Society too much praise could not be given. The acting was absolutely "top hole," and no trouble was spared to make each play a huge success.

The production of F. W. Sydney's *The Brixton Burglary* was excellently staged and acted, and if reproduced by the same company in London would, I am sure, attract a crowded house. Our famous *troupe*, "The Chierrots," contained first-class talent, ranging from the classical baritone to the giddy young flapper, and two choice comedians in Lieut. Martin and Hills. The first-named was the funniest comedian I have seen on the stage for some years. Lieut. J. E. Day, who unearthed the "Chierrots," deserves great praise for his selection.

The programmes for these entertainments had to be submitted to the *kommandant* for censor, and when approved by "His Mightiness" were, with his permission, sent to the nearest town to be printed. At each entertainment a German officer and an interpreter had to be present. But in spite of these precautions many hits were made at "Old Harry," and generally appreciated by the Hun officers, for most of them hated him almost as much as we did. The costumes for the different plays had to be hired from outside, but all the scenery was made and painted by the prisoners. The advertisement drop curtain was a thing of beauty and a joy for ever.

Some of the programmes of our entertainments I am cherishing as souvenirs, and those of the pantomime, *Sinbad the Sailor*, and the drama, *Captain Bon-bon*, recall many happy recollections. At Heidelberg our opportunities for this sort of thing were greater, but even at Clausthal the performances were cheerful. One programme of a concert arranged by the "Chierrots" on October 9th, 1918, was as follows on the next page:—

THE CHIERROTS.

PRODUCED BY JULIUS E. DAY

(WHERE FROM???).

CLAUSTHAL, OCTOBER 9th, 1918.

N.B.—The Troupe can be booked by the minute, hour, day, week, month, year, or century—or even till the end of the war.

All applications must be addressed to

A. A. DIDD, Chierrot Manager.

Piano by "Instalments." Tunnelweg Zimmer, Neutral Zone.

PART I.

1. "The Opening Chorus" seven-thirty o'clock, so
   We start off with Bullock's best musical oxo.

2. G. S. Deane sings a song about "Two Eyes of Grey"; His favourite motto's "Itch Deane," so they say.

3. A duet is sung, "First and Last Love's" the name, By Pierrots of Billiards and Almanack fame.

4. The next is a song by a bounding young binger, Who's "Going to Grow a Moustache"—'twill be ginger!

5. A quartette by Blackall, Dodd. Roberts and Ely, May please you or not, but I think it will, really.

6. Here Martin explains why he's looking so leno; With no "Apple Dumplings" he can't have a beano.

7. Dodd sings of a "Watchmann" who's up bright and early, He always goes down 'cos his hair is curly.

8. A parody rendered by Blackie, nee Snowy, You'll never believe me, but, well, it is Goey.

9. Both Bullock and Dood have a job to be nowski, They thump side by side "Spanish Dances" moskowski.

10. Here Cupid appears with his arrows. Ha! Ha! Just watch his get-off with "The Girl at the Bar."

   10 Minutes Interval.

   Carriages: 9.30 p.m.
   Escapes: 9.45 p.m.
   Appels: 12 to 1 a.m.

During the interval, ices will be served in the barracks. Other refreshment can be had second turning on the left up the corridor.

PART II.

1. Number one of part two is a skit, "The Translator"; It's written by Clarke, and is quite a first-rater.

2. The troupe tries to dance (you will get some fun from it),
   And sings slopps words about "My Fairy Comet."

3. F. E. Hills (i.e., Ginger, as everyone knows), Though there aren't any girls, tells us "How to Propose."

4. Tommy Dodd sings a song that is always expected, You'll find it on every programme—"Selected."

5. Blackie sings again, "What a Big Girl now I'm Getting" (Is Blackie a girl or a boy? What's the betting?).

6. Here Martin, no, Mills—"Beg yer Pardon"—that's wrong, I mean Martin and Hills, raise their voices in song.

7. "Tom o' Devon," by G. S. Deane, rendered with verve is.
   (G. S., we presume, stands for General Service.)

8. Now Martin disports in "The Silvery Sea." The water's so bracing, he hops like a flea.

9. Ely sings us a song of "A Fat L'il Feller," Whose parents are coloured—one black and one yeller.

10. The programme concludes in appropriate style,
    With a trip by the troupe in "Some Automobile."

OUR ADVERTISEMENT PAGE.

CHAPTER 27

How the End Came

The Germans by this time saw that their game was up. Their armies were everywhere being driven back, and they had no more men to send to the front. "Old Harry" knew that his day of reckoning was drawing near, and instead of sticking to his gams like a man, turned round and absolutely crawled to us. Finally, a few days after the Armistice was signed, he was seen, early one morning, driving to the station in the parcel cart, in mufti. This was the last we ever saw or heard of him.

About a week after the Armistice we were permitted to leave the camp from 10 a.m. to 4.30 p.m. on parole. We were not permitted to enter any of the villages in the neighbourhood, but that did not worry us, as a hard frost had set in, and we enjoyed some excellent skating on the numerous lakes which are to be found all over the top of the Hartz Mountains.

On the 9th December we received the good news that we would leave the camp on the 11th for home, *via* Warnemunde and Copenhagen. We entrained at Clausthal station at 4 p.m. on the 11th December and reached Warnemunde on the 12th at 3 p.m. I embarked on the small Danish steamer *Cimbria*, but it was too late to make a start that night, as there were several mine fields to be negotiated.

A few days before a British light cruiser had been blown up on the mines, also a Russian transport with 800 Russian prisoners had shared a similar fate.

On board the *Cimbria* everything possible was done to make us comfortable. There were four charming Danish nurses to look after any wounded prisoners. They all spoke English fluently, and we monopolised every moment of their spare time, as we had not spoken to a woman for many weary months. We arrived at Copenhagen safely at 3 p.m. on the 13th December, and disembarked with many regrets from the little *Cimbria*.

I have never experienced such hospitality as shown us by the Danish people. Every one of them seemed so pleased to see us, and to do everything they possibly could to make our stay in their capital as pleasant as possible, and I am afraid most of the young officers lost their hearts to the beautiful Danish girls, whose complexions are absolutely matchless.

I would like to say a few words in praise of Miss M. E. Chumley, head of the Australian Red Cross organisation in London. This lady, who is a resident of Melbourne, performed wonderful work for the Australian prisoners of war, and if anyone merits a decoration for distinguished and noble services it is Miss Chumley. I can never forget her kindness when we were immured at Clausthal. We frequently wrote to the Red Cross for various articles, and no trouble ever deterred her from obtaining what we desired. Our least request was faithfully attended to, and the assistance we received through this good lady's offices made life endurable to us.

On my return to London I called upon Miss Chumley to personally thank her for her great kindness. I found her absolutely run down in health and worn out by her untiring labours, but refusing resolutely to take the rest of which she was so obviously in need. While I was at her office a number of Australian soldiers came in. She met them personally. "Numbers, please, and full names. Yes, here's a letter for you, and you, and you. Now, boys, where are you going for Xmas? What? Nowhere! Now just wait a moment," and she went to the telephone. Various folk having house parties were rung up, and in five minutes the happy soldiers were sent to different English homes to spend a merry Christmas. Miss Chumley appeared to prefer doing things herself than to entrust them to her assistants.

If we did not receive all the parcels sent to us it was not Miss Chumley's fault. As a matter of fact, when we were at Clausthal the percentage of parcels lost up to the time of the armistice was about forty-five, and after that about eighty-five. There is no doubt that "Old Harry" received his share, but the bulk went to an N.C.O. named Nella, who was a sort of quartermaster. This Nella also conducted a general store in the neighbouring village, and when the parcel cart came from the station each day, it halted outside this establishment, and half its contents were generally unloaded. In fact, after the armistice was signed, and we could move about, we discovered that

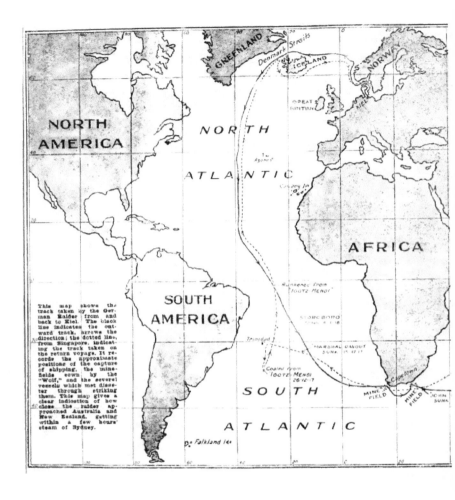

This map shows the track taken by the German Raider from and back to Kiel. The black line indicates the outward track, arrows the direction; the dotted line, from Singapore, indicating the track taken on the return voyage. It records the approximate positions of the capture of shipping, the mine-fields sown by the "Wolf," and the several vessels which met disaster through striking them. This map gives a clear indication of how close the raider approached Australia and New Zealand, getting within a few hours' steam of Sydney.

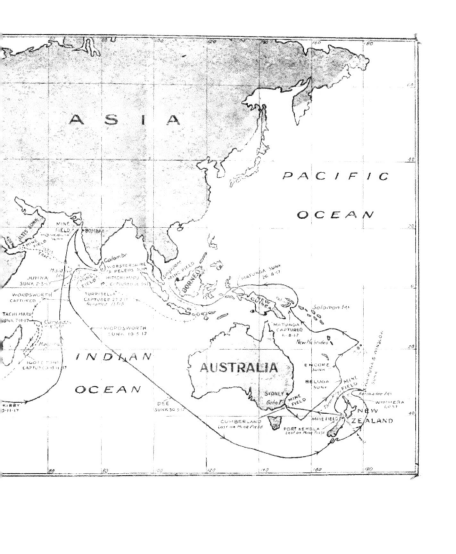

in numerous villages in the neighbourhood proprietors of shops had been supplied with Australian butter, jam, tinned meat, and clothing by Nella's central store. He must have made a substantial fortune out of the parcels looted in this fashion.

On December 16th I embarked on H.M.T. *Plassey*, and sailed for Leith, escorted by H.M.S. *Centaur*. Crossing the North Sea, we passed numerous floating mines, several of which the *Centaur* exploded by gun-fire.

We arrived at Leith on the afternoon of the 19th, and were greeted with the skirl of the bagpipes and school children singing songs and waving flags.

I arrived in London on the morning of the 20th, and was lucky in procuring a berth on H.M.A.T. *Barambah*, sailing for Australia on Christmas Eve. On boarding the *Barambah*, I found that Germany was still dogging me, for the vessel proved to be the late German-Australian liner *Hobart* So I returned as I was taken away—on a vessel "Made in Germany."

A Captive on a German Raider

Contents

Chapter 1

The S. S. *Hitachi Maru*, 6,916 tons, of the Nippon Yushen Kaisha (Japan Mail Steamship Co.) left Colombo on September twenty-fourth, 1917, her entire ship's company being Japanese. Once outside the breakwater the rough weather made itself felt, the ship rolled a good deal and the storms of wind and heavy rain continued more or less all day. The next day the weather had moderated, and on the succeeding day, Wednesday the twenty-sixth, fine and bright weather prevailed, but the storm had left behind a long rolling swell.

My wife and I had joined the ship at Singapore on the fifteenth, having left Bangkok, the capital of Siam, a week earlier. Passengers who had embarked at Colombo were beginning to recover from their seasickness, and had begun to indulge in deck games, and there seemed every prospect of a pleasant and undisturbed voyage to Delagoa Bay, where we were due on October seventh.

The chart at noon on the twenty-sixth marked five hundred and eight miles from Colombo, two thousand, nine hundred and twelve to Delagoa Bay, and one hundred and ninety to the Equator; only position, not the course, being marked after the ship left Colombo. Most of the passengers had, as usual, either dozed on the deck or in their cabins after *tiffin*, my wife and I being in deck chairs on the port side. When I woke up at one forty-five I saw far off on the horizon on the port bow, smoke from a steamer. I was the only person awake on the deck at the time, and I believe no other passenger had seen the smoke.

It was so far away that it was impossible to tell whether we were meeting or overtaking the ship. Immediately thoughts of a raider sprang to my mind, though I did not know one was out. It is generally understood that instructions to captains in these times are to suspect every vessel seen at sea, and to run away from all signs of smoke. The officer on the bridge with his glass must have seen the smoke long before I did, so my suspicions of a raider were gradually disarmed as we did not alter our course a single point, but proceeded to meet the stranger whose course towards us formed a diagonal one with ours. If nothing had happened she would have crossed our track slightly astern of us.

But something did happen. More passengers were now awake, discussing the nationality of the ship bearing down on us. Still no alteration was made in our course, and we and she had made no sign of recognition. Surely, everything was all right, and there was nothing to fear. Even the Japanese commander of the gun crew betrayed no anxiety in the matter, but stood with the passengers on the deck watching the oncoming stranger. Five bells had just gone when the vessel, then about seven hundred yards away from us, took a sudden turn to port and ran up signals and the German Imperial Navy flag.

There was no longer any doubt—the worst had happened. We had walked blindly into the open arms of the enemy. The signals were to tell us to stop. We did not stop. The raider fired two shots across our bows. They fell into the sea quite close to where most of the passengers were standing. Still we did not stop. It was wicked to ignore these orders and warnings. Most of the passengers went to their cabins for lifebelts and life-saving waistcoats, and at once returned to the deck watching the raider. As we were still steaming and had not obeyed the order to stop, the raider opened fire on us, firing a broadside.

While the firing was going on, a seaplane appeared above the raider; some assert that she dropped bombs in front of us, but personally I did not see this.

The greatest alarm now prevailed on our ship. My wife and I returned to our cabin to fetch an extra pair of spectacles, our passports and my pocketbook, and at the same time picked up her jewel case. The alleyway between the companion-way and our cabin was by this time strewn with splinters of wood, glass and wreckage; pieces of shell had been embedded in the panelling, and a large hole had been made in the funnel.

We returned once more to the port deck where most of the first class passengers had assembled waiting for orders—which never came. No instructions came from the captain or officers or crew; in fact, we never saw any of the ship's officers until long after all the lifeboats were afloat on the sea.

The ship had now stopped and the firing had apparently ceased, but we did not know whether it would recommence, and of course imagined the Germans were firing to sink the ship. It was useless trying to escape the shots, as we did not know then at what part of the ship the Germans were firing, so there was only one thing for the passengers to do—to leave the ship, as we all thought she was sinking. Some of the passengers attempted to go on the bridge to get on the boat deck and help lower the boats, as it seemed nothing was being done, but were ordered back by the Second Steward, who, apparently alone among the ship's officers, kept his head throughout.

The number one boat was now being lowered on the port side; it was full of Japanese and Asiatics. When it was flush with the deck the falls broke, the boat capsized, and with all its occupants was thrown into the sea. One or two, we afterwards heard, were drowned. The passengers now went over to the starboard side, as apparently no more boats were being lowered from the port side, and we did not know whether the raider would start firing again. The number one starboard boat was being lowered; still there was no one to give orders. The passengers themselves saw to it that the women got into this boat first, and helped them in, only the second steward standing by to help.

The women had to climb the rail and gangway which was lashed thereto, and the boat was so full of gear and tackle that at first it was quite impossible for anyone to find a seat in the boat. It was a difficult task for any woman to get into this boat; my wife fell in, and in so doing dropped her jewel case out of her handbag into the bottom of the boat, and it was seen no more that day. The husbands followed their wives into the boat and several other men among the first-class passengers also clambered in.

Directly after the order to lower away was given, and before anyone could settle in the boat the stern falls broke, and for a second the boat hung from the bow falls vertically, the occupants hanging on to anything they could. Then, immediately afterwards, the bow falls broke, or were cut, and the boat dropped into the water and righted itself. We were still alongside the ship when another boat was swung out and lowered immediately on to our heads. We managed to push off just in time before the other boat, the falls of which also broke, reached the water.

Thus, there had been no preparation made for accidents—we might have been living in the times of profoundest peace for all the trouble that had been taken to see that everything was ready in case of accident. Some passengers had asked for boat drill when the ship left Singapore, but were told there was no need for it, or for any preparations till after Cape Town, which, alas! never was reached. Accordingly, passengers had no places given to them in the boats, the boats were not ready, and confusion instead of order prevailed. It was nothing short of a miracle that more people were not drowned. If the ship had only stopped when ordered by signals to do so, there would have been no firing at all. Even if she had stopped after the warning shots had been fired no more firing would have taken place, and nobody need have left the ship at all.

It seemed too, at the time, that if only the *Hitachi* had turned tail and bolted directly the *Wolf's* smoke was seen on the horizon by the officer on watch on the bridge—at the latest, this must have been about one-thirty—she might have escaped altogether, as she was a much quicker boat than the *Wolf*. At any rate, she might have tried. Her fate would have been no worse if she had failed to escape—for surely even the Germans could not deny any ship the right to escape if she could effect it. Certainly the seaplane might have taken up the chase, and ordered the *Hitachi* to stop. We heard afterwards that one ship—the *Laruna*, from New Zealand to San Francisco—had been caught in this way. The seaplane had hovered over her and dropped messages on her deck ordering her to follow the plane to a concealed harbour nearby, failing which, bombs would be dropped to blow up the ship. Needless to say, the ship followed these instructions.

"There was no panic, and the women were splendid"—how often one has read that in these days of atrocity at sea! We were to realise it now; the women were indeed splendid. There was no crying or screaming or hysteria, or wild enquiries. They were perfectly calm and collected, none of them showed the least fear, even under fire.

As we thought the ship was slowly sinking, we pushed oil from her side as quickly as possible. There were now four lifeboats in the water at some distance from each other. The one in which we were contained about twenty-four persons. There was no officer or member of the crew with us, while another boat contained officers and sailors only. No one in our boat knew where we were to go, or what we were to do. One passenger wildly suggested that we should hoist a sail and set sail for Colombo, two days' *steaming* away! Search was made for provisions and water in our boat, but she was so full of people and impedimenta that nothing could be found. It was found, however, that water was rapidly coming into the boat, and before long it reached to our knees.

The hole which should have been plugged could not be found, so for more than an hour some of the men took turns at pulling and bailing the water out with their sun-helmets. This was very hot work, as it must be remembered we were not far from the Equator. Ultimately, however, the hole was found and plugged. An Irish Tommy going home from Singapore was in our boat. He was most cheerful and in every way helpful, working hard and pulling all the time. It was he who plugged the hole, and as he was almost the only one among us who seemed to have any useful knowledge about the management of lifeboats, we were very glad to reckon him among our company.

The four boats were now drifting aimlessly about over the sea, when an order was shouted to us, apparently from a Japanese officer in one of the other boats, to tie up with the other three boats. After some time, this was accomplished and the four boats in line drifted on the water. The two steamers had stopped, so we did not know what was happening on board either of them, but saw the raider's motor-launch going between her and her prize, and picking up some of the men who had fallen into the sea when the boat capsized.

Luckily, the sharks with which these waters are infested had been scared off by the gunfire. We realised, when we were in the lifeboats, what a heavy swell there was on the sea, as both steamers were occasionally hidden from us when we were in the trough of the waves. There was no one in command of any of the boats, and we simply waited to see what was going to happen.

Chapter 2

Escape in any way was obviously out of the question. At last the raider got under way and began to bear down on us. Most of us thought that the end had come and that we were up against an apostle of the "*sink the ship and leave no trace*" theory—which we had read about in Colombo only a couple of days before—the latest development of frightfulness. Our minds were not made easier by the seaplane circling above us, ready, as we thought, to administer the final blow to any who might survive being fired on by the raider's guns. It was a most anxious moment for us all, and opinions were very divided as to what was going to happen. One of the ladies remarked that she had no fear, and reminded us that we were all in God's hands, which cheered up some of the drooping hearts and anxious minds.

Certainly most of us thought we were soon to look our last upon the world—what other thoughts were in our minds as we imagined our last moments were so near, will remain unrecorded.

However, to our intense relief, nothing of the sort happened, and as the raider came slowly nearer to us, an officer on the bridge megaphoned us to come alongside. This we did; three boats went astern, and the one in which we were remained near the raider's bows. An officer appeared at the bulwarks and told us to come aboard; women first, then their husbands, then the single men. There was no choice but to obey, but we all felt uneasy in our minds as to what kind of treatment our women were to receive at the hands of the Germans on board.

The ship was rolling considerably, and it is never a pleasant or easy task for a landsman, much less a landswoman, to clamber up a rope ladder some twenty feet up the side of a rolling ship. However, all the ladies acquitted themselves nobly, some even going up without a rope round their waists. The little Japanese stewardess, terrified, but showing a brave front to the enemy, was the last woman to go up before the men's ascent began. Two German sailors stood at the bulwarks to help us off the rope ladder into the well deck forward, and by five-twenty we were all aboard, after having spent a very anxious two hours, possibly the most anxious in the lives of most of us.

It was at once evident, directly we got on board, that we were in for kindly treatment. The ship's doctor came forward, saluted, and asked who was wounded and required his attention. Most of the passengers—there were only twenty first, and about a dozen second class—were in our boat. Among the second class passengers with us were a few Portuguese soldiers going from Macao to Delagoa Bay.

Some of us were slightly bruised, and all were shaken, but luckily none required medical treatment. Chairs were quickly found for the ladies, the men seated themselves on the hatch, and the German sailors busied themselves bringing tea and cigarettes to their latest captives. We were then left to ourselves for a short time on deck, and just before dark, a spruce young lieutenant came up to me, saluted, and asked me to tell all the passengers that we were to follow him and go aft. We followed him along the ship, which seemed to be very crowded, to the well deck aft, where we met the remaining few passengers and some of the crew of the "Hitachi."

We had evidently come across a new type of Hun. The young lieutenant was most polite and courteous and attentive. He apologised profusely for the discomfort which the ladies and ourselves would have to put up with—"But it is war, you know, and your government is to blame for allowing you to travel when they know a raider is out"—assured us he would do what he could to make us as comfortable as possible, and that we should not be detained more than three or four days. This was the first of a countless number of lies told us by the Germans as to their intentions concerning us.

We had had nothing to eat since *tiffin*, so we were ordered below to the 'tween decks. We clambered down a ladder to partake of our first meal as prisoners. What a contrast to the last meal we enjoyed on the *Hitachi*, taken in comfort and apparent security! (But, had we known it, we were doomed even then, for the raider's seaplane had been up and seen us at eleven a. m., had reported our position to the raider, and announced three p. m. as the time for our capture. Our captors were not far out! It was between two-thirty and three when we were taken.) The meal consisted of black bread and raw ham, with hot tea served out of a tin can.

We sat around on wooden benches, and noticed that the crockery on which the food was served had been taken from other ships captured—one of the Burns Philp Line, and one of the Union Steamship Company of New Zealand. Some of the Japanese officers and crew were also in the 'tween decks—later on the Japanese captain appeared, (we had not seen him since he left the saloon after *tiffin*) and he was naturally very down and distressed—and some of the German sailors came and spoke to us.

Later on the young lieutenant came down and explained why the raider, which the German sailors told us was the *Wolf*, had fired on us. We then learnt for the first time that many persons had been killed outright by the firing—another direct result of the *Hitachi's* failure to obey the raider's orders to stop. It was impossible to discover how many. There must have been about a dozen, as the total deaths numbered sixteen, all Japanese or Indians; the latest deaths from wounds occurred on October twenty-eighth, while one or two died while we were on the *Wolf.* The lieutenant, who we afterwards learnt was in charge of the prisoners, told us that the *Wolf* had signalled us to stop, and not to use our wireless or our guns, for the *Hitachi* mounted a gun on her poop for the submarine zone. He asserted that the *Hitachi* hoisted a signal that she understood the order, but that she tried to use her wireless, that she brought herself into position to fire on the *Wolf* and that preparations were being made to use her gun.

The Germans professed deep regret at this, and at the loss of life caused, the first occasion on which lives had been lost since the *Wolf's* cruise began. The *Wolf*, however, they said, had no choice but to fire and put the *Hitachi's* gun out of action. This she failed to do, as the shooting was distinctly poor, with the exception of the shot aimed at the wireless room, which went straight through without exploding there or touching the operator, and exploded near the funnel, killing most of the crew who were running to help lower the boats. The other shots had all struck the ship in the second-class quarters astern. One had gone right through the cabin of the second steward, passing just over his bunk—where he had been asleep a minute before—and through the side of the ship.

Others had done great damage to the ship's structure aft, but none had gone anywhere near the gun or ammunition-house on the poop. I saw afterwards some photos the Germans had taken of the gun, as they said they found it when they went on boards These photos showed the gun with the breech open, thus proving, so the Germans said, that the Japanese had been preparing to use the gun. In reality, of course, it proved nothing of the sort; it is more than likely that the Germans opened the breech themselves before they took the photograph, as they had to produce some evidence to justify their firing on the *Hitachi*. But whether the Japanese opened the gun breech and prepared to use the gun or not, it is quite certain that the *Hitachi* never fired a shot at the *Wolf*, though the Germans have since asserted that she did so. It was indeed very lucky for us that she did not fire—had she done so and even missed the *Wolf*, it is quite certain the *Wolf* would have torpedoed the *Hitachi* and sent us to the bottom.

It was very hot in the 'tween decks, and after our meal we were all allowed to go on deck for some fresh air. About eight o'clock, however, the single men of military age were again sent below for the night, while the married couples and a few sick and elderly men were allowed to remain on deck. It was a, cool moonlight night, and armed guards patrolled the deck all night. We had nothing but what we stood up in, so we lay down in chairs as we were, and that night slept, or rather did not sleep, under one of the *Wolf's* guns. Throughout the night we were steaming gently, and from time to time we saw the *Hitachi* still afloat, and steaming along at a considerable distance from us.

Soon after daybreak next morning, the men were allowed to go aft under the poop for a wash, with a very limited supply of water, and the ladies had a portion of the 'tween decks to themselves for a short time. The commander sent down a message conveying his compliments to the ladies, saying he hoped they had had a good night and were none the worse for their experiences. He assured us all that we should be in no danger on his ship and that he would do what he could to make us as comfortable as possible under the circumstances. But, we were reminded again, this was war. Indeed, it was, and we had good reason to know it now, even if the war had not touched us closely before. Breakfast, consisting of black bread, canned meat and tea, was then brought to us on deck by the German sailors, and we were left to ourselves on the well deck for some time.

There seemed to be literally hundreds of prisoners on and under the poop, and the whole ship, as far as we could see, presented a scene of the greatest activity. Smiths were at work on the well deck, hammering and cutting steel plates with which to repair the *Hitachi*, mechanics were working at the seaplane, called the *Wolfchen*, which was kept on the well deck between her flights; prisoners were exercising on the poop, and the armed guards were patrolling constantly among them and near us on the well deck. The guards wore revolvers and side-arms, but did not appear at all particular in the matter of uniform. Names of various ships appeared on their caps, some had on them only the words "*Kaiserliche Marine.*" Some were barefoot, some wore singlets and shorts, while some even dispensed with the former. Most of the crew at work wore only shorts, and, as one of the lady prisoners remarked, the ship presented a rather unusual exhibition of the European male torso!

Some German officers came aft to interrogate us; they were all courteous and sympathetic, and I took the opportunity of mentioning to the young lieutenant the loss of my wife's jewels in the lifeboat, and he assured me he would have the boat searched, and if the jewels were found they should be restored.

The Japanese *dhobi* had died from wounds during the night and was buried in the morning, nearly all the German officers, from the commander downwards, attending in full uniform. The Japanese captain and officers also attended, and some kind of funeral service in Japanese was held.

Officers and men were very busy on the upper deck—we were much impressed by the great number of men on board—and we noticed a lady prisoner, a little girl, evidently a great pet with the German sailors and officers, some civilian prisoners and some military prisoners in khaki on the upper deck, but we were not allowed to communicate with them. There were also a few Tommies in khaki among the prisoners aft. It was very hot on the well deck, and for some hours we had no shelter from the blazing sun. Later on, a small awning was rigged up and we got a little protection, and one or two parasols were forthcoming for the use of the ladies.

During the morning the sailors were allowed to bring us cooling drinks from time to time, and both officers and men did all they could to render our position as bearable as possible. The men amongst us were also allowed to go to the ship's canteen and buy smokes. We were steaming gently in a westerly direction all day, occasionally passing quite close to some small islands and banks of sand, a quite picturesque scene. The sea was beautifully calm and blue, and on the shores of these banks, to which we sailed quite close, the water took on colours of exquisite hues of the palest and tenderest blue and green, as it rippled gently over coral and golden sands.

Tiffin, consisting of rice, bacon and beans was dealt out to us on deck at midday, and the afternoon passed in the same way as the morning. The *Wolf's* chief officer, a hearty, elderly man came aft to speak to us. He chaffed us about our oarsmanship in the lifeboats, saying the appearance of our oars wildly waving reminded him of the sails of a windmill. "Never use your wireless or your gun," he said, "and you'll come to no harm from a German raider."

By about five o'clock the two ships arrived in an atoll, consisting of about fifteen small islands, and the *Hitachi* there dropped anchor. The *Wolf* moved up alongside, and the two ships were lashed together. Supper, consisting of tinned fruit and rice was served out at five-thirty and we were then told that the married couples and one or two elderly men were to return to the *Hitachi* that night. So with some difficulty we clambered from the upper deck of the *Wolf* to the boat deck of the *Hitachi* and returned to find our cabins just as we had left them in a great hurry the day before.

We had not expected to go on board the *Hitachi* again, and never thought we should renew acquaintance with our personal belongings. We ourselves were particularly sad about this as we had brought away from Siam after twenty years' residence there, many things which would be quite irreplaceable. We were therefore very glad to know they were not all lost to us. But we congratulated ourselves that the greater part of our treasures gathered there had been left behind safely stored in the bank and in a *godown* in Bangkok.

Chapter 3

The *Hitachi* was now a German ship, the prize captain was in command, and German sailors replaced the Japanese, who had all been transferred to the *Wolf.* The German captain spoke excellent English and expressed a wish to do all he could to make us as comfortable on board as we had been before. There was of course considerable confusion on board, and we found next morning that the bathrooms and lavatories were not in working order. This state of affairs prevailed for the next few days, and the men passengers themselves had to do what was necessary in these quarters and haul sea-water aboard. The next morning the transference of coal, cargo, and ship's stores from the *Hitachi* to the *Wolf* began, and went on without cessation for the next five days. One of the German officers came over and took photos of the passengers in groups, and others frequently took snapshots of various incidents and of each other on different parts of the ship.

We know now that we were then anchored in a British possession, one of the Southernmost groups of the Maldive Islands. Some of the islands were inhabited, and small sailing boats came out to the *Wolf,* presumably with provisions of some kind. We were of course not allowed to speak to any of the islanders who came alongside the *Wolf,* and were not allowed alongside the *Hitachi.* On one occasion even, the doctor of the *Wolf* went in the ship's motor-launch to one of the islands to attend the wife of one of the native chiefs!

On the next day—the twenty-eighth—all the *Hitachi's* passengers returned on board her, and at the same time some of the Japanese stewards returned, but they showed no inclination to work as formerly. Indeed, the German officers had no little difficulty in dealing with them. They naturally felt very sore at the deaths of so many of their countrymen at the hands of the Germans, and they did as little work as possible.

With their usual thoroughness the Germans one day examined all our passports and took notes of our names, ages, professions, maiden names of married ladies, addresses, and various other details. One young man who had on his passport his photo taken in military uniform was, however, detained on the *Wolf* as a military prisoner. He was asked by a German officer if he were going home to fight. He replied that he certainly was and pluckily added, "I wish I were fighting now."

On October first the married prisoners from the *Wolf*, together with three Australian civilian prisoners over military age, a colonel of the Australian A. M. C., a major of the same corps, with his wife, an Australian stewardess, some young boys, and a few old mates and sea-captains were sent on board the *Hitachi*. They had all been taken off earlier prizes captured and sunk by the *Wolf*. The Australians had been captured on August sixth from the S.S. *Matunga*, from Sydney to what was formerly German New Guinea, from which latter place they had been only a few hours distant.

An American captain, with his wife and little girl, had been captured on the barque *Beluga*, from San Francisco to Newcastle, N. S.W., on July ninth, both of these ships having been sunk by the Germans. All the passengers transferred were given cabins on board the *Hitachi*. We learnt from these passengers that the *Wolf* was primarily a mine-layer, that she had laid mines at Cape Town, Bombay, Colombo and off the Australian and New Zealand coasts. She had sown her last crop of mines, one hundred and ten in number, off the approaches to Singapore before she proceeded to the Indian Ocean to lie in wait for the *Hitachi*. Altogether she had sown five hundred mines.

During her stay in the Maldives the *Wolf* sent up her seaplane—or, as the Germans said "the bird"—every morning about six, and she returned about eight. Everything was apparently all clear, and the *Wolf* evidently anticipated no interference or unwelcome attention from any of our cruisers. Two of them, the *Venus* and the *Doris*, we had seen at anchor in Colombo harbour during our stay there, but it was apparently thought not worthwhile to send any escort with the *Hitachi*, though the value of her cargo was said to run into millions sterling; and evidently the convoy system had not yet been adopted in Eastern waters.

The *Wolf* remained alongside us till the morning of October third, when she sailed away at daybreak, leaving us anchored in the centre of the atoll. It was a great relief to us when she departed; she kept all the breeze off our side of the ship, so that the heat in our cabin was stifling, and it was in addition very dark; the noise of coaling and shifting cargo was incessant, and the roaring of the water between the two ships most disturbing. Before she sailed away the prize captain handed to my wife most of her jewels which had been recovered from the bottom of our lifeboat. As many of these were Siamese jewellery and unobtainable now, we were very rejoiced to obtain possession of them again, but many rings were missing and were never recovered.

The falls of the lifeboats were all renewed, and on October fifth we had places assigned to us in the lifeboats, and rules and regulations were drawn up for the "detained enemy subjects" on board the *Hitachi*. They were as follows:—

RULES AND REGULATIONS FOR ON BOARD THE GERMAN AUXILIARY
SHIP *HITACHI MARU* DETAINED ENEMY SUBJECTS

1. Everybody on board is under martial law and any offence is liable to be punished by same.

2. All orders given by the Commander, First Officer or any of the German crew on duty are to be strictly obeyed.

3. After the order "*Schiff abblenden*" every evening at sunset no lights may be shown on deck or through portholes etc. that are visible from outside.

4. The order "*Allemann in die Boote*" will be made known by continuous ringing of the ship's bell and sounding the gongs. Everybody hurries to his boat with the lifebelt and leaves the ship. Everybody is allowed to take one small bag preciously packed.

5. Nobody is allowed to go on the boatdeck beyond the smoke-room. All persons living in first class cabins are to stay amidships and are not allowed to go aft without special permission; all persons living aft are to stay aft.

6. The Japanese crew is kept only for the comfort of the one-time passengers and is to be treated considerately as they are also d. e. s.

7. The d. e. s. are not allowed to talk with the crew.

At sea, October 6th, 1917.

Kommando S.M.H. *Hitachi Maru*
C. Rose,
Lt.z.See & Kommandant.

Lieutenant Rose very kindly told me that as I was leaving the East for good and therefore somewhat differently situated from the other passengers, he would allow me to take in the lifeboat, in addition to a handbag, a cabin trunk packed with the articles from Siam I most wanted to save.

It was evident from this that the Germans intended sinking the ship if we came across a British or Allied war vessel. We were of course unarmed, as the Germans had removed the *Hitachi's* gun to the *Wolf*, but the German captain anticipated no difficulty on this score, and assured me that it was the intention of the commander of the *Wolf* that we should be landed in a short time with all our baggage at a neutral port with a stone pier. We took this to mean a port in either Sumatra or Java—and we were buoyed up with this hope for quite a considerable time. But, alas! like many more of the assurances given to us, it was quite untrue.

There were now on board one hundred and thirty-one souls, of whom twenty-nine were passengers. On Saturday, October sixth, the seaplane returned in the afternoon and remained about half an hour, when she again flew away. She brought a message of evidently great importance, for whereas it had been the intention of our captain to sail away on the following afternoon, he weighed anchor the next morning, and left the atoll. He had considerable trouble with the anchor before starting, and did not get away till nearly eight o'clock, instead of at daybreak. Evidently something was coming to visit the atoll; though it was certain nothing could be looking for us, as our capture could not then have been known, and there could have been no communication between the Maldives and Ceylon or the mainland.

The ship was cleaned and put in order, the cargo properly stowed, and the bunkers trimmed by the German crew, aided by some neutrals who had been taken prisoner from other ships before and for some days after we sailed. Some of the sailors among the prize crew were good enough to give us some pieces of the *Wolf's* shrapnel found on the *Hitachi*, relics which were eagerly sought after by the passengers. The passengers were now under armed guards, but were at perfect liberty to do as they pleased, and the relations between them and the German officers and crew were quite friendly.

Deck games were indulged in as before our capture, and the German captain took part in them. Time, nevertheless, hung heavily on our hands, but many a pleasant hour was spent in the saloon with music and singing. One of the Australian prisoners was a very good singer and pianist, and provided very enjoyable entertainment for us. On Sunday evenings, after the six o'clock "supper," a small party met in the saloon to sing a few favourite hymns, each one choosing the ones he or she liked best. This little gathering was looked forward to by those who took part in it, as it formed a welcome break in the ordinary monotonous life on board.

The only Japanese left on board were some stewards, cooks, and the stewardess. A German chief mate and chief engineer replaced the Japanese, and other posts previously held by the Japanese were filled by Germans and neutrals. The times of meals were changed, and we no longer enjoyed the good meals we had had before our capture, as most of the good food had been transferred to the *Wolf*. *Chota hazri* was done away with, except for the ladies; the meals became much simpler, menus were no longer necessary, and the Japanese cooks took no more trouble with the preparation of the food.

However, on the whole we were not so badly off, though on a few occasions there was really not enough to eat, and some of the meat was tainted, as the freezing apparatus had got out of order soon after the ship was captured.

We steamed gently on a south-westerly course for about five days, and on the succeeding day, October twelfth, changed our course many times, going northeast at six-thirty a.m., southeast at twelve-thirty p.m., northeast again at four p.m., and north at six-thirty p.m., evidently waiting for something and killing time, as we were going dead slow all day.

The next morning, we had stopped entirely, and sighted smoke at ten twenty a.m.—it was, of course, the *Wolf*, met by appointment at that particular time and place. She came abreast of us about eleven-twenty a.m. and we sailed on parallel courses for the rest of the day. She was unaccompanied by a new prize, and we were glad to think she had been unsuccessful in her hunt for further prey. She remained in company with us all next day, Sunday, and about five p.m. moved closer up, and after an exchange of signals we both changed courses and the *Wolf* sheered off, and to our great relief we saw her no more for several days. There was always the hope that when away from us she would be seen and sunk by an Allied cruiser, and always the fear that when she came back to us we might again be put on board her.

The Germans seemed to have a perfect mania for taking photographs—we were of course not allowed to take any and cameras were even taken away from us—and one day Lieut. Rose showed me photos of various incidents of the *Wolf's* cruise, including those of the sinkings of various ships. (I saw, too, on this day a photo of the *Hitachi* flying the German flag and one showing the damage sustained by her from the *Wolf's* firing. There were ugly holes in the stern quarters, but all above the water-line.) The German officers would take with them to Germany hundreds of pictures giving a complete photographic record of the *Wolf's* expedition.

We cruised about again after the *Wolf* had left us for a couple of days, and on the seventeenth were stationary all day. Several sharks were seen around the ship, and the German sailors caught two or three fairly large ones during the day and got them on board. On the eighteenth the sea was rough and we were gently steaming to keep the ship's head to the seas, and on the following day we again changed our course many times. Saturday morning, October twentieth, again saw the *Wolf* in sight at six-thirty. She was still alone, and we proceeded on parallel courses, passing about midday a few white reefs with breakers sweeping over them.

Shortly afterwards we came in sight of many other reefs, and at two p. m. we anchored, and the *Wolf* tied up alongside us within a snug and sheltered spot. We were almost surrounded by large and small coral reefs, against which we could see and hear the breakers dashing. It was a beautiful anchorage, and the waters were evidently well known to the Germans. Some of the seafaring men amongst us told us we were in the Cargados Carajos Reef, southeast of the Seychelles, and that we were anchored near the Nazareth Bank.

Chapter 4

So confident did the Germans feel of their security that they stayed in this neighbourhood from October twentieth to November seventh, only once—on October twenty-eighth—moving a few hundred yards away from their original anchorage, and although a most vigilant lookout was kept from the crow's nest on the *Wolf*, the seaplane was not sent up once to scout during the whole of that time. Coal, cargo and stores were transferred from the *Hitachi* to the *Wolf*, and the work went on day and night with just as much prospect of interference as there would have been if the *Wolf* had been loading cargo from a wharf in Hamburg in peace time. The coolness and impudence of the whole thing amazed us.

But one day, October twenty-second, was observed as a holiday. It was Lieutenant Rose's birthday, and, incidentally, the *Kaiserin's* also. So no loading or coaling was done, but the band on the *Wolf*— most of the members with the minimum of clothing and nearly all with faces and bodies black with coal-dust—lined up and gave a musical performance of German patriotic airs.

Every day we looked, but in vain, for signs of help in the shape of a friendly cruiser, but the Germans proceeded with their high-seas robbery undisturbed and unalarmed. The *Hitachi* had a valuable cargo of rubber, tea, tin, copper, antimony, hides, cocoanut and general stores, and it was indeed maddening to see all these cases marked for Liverpool and London being transferred to the capacious maw of the *Wolf* for the use of our enemies.

On October twenty-eighth a Japanese sailor wounded at the time of the *Hitachi's* capture, died on the *Wolf*. This was the last death from wounds inflicted on that day. His body was brought over to the *Hitachi*—once again all the German officers from the commander downwards, including the two doctors, appeared in full uniform to attend the funeral service. The Japanese captain and officers also came over from the *Wolf*, and the body was committed to the sea from the poop of the "*Hitachi*."

Various rumours came into circulation about this time as to what was to happen to us. The most likely thing was, if the *Wolf* did not secure another prize, that the *Hitachi* would be sunk and all of us transferred to the *Wolf* once more. It was certain, however, that the Germans did not want us on the *Wolf* again, and still more certain that we did not want to go. They regarded us, especially the women, as a nuisance on board their ship, which was already more than comfortably full. In addition, some of the German officers who had before given up their cabins to some of the married couple prisoners, naturally did not want to do so again, as it meant that all the officers' quarters would become very cramped. The German doctor, too, protested against further crowding of the *Wolf*, but these protests were overruled.

There was talk of their leaving the *Hitachi* where she was, with some weeks' stores on board, with her coal exhausted and her wireless dismantled, the *Wolf* to send out a wireless in a few weeks' time as to our condition and whereabouts. If this had happened, there was talk among us of a boat expedition to the Seychelles to effect an earlier rescue. There was also mentioned another scheme of taking the *Hitachi* near Mauritius, sending all her prisoners and German officers and crew off in boats at nightfall to the island, and then blowing up the ship. But all these plans came to nothing, and as day by day went by and the *Wolf*, for reasons best known to herself, did not go out after another prize, though the Germans knew and told us what steamers were about—and in more than one case we knew they were correct—it became evident that the *Hitachi* would have to be destroyed, as she had not enough coal to carry on with, and we should all have to be sent on to the *Wolf*.

But the married men protested vigorously against having their wives put in danger of shell fire from a British or Allied cruiser, and on October thirtieth sent the following petition to the commander of the *Wolf*:

We, the undersigned detained enemy subjects traveling with our wives, some of whom have already been exposed to shell fire, and the remainder to the risk thereof, and have suffered many weeks' detention on board, respectfully beg that no women be transferred to the auxiliary cruiser, thereby exposing them to a repetition of the grave dangers they have already run. We earnestly trust that some means may be found by which consideration may be shown to all the women on board by landing them safely without their incurring further peril. We take this opportunity of expressing our gratitude for the treatment we have received since our capture, and our sincere appreciation of the courtesy and consideration shown us by every officer and man from your ship with whom we have been brought in contact.

He sent back a verbal message that there was no alternative but to put us all, women included, on the *Wolf*, as the *Hitachi* had no coal, but that they should be landed at a neutral port from the next boat caught, if she had any coal.

We were still not satisfied with this, and I again protested to our captain against what was equivalent to putting women out in a German first line trench to be shot by our own people. He replied that we need have no anxiety on that score:

We know exactly where all your cruisers are, we pick up all their wireless messages, and we shall never see or go anywhere near one of them.

Whether the Germans did know this, or hear our ships' wireless I cannot tell, but it is certainly true that we never, between September and February, saw a British or Allied vessel of any sort or kind, or even the smoke of one, although during that time we travelled from Ceylon to the Cape, and the whole length of the Atlantic Ocean.

The food on the *Hitachi* was now getting poorer and poorer. There was no longer any fruit, cheese, vegetables, coffee or jam. All the eggs were bad, only a very little butter remained, the beer was reserved for the ship's officers, iced water and drinks were no longer obtainable, and the meat became more and more unpleasant. On the *Wolf* the food was still poorer, and *beriberi* broke out on the raider. A case of typhoid also appeared on the *Wolf* and the German doctors thereupon inoculated every man, woman and child on both ships against typhoid. We had heard before of German "inoculations" and some of us had nasty forebodings as to the results. But protests were of no avail—everyone had to submit. The first inoculation took place on November first, the next on November eleventh, and some of the people were inoculated a third time.

One night while the ships were lashed alongside a great uproar arose on both ships. The alarm was given, orders were shouted, revolvers and side arms were hastily assumed and sailors commenced rushing and shouting from all parts of both ships. Most of us were scared, not knowing what had happened. It appeared that a German sailor had fallen down between the two ships; his cries, of course, added to the tumult, but luckily he was dragged up without being much injured. We could not help wondering if such a commotion were made at such a small accident, what would happen if a cruiser came along and the real alarm were given. The ship would bid fair to become a veritable madhouse—evidently the nerves of all the Germans were very much on edge. The only thing for the prisoners to do was to get out of the way as much as possible, and retire to their cabins.

In addition to the transference of coal and cargo which went on without cessation, day and night, our ship was gradually being stripped. Bunks and cabin fittings, heating apparatus, pianos, bookcases, brass and rubber stair-treads, bed and table linen, ceiling and table electric fans, clocks and all movable fittings were transferred to the *Wolf*, and our ship presented a scene of greater destruction every day. The Germans were excellent shipbreakers. Much of the cargo could not be taken on board the *Wolf*, it was not wanted, and there was no room for it, and some of this, especially some fancy Japanese goods, clothes, gloves and toys, was broached by the sailors, and some was left untouched in the holds. The prize captain secured for himself as a trophy, a large picture placed at the head of the saloon stairs of the *Hitachi*. This represented a beautiful Japanese woodland scene, embossed and painted on velvet.

Longing eyes had been cast on the notice published by the Germans concerning rules and regulations on board, and most of us determined to get possession of it. When first fixed on the notice board it had been blown down, and recovered by a German sailor. It was then framed and again exhibited. Later on it was again taken out of its frame and again pinned up. It remained on the notice board till the day before the *Hitachi* was sunk. After supper that evening I was lucky enough to find it still there, so removed it and have kept it as a memento of the time when I was a "detained enemy subject!"

The boats were all lashed down, the hatches the same, and every precaution taken to prevent wreckage floating away when the vessel was sunk. On the afternoon of November fifth the Germans shifted all the passengers' heavy luggage on to the *Wolf*, and we were told we should have to leave the *Hitachi* and go on board the *Wolf* at one p.m. the next day. The *Hitachi* was now in a sad condition, her glory was indeed departed and her end very near. We had our last meal in her stripped saloon that day at noon, and at one o'clock moved over on to the *Wolf*, the German sailors carrying our light cabin luggage for us. The crew and their belongings, the Japanese stewards and theirs, moved over to the *Wolf* in the afternoon, and at five p.m. on November sixth the *Wolf* sheered off, leaving the *Hitachi* deserted, but for the German captain and officers, and the bombing party who were to send her to the bottom next day.

Both ships remained where they were for the night, abreast of and about four hundred yards distant from each other. At nine a.m. on November seventh they moved off and manoeuvred. The Germans did not intend to sink the *Hitachi* where she was, but in deep water. To do this they had to sail some distance from the Nazareth Bank. The *Hitachi* hoisted the German Imperial Navy flag, and performed a kind of naval goosestep for the delectation of the *Wolf*. At one p.m. the flag was hauled down, both ships stopped, and the *Hitachi* blew off steam for the last time.

There were still a few people on her, and the *Wolf's* motor-launch made three trips between the two ships before the German captain and bombing officer left the *Hitachi*. Three bombs had been placed for her destruction, one forward outside the ship on the starboard side, one amidships inside, and one aft on the port side outside the ship. At one thirty-three p.m. the captain arrived alongside the *Wolf*, and at one thirty-four the first bomb exploded with a dull subdued roar and a high column of water; the explosion of the other bomb followed at intervals of a minute, so that by one thirty-six the last bomb had exploded. All on the *Wolf* now stood watching the *Hitachi's* last struggle with the waves, a struggle which, thanks to her murderers, could have but one end; and the German officers stood on the *Wolf's* deck taking photos at different stages of the tragedy.

The struggle was a long one—it was pathetic beyond words to watch it—for some time it even seemed as if the *Hitachi* were going to snatch one more victory from the sea, but just before two o'clock there were signs that she was settling fast. Her well deck forward was awash; exactly at two o'clock her bows went under, soon her funnel was surrounded with swirling water; it disappeared, and with her propellers high in the air she dived slantingly down to her great grave, and at one minute past two the sea closed over her. Twenty-five minutes had elapsed since the explosion of the last bomb. The Germans said she and her cargo were worth a million sterling when she went down.

There was great turmoil on the sea for some time after the ship disappeared; the ammunition-house on the poop floated away, a fair amount of wreckage also came away, an oar shot up high into the air from one of the hatches, the sodium lights attached to the lifebuoys ignited and ran along the water, and the *Wolf*, exactly like a murderer making sure that the struggles of his victim had finally ceased, moved away from the scene of her latest crime.

Thus came to an end the second of the Nippon Yushen Kaisha fleet bearing the name of *Hitachi Maru*. The original ship of that name had been sunk by the Russians in the Russo-Japanese war. Our ill-fated vessel had taken her place. It will savour of tempting Providence if another ship ever bears her unfortunate name, and no sailor could be blamed for refusing to sail in her.

Chapter 5

Life on the *Wolf* was very different to life on the *Hitachi*. To begin with, all the single men of military age from the *Hitachi* were accommodated on the 'tween decks, and slept in hammocks which they had to sling themselves. The elder men among them slept in bunks taken from the *Hitachi*, but the quarters of all in the 'tween decks were very restricted; there was no privacy, no convenience, and only a screen divided the European and Japanese quarters. The condition of our fellow-countrymen from the *Hitachi* was now the reverse of enviable, though it was a great deal better than that of the crews of the captured ships, who were "accommodated" under the poop—where the captains and officers captured had quarters to themselves—and exercised on the poop and well deck, the port side of which was reserved for the Japanese.

There were now more than four hundred prisoners on board, mostly British, some of whom had been captured in the February previous, as the *Wolf* had left Germany in November, 1916, the *Hitachi* being the tenth prize taken. The condition in which these prisoners lived cannot be too strongly condemned. The heat in the tropics was insufferable, the overcrowding abominable, and on the poop there was hardly room to move. While anchored near Sunday Island, in the Pacific some months earlier, two of the British prisoners taken from the first prize captured managed to escape. Their absence was not noticed by the Germans till a fortnight later, as up to then there had been no daily rollcall, an omission which was at once rectified directly these two men were noted missing.

As a punishment, the prisoners aft were no longer allowed to exercise on the poop, but were kept below. The heat and stifling atmosphere were inconceivable and cruel. The iron deck below presented the appearance of having been hosed—in reality it was merely the perspiration streaming off these poor persecuted captives that drenched the deck. The attention of the ship's doctor was one day called to this and he at once forbade this inhuman confinement in future. From then onwards, batches of the prisoners were allowed on the poop at a time, so that every man could obtain at least a little fresh air a day—surely the smallest concession that could possibly be made to men living under wretched conditions.

But notwithstanding these hardships the men seemed to be merry and bright and showed smiling faces to their captors. They had all evidently made up their minds to keep their end up to the last, and were not to be downed by any bad news or bad treatment the Germans might give them.

The *Wolf* of course picked up wireless news every day, printed it, and circulated it throughout the ship in German and English. We did not, however, hear all the news that was picked up, but felt that what we did hear kept us at least a little in touch with the outside world, and we have since been able to verify that, and also to discover that we missed a great deal, too.

The accommodation provided for the married couples on the *Wolf* was situated on the upper deck on the port side. Some "cabins" had been improvised when the first women and civilian prisoners had been captured, some had been vacated by the officers, and others had been carved out as the number of these prisoners increased. The cabins of course—small—there was very little room to spare on the *Wolf*—and, at the best, makeshift contrivances, but it must be admitted that our German captors did all they could to make us as comfortable as possible under the conditions prevailing. The married couples, the Australian military officers and a few elderly civilians messed together in the officers' ward-room, quite a tiny saloon, which was placed at our disposal after the officers had finished their meals.

The food on the *Wolf* was better cooked than it had been on the *Hitachi*, but there was of course no fresh food of any kind. Even the potatoes we had were dried and had to be soaked many hours before they were cooked, and even then they did not much resemble the original article; the same remark applies to the other vegetables we had. Occasionally our meals satisfied us as far as quantity went, but in the main we left the table feeling we could with ease dispose of a great deal more. This was especially the case after breakfast, which consisted of bread and jam only. Each cabin had a German orderly to look after and wait on its occupants, two German stewards waited on us at meals,

185

and a Japanese steward had two or three cabins to look after and clean.

The deck—we were only allowed the port side—was only about six feet wide, and part of this was occupied by spare spars. Sailors and officers, and prisoners to fetch their food were passing along this deck incessantly all day, so it can be easily imagined there was not much room for sitting about in deck chairs. On this deck, too, was the prisoners' cell, usually called the "calaboose," very rarely without an occupant with an armed sentry on guard outside. It was not a cheerful abode, being very small and dark; and the prisoner, if his sentence were a long one, served it in instalments of a few days at a time.

We were allowed to go down to the well deck to see our friends and sit on the hatch with them during the daytime. They had their meals in the 'tween decks at different times from us, but the food provided was usually just the same. The evenings were the deadliest times of all on the *Wolf*. At dusk the order "*Schiff Abblenden*" resounded all through the ship, sailors came round to put tin plates over all the portholes, and from thence onward throughout the night complete darkness prevailed on deck, not a glint of light showing anywhere on the ship.

When the *Wolf* considered herself in dangerous waters, and when she was laying mines, even smoking was forbidden on deck. All the cabins had a device by which directly the door was open the light went out, only to be relit directly the door closed. So it was impossible for anyone to leave his cabin with the door open and the light on. There was nothing to do in the evenings after the last meal, which was over before eight o'clock. There was nowhere to sit except on the dark deck or in the dark cabins; it was so hot that the cabin doors had to be kept open, and the evenings spent on the *Wolf* were certainly very dreary. Most of us felt we would rather be in gaol on shore, for then we should be in no risk of being killed at any moment by our own people, our cells would have been larger than our cabins, our food possibly not much worse, and our gaol would at least have been stationary and not rolling about, though it must be confessed that the *Wolf* was a good sea boat.

She had been one of the Hansa line before the war, and was about six thousand tons, with a speed of about ten knots at the outside. She had been thoroughly adapted for her work as a raider, had four torpedo tubes and six guns (said to be 4.7) with concrete emplacements, not to mention machine and smaller guns, none of which could be seen by a passing ship, to which the *Wolf* looked, as she was intended to look, exactly like an innocent tramp. When in action her bulwarks dropped, giving free play to her guns and torpedoes. There was telephone communication between her bridge and every gun and every part of the ship; she carried a huge searchlight, her masts and funnel were telescopic, and she could rig an extra funnel. She carried large supplies of bombs, hand grenades, rifles and small arms, had hospitals with two doctors on board; among her crew of more than three hundred were representatives of every trade, she was thoroughly well equipped in every way, the officers had the best and most powerful binoculars, and absolutely nothing seemed to have been forgotten.

There were, it was said, only three of the officers who were Imperial Navy men, the commander, the artillery officer, and the lieutenant in charge of the prisoners. All the other officers and a great many of the crew were from the German mercantile marine, who had travelled with, mixed with and lived with Englishmen in many parts of the world. To this we undoubtedly owed the kindly treatment we received on board, treatment which was infinitely better than we expected to receive. The majority of the officers and men were certainly kindly disposed towards us. There is no doubt, however, that the fear we might be taken by a British cruiser also had something to do with this treatment, for if we had been treated badly the Germans knew they would have had cause to regret it had they been captured.

In a conversation with the lieutenant in charge of the prisoners—who, by the way, had a Scottish mother—I remarked that it was very hard on our relatives and friends not knowing what had become of us. He agreed that it was, but added it was no worse for my relations than it was for his! They did not know where he was either! I replied:

No, but you are out doing your duty and serving your country, and when you left home your people knew they would have no news of you for many months. It is quite different with us. We were not out to be taken prisoner, we were simply travelling on business, being compelled to do so. We are not serving our country by being caught and kept in this way, and our relatives did not expect us to disappear and send them no news of ourselves for a long time.

However, he affected not to see the difference between our case and his; just as the sailors often told the prisoners aft that in case of the *Wolf* going into action, it would be no worse for the prisoners than it was for the fighting crew.

We were forbidden to talk to the crew, but under cover of the darkness some of them, a great number of whom spoke English, were only too glad to speak to us. We learnt from them that the *Wolf* had been out a year, and that they were all very "fed up" with it all, tired of the life, tired of the sea, tired of the food, longing to get home, and longing for the war to end. They had, too, no doubts as to how it would end, and were certain that the *Wolf* would get back to Germany whenever she wished to do so.

They were certain three things would bring them victory; their submarines, the defection of Russia who would soon be made to conclude peace with Germany, and the fact that in their opinion America had entered the war too late.

The interests of the *Wolf* were now, to a certain extent, identical with our own—that we should not meet an Allied cruiser. A notice was posted in some of our cabins saying that in that event the women with their husbands, and some other prisoners would be put into boats with a white flag, "if weather and other conditions permitted." The other prisoners, however, *viz:*—those under the poop and on the 'tween decks, would have had no chance of being saved. They would all have been battened down under hatches (this indeed was done whenever the *Wolf* sighted or captured a ship, when mines were being sown, and when and other drill was carried on) and armed guards with hand grenades sent among them. Their fate, if the *Wolf* had gone into action, would have been too terrible to contemplate, and it is certain very few of them could have been saved.

The *Wolf* with a company of over seven hundred on board sailed away on a south-westerly course for the next two days, and the usual routine of the ship went on, but no further drills took place. Soon after daybreak on November tenth a sailor came along and locked us all in our cabins, armed guards patrolled the deck, and a short time after an officer came to each cabin and informed us there was a steamer on the starboard side which the *Wolf* intended to capture. He told us the *Wolf* would fire on her to make her stop, and provided all of us with cotton wool to insert in our ears while the guns were being fired! We waited for the sound of the guns, but nothing happened, and in about half an hour the same officer came along and said to us, "Don't be fearful, the other ship has stopped and there will be no firing!"

Our cabin doors were unlocked, the men on the upper deck were allowed out, the ladies were requested not to show themselves on deck, and another officer ran along the deck saying "We've catched her, we've catched her, a neutral this time!"

The "catched" vessel had stopped and was lying very near the *Wolf*. The name on her stern proclaimed her to be the *Igotz Mendi* of Bilbao, and she was flying the Spanish flag. In a short time, a prize crew left the *Wolf* in her motor-launch, and proceeded to the other ship. After they had been aboard her a few minutes, a message came back that the Spanish ship was from Delagoa Bay to Colombo with a cargo of fifty-eight hundred tons of coal for the British Admiralty authorities in Ceylon. The chagrin of the Germans may be imagined when they realized that they had captured this ship just three days too late to save the *Hitachi*. Here was a ship with ample coal, which, had it been captured a few days before, would have enabled the Germans to save the *Hitachi* and take her as a prize to Germany as they had always desired to do.

The *Igotz Mendi* had left Lourenco, Marquez, on November fifth and was due at Colombo on the twenty-second. Before nine a.m. on the morning of the capture, both ships had turned about, the prize now being in command of the Germans, and were going back on the course the *Wolf* had followed since the destruction of the *Hitachi*. Discussion was rife among the prisoners as to what would be done with the new capture, and whether the commander of the *Wolf* would redeem his promise to transfer the married couples to the "next ship caught."

Chapter 6

The two ships steamed along in company for the next three days, usually stopping towards sunset for communications and sending orders. On Sunday the eleventh we were invited to a band performance on the well deck forward. It was quite a good one. The first mate came along and jokingly said to us, "What more can you want? We give you a free passage, free food, and even free music."

I replied, "We only want one more thing free."

"What is that?" he asked.

"Freedom," I answered.

"Ah!" he said, smiling. "I am afraid you can't."

I had asked him earlier in the day, if he would allow us the use of a room and a piano for a short time in the afternoon, so that we could keep up our custom of singing a few hymns on Sunday. Later on, he told me we might, with the permission of the officers, have their wardroom for half an hour. The officers and he had kindly agreed to this, a concession we much appreciated, and the little wardroom was crowded indeed on that occasion.

At daybreak on the thirteenth both ships arrived at the Nazareth Bank, and before nine a.m. were lashed together. On such occasions the *Wolf* never dropped anchor, for she might have to be up and away at the slightest warning; the prize ship was always the one to drop anchor. On the previous Tuesday the *Wolf* had been lashed alongside the *Hitachi*; here, on this Tuesday, the *Wolf* was lashed alongside another captured ship in the very same place! Again the daring and coolness of our captors amazed us.

Coaling from the *Igotz Mendi* to the *Wolf* at once began, and a wireless installation was immediately rigged up by the Germans on the Spanish ship. Coaling proceeded all that day, and the German officers and crews on both ships were very busy. The prisoners aft were also very busy catching fish over the side. No sooner had the ships stopped than lines were dropped overboard and many fine fish were caught. The prisoners aft wore very little clothing and often no headgear at all, though we were in the tropics, where we had always thought a sun-helmet was a *sine qua non*. But the prisoners got on quite well without one.

On the morning of the fourteenth orders were given to the married couples on the *Wolf* to get their light baggage ready at once for transference to the Spanish ship, as she and the *Wolf* might have to separate at any moment. Our heavy baggage would be transferred if time allowed. Evidently something was in the air, some wireless message had been picked up, as the seaplane was being brought up from the 'tween decks, and assembled in great haste on the well deck. The *Wolfchen* went up about four-twenty and returned about five-thirty and in the interval our heavy baggage had been brought up from the *Wolf's* hold ready to be transhipped to the *Igotz Mendi*. We did not understand at the time why the Germans were so considerate to us in the matter of baggage—but later on, a great deal later on, light dawned on us!

At dusk that evening the married people were transferred to the Spanish ship. The next morning, we were still alongside the *Wolf* and remained there till the morning of the seventeenth, our heavy baggage being transhipped in the interval. There had also been transferred the colonel of the A.A.M.C. already mentioned, and three other men— including the second mate of one ship previously captured—who were in ill-health. One of the *Hitachi* prisoners, a man over military age, who had come on board at Colombo straight from hospital, and was going for a health voyage to South Africa, had been told in the morning that he was to be transferred to the Spanish ship. But later on, much to the regret of everyone, it was found that the Germans would not release him. A German officer came up to him and said in my hearing, "Were you not told this morning that you were to go on the *Igotz Mendi?*"

"Yes," he replied.

"Well," said the officer, "you're not to."

Comment on the brutal manner of this remark is unnecessary.

The message the seaplane had brought back had evidently been a reassuring one, and we heard a long time afterwards that the *Wolf* had picked up a wireless from a Japanese cruiser, presumably looking for the *Hitachi*, only thirty miles away. Hence the alarm! Unfortunately for us, if this report were true, the cruiser did not turn aside to look in the most obvious place where a ship like the *Wolf* would hide, so once more the *Wolf* was safe.

If only there had been a couple of cruisers disguised, like the *Wolf*, as tramps, each one carrying a seaplane or two, in each ocean free from submarine attentions, the *Wolf* could have been seen and her career brought to an end long before. The same end would probably have been attained on this occasion if a wireless message had been sent from Delagoa Bay to Colombo saying that the *Igotz Mendi* had left the former port for the latter with five thousand tons of coal on board. The strong wireless installation on the *Wolf*, which picked up every message within a large radius, but of course never sent any, would have picked up this message, and the *Wolf* would probably have risen to the bait, with the result that she could have been caught by an armed vessel sent in search of her on that track. For it must have been known that a raider was out in those waters, as the disappearance of the *Hitachi* could only have been due to the presence of one.

Coaling proceeded without cessation till the morning of the seventeenth, when the *Wolf* moved off a short distance. Passengers on mail boats familiar with the process of coaling ship at Port Said, Colombo, or any other port, can imagine the condition of these ships, after three or four days' incessant coaling day and night. The appearance of the *Igotz Mendi* was meanwhile undergoing another change. When captured she was painted white and had a buff funnel with her Company's distinguishing mark. She was now painted the Allied grey colour, and when her sides and funnel had been transformed the two ships sailed away, and on the evening of the seventeenth, after final orders and instructions had been given, parted company. For some days after this painting was the order of the day on the Spanish ship, which was now grey on every part visible.

The captain of the Spanish ship was now relieved of his duties—and also of his cabin, which the German captain had annexed, leaving the owner thereof the chartroom to sleep in—and was naturally very chagrined at the course events had taken, especially as he said he had been told by the consul at Lourenco Marquez that the course between there and Colombo was quite clear, and had not even been informed of the disappearance of the *Hitachi*, though she had been overdue at Delagoa Bay about a month.

Consequently, he had been showing his navigation lights at sea, and without them the *Wolf* would probably not have seen him, as it was about one a.m. when the *Wolf* picked him up. The remaining Spanish officers took their watch on the bridge, always with a member of the prize crew in attendance, the Spanish engineers remained in charge of the engine-room, again with a German always present, and the Spanish crew remained on duty as before. There was a prize crew of nine Germans on board; the captain, Lieutenant Rose, who had also been in charge of the *Hitachi* after her capture, and the first officer, who had also filled that post on the *Hitachi*, being the only officers. Lieutenant Rose spoke Spanish in addition to English and French, and the Spanish captain also spoke very good English. Some of the Spanish officers also spoke English, but the knowledge of it was not so general as it was on the *Wolf*, where every officer we met spoke our language, and most of the prize crew spoke quite enough to get on with.

The *Igotz Mendi* had been completed in 1916, and was a ship admirably fitted for her purpose, which, however, was not that of carrying passengers. Ordinarily she was a collier, or carried iron ore. Her decks were of iron, scorchingly hot in the tropics, and icy cold in northern latitudes. There was no place sheltered from the sun in which to sit on the small deck space, and the small awnings which were spasmodically rigged up were quite insufficient for the purpose. There were no cabins except those provided for the officers, who generously gave them up to the married couples on board, the officers taking quarters much more crowded and much less desirable.

The cabins were quite suitable for one occupant each, but very cramped for two; the one occupied by my wife and myself being only seven and a half feet square. Each contained one bunk and one settee, the latter being a sleeping place far from comfortable, as it was only five and a half feet long by about twenty inches wide, and the floor space was very narrow and restricted. There were four cabins, two on each side of a narrow alleyway about two feet wide, while one married couple occupied the chief engineer's cabin further aft on the starboard side, quite a roomy apartment. The port cabin opposite to it was occupied by an old Mauritius-Indian woman and her little granddaughter, the Japanese stewardess, the Australian stewardess already mentioned, and a coloured man going to South Africa with his Chinese wife. Rather crowded quarters, not to mention somewhat unseemly conditions!

The Asiatic passengers had been "intermediate" passengers on the *Hitachi*—*i.e.* between the second-class and deck passengers. The four men above mentioned occupied a space under the poop, it could not be dignified with the name of cabin. It was very small, only one occupant could dress at a time, and immediately in front of it was a reeking pigsty with three full-sized occupants. The passage to it from the saloon on the upper deck was often a perilous one in rough weather and on dark nights, for there was never any light showing on board at night during the whole cruise. The prize crew had quarters on the starboard side under the poop; they were exceedingly small, cramped, and in every way inconvenient and uncomfortable. This, then, was to be our home for the next few months. We did not know for how long, but we regarded the prospect with a certain amount of equanimity, as the ship was unarmed, and we knew we should not be fired on by a hostile cruiser, as might have been the case if we had remained on the *Wolf*.

When we arrived on the Spanish boat we were served with meals at the same time to which the Spanish officers had been accustomed, *i.e.* breakfast at nine and supper at four, but these times were soon afterwards changed to breakfast at eight-thirty, *tiffin* at twelve-thirty and supper at five-thirty. We were lucky to get fresh food for some days. But this soon came to an end, though the stock of muscatels, a quince preserve—called *membrillo*—and Spanish wine lasted very much longer. There was on board a certain amount of livestock; some chickens, and a couple of cows each of which had a calf born on board; these all met the usual fate of such things on appropriate occasions.

For many days after we parted company with the *Wolf* we ambled and dawdled through the sea on a south-westerly course, sometimes stopping altogether for an hour or two, sometimes for half a day, sometimes for a whole day. The monotony of this performance was deadly beyond words. On one of these days, the captain offered to land us at Mauritius on the following morning and give himself up with the crew and ship if we could raise £100,000 for him. Unfortunately, we couldn't!

On the afternoon of the twenty-third the Germans became very agitated at the sight of smoke on the horizon. At first we all thought it was the *Wolf*, but before long we could see two columns of smoke, evidently coming from two steamers traveling together. The prisoners then became very agitated also, as help might be at hand. But the Germans at once changed the course, and manoeuvred at full speed in such a way that we soon got out of sight of the smoke, when we resumed our original course again, after having boxed the compass more than once, and the German captain came down from the bridge and told us there was no relief for us yet. We all felt that if the *Hitachi* had only avoided distant smoke as the German captain had done, we need never have made the acquaintance of the *Wolf*.

On the twenty-fourth we again met the *Wolf* in the evening. Whenever the *Wolf* had an appointment to meet her prize at a certain time and place, the prize always hoisted recognition signals directly she saw the *Wolf* on the horizon. These were made of wicker, and varied in shape on different occasions.

We were now well to the south of Africa, in the roaring forties, and we saw many schools of whales, and albatrosses accompanied us for many days. By December first we had begun to steer northwest, and on the third the captain informed us we were the nearest we should ever be to Cape Town, the port to which I had set out. We were then one hundred and fifty miles off. We met the *Wolf* again on the fifth and travelled in her company during the remainder of that day and the next two, stopping as usual for communication and the sending of stores to us in the evenings just before sunset.

Often, when the ship stopped, Lieutenant Rose would go aboard the *Wolf*, another lieutenant boarding us and remaining in charge during his absence. The *Wolf* on this occasion told us she had sunk the American sailing vessel *John H. Kirby*, from America to East London with a cargo of four hundred motorcars on board, when two days from her destination, the officers and crew being taken on board the *Wolf*. Many people in South Africa would have to dispense with their motor joy-rides at Christmas in consequence.

The evening of December seventh was the last occasion on which we saw the *Wolf* for many days. The two ships now shaped a course for the Brazilian Island of Trinidad, where it was understood the *Wolf* would coal from her prize, and with her spend the Christmas holidays.

Chapter 7

It must not be supposed that the life of the prisoners on the *Igotz Mendi* in any way approximated to that of passengers on an ordinary passenger ship. To begin with, there were no ship's servants to wait on us with the exception of the Spanish steward, a youth who "waited" at table and excelled in breaking ship's crockery. If the cabins were to be kept clean, we had to do it ourselves. Every morning saw the occupants sweeping out and cleaning up their cabins, as no ship's servant ever entered them. The water supply was very limited, and had to be fetched by ourselves—no matter what the weather—sometimes from the fore peak, and sometimes from a pump near the ship's galley.

Washing water and drinking water were served out twice a day, at 8 a.m. and 4 p.m., an ordinary water can being the allowance of the former, and a water bottle that of the latter. The supply of washing water was very inadequate, and no hot water was ever available. After washing ourselves, we had to wash our clothes in the same water—for there was of course no laundry on board—and then the cabin floor after that. By this time the water was mud. It was impossible to have a proper bath all the time we were on board, for there was no water supply in the bathroom, and it was kept in an extremely dirty condition.

The saloon, about eighteen feet square, in which all the meals were served in two sittings, was very rarely clean, and the habits of the captain's pup did not improve matters. The pup, born on the *Wolf*, rejoiced in the name of "Luchs" and as his presence was so evident in the saloon, it was often appropriately named the "*Salon de luxe*." The table "appointments" were often disgusting. The table cloth was filthy after the first meal or so, thanks to the rolling of the ship, but was only changed twice, sometimes only once a week. Cups were used without saucers, and spoons gradually disappeared, so that towards the end one had to suffice between four or five persons.

We got thoroughly sick of the food provided, but the German officers and crew had just the same. The *Hitachi* had been carrying ten thousand cases of canned crab to England. A great part of this was saved, and divided between the *Wolf* and her prize. None of us ever want to see or hear of this commodity again; we were fed on it till most of us loathed it, but as there was nothing else to eat when it was served, we perforce had to eat that, or dry bread, and several of us chose the latter. Bully beef, every variety of bean, dried vegetables, dried fish that audibly announced its advent to the table, bean soup, and pea soup we got just as sick of, till, long before the end, all the food served nauseated us. Tea, sometimes made in a coffee pot, sometimes even with salt water, was the usual hot drink provided, but coffee was for some time available once a day.

We owe a great debt to one of our fellow-prisoners, a ship's cook, captured from one of the other ships, who in return for his offer to work as baker was promised his liberty, which fortunately he has now secured, though no thanks to the Germans. He baked, under the most difficult conditions, extraordinarily good bread, and over and over again we should have gone without food but for this. We were often very hungry, for there was nothing to eat between "supper" at 5.30, and breakfast next morning at 8.30. The captain had given each lady a large box of biscuits from the *Hitachi*, and my wife and I used to eat a quarter of a biscuit each before turning in for the night. We could not afford more—the box might have to last us for many months.

Mention has been made of the ship's rolling. Her capacity for this was incredible—in the smoothest sea, whether stopped or under steam, she rolled heavily from side to side, and caused great discomfort, inconvenience, and often alarm to all on board. The remark, "The *Mendi* roll, fresh every day for every meal, for breakfast, dinner and tea," was made by someone at almost every meal time, as we clutched at our food, gliding or jumping from end to end of the saloon table, accompanied by the smashing of crockery and upsetting of liquids and soup. Even the captain was astonished at the rolling of the ship, as he well might have been, when one night he, in common with most of us, was flung out of his berth. No ship ever rolled like it—the bath in the bathroom even got loose and slid about in its socket, adding to the great din on board.

As may be imagined there was not much to do on board. The few books we had between us were passed round and read over and over again. Some were also sent over from the *Wolf* for us. Card games of various kinds also helped to pass the time, and the captain and some of the prisoners held a "poker school" morning, afternoon and evening in the saloon. But time, nevertheless, dragged very heavily.

We were at liberty to go practically where we liked on board, but we were never able to get far away from the German sailors, who always appeared to be listening to our conversation, no matter where we were. As on the *Wolf* they were sometimes caught spying on us, and listening at the portholes or ventilators of our cabins.

We next picked up the *Wolf* on the afternoon of December nineteenth and heard that since we had last seen her she had sunk a French sailing vessel loaded with grain for Europe. The two ships proceeded on parallel courses for Trinidad, but about eight p.m. both ships turned sharply round and doubled on their tracks, proceeding on a south-easterly course at full speed. We learnt the reason for this the next day. German raiders had previously coaled and hidden at Trinidad but Brazil was now in the war, so that hole was stopped, and the *Wolf* had intercepted a wireless from the commander of a Brazilian cruiser to the garrison on Trinidad. Hence her rapid flight! But for that wireless message the *Wolf* would have walked right into the trap, and we should have been free within twelve hours from the time she picked up the message.

Once again wireless had been our undoing. The *Hitachi* had wirelessed the hour of her arrival at, and departure from Singapore and Colombo, the *Wolf* of course had picked up the messages and was ready waiting for her. One other ship, if not more, was caught in just the same way. The *Matunga* had wirelessed, not even in code, her departure, with the nature of her cargo, from Sydney to New Guinea, and she wirelessed again when within a few hours of her destination. The *Wolf* waited for her, informed her that she had on board just the cargo the *Wolf* needed, captured, and afterwards sunk her. The *Wolf's* success in capturing ships and evading hostile cruisers was certainly due to her intercepting apparently indiscriminate wirelessing between ships, and between ships and shore—at one time in the Indian Ocean the *Wolf* was picking up news in four languages—and to her seaplane which enabled her to scout thoroughly and to spot an enemy ship long before she could have been seen by the enemy.

Soon after leaving the Indian Ocean, the seaplane had been taken to pieces and placed in the 'tween decks, so that if the *Wolf* had been seen by another steamer, her possession of a seaplane would not be revealed.

The two ships proceeded on their new course at full speed for the next two days. On the twenty-first they slowed down, hoping to coal in the open sea. The next day both ships stopped, but the condition of the sea would not admit of coaling; we were then said to be about seven hundred miles east of Montevideo. It was a great disappointment to the Germans that they were prevented from coaling and spending their Christmas under the shelter of Trinidad, but it became quite clear that all the holes for German raiders in this part of the ocean had now been stopped, and that they would have to coal in the open sea or not at all. Some of us thought the Germans might go back to Tristan da Cunha or even to Gough Island—both British possessions in the South Atlantic—but the Germans would not risk this. Even St. Helena was mentioned as a possible coaling place but the Germans said that was impracticable, as it would mean an attack on an unfortified place, as if this would have been a new procedure for German armed forces!

But the disappointment about Trinidad was mitigated by other wireless news received. The commander of the *Wolf* called all his men together, and harangued them to the effect that the latest news was that Russia and Rumania were now out of the war, having given in to Germany, that the war would certainly be over in six months, and that the *Wolf* would then go home in safety to a victorious, grateful and appreciative Fatherland. Some such spur as this was very necessary to the men, who were getting very discontented with the length of the cruise and conditions prevailing, notably the monotony of the cruise and threatened shortage of food, drink and tobacco. The *Wolf* had brought out from Germany enormous stores of provisions for the cruise, which was expected to last about a year. In fact, her cargo from Germany consisted of coal, stores, ammunition and mines only. She replenished her stores solely from the prizes she took.

Christmas Eve was still too rough for the ships to tie up alongside, and our Christmas the next day was the reverse of merry. The Germans had held a Christmas service on the *Wolf* on Christmas Eve, and sounds of the band and singing were wafted to us over the waters. We could hold no service on the *Igotz Mendi* as we had no piano, but our friends on the *Wolf*, so we heard afterwards, gathered together in the 'tween decks and joined in some Christmas music. On Christmas morning the Spanish captain regaled the ladies with some choice brand of Spanish wine, and offered first-class cigars to the men prisoners, rather better than the "*Stinkadoros*" sometimes offered us by the crew. German officers on the ships exchanged visits and we all tried to feel the day was not quite ordinary.

Our thoughts and wishes on this sad Christmas Day may perhaps be "better imagined than described." The German officers had a great feast and a jolly time on the *Wolf.* One cow and three pigs had been killed for the Christmas feast, but they did not go far between nearly eight hundred people and all the prisoners, at least, were glad when the dismal farce of Christmas under such conditions was over.

The weather on Boxing Day was only a little more favourable than that on Christmas Day, but the Germans decided to wait no longer to coal the *Wolf.* They had previously conveyed water to our ship from the *Wolf* in boats. The same method of transferring coal was discussed, but that idea was abandoned. At five p.m. she tied up alongside us. She bumped into us with considerable force when she came up, and not many of us on board the *Igotz Mendi* will ever forget that night. Both ships were rolling heavily, and repeatedly bumping into each other, each ship quivering from end to end, and the funnel of the *Igotz Mendi* was visibly shaking at every fresh collision. Sleep was impossible for anyone on our boat; in fact, many feared to turn in at all as they thought some of the plates of the boats might be stove in.

The next day was no better, but rather worse. About six p.m. there was a great crash which alarmed all it was due to the *Wolf's* crashing into and completely smashing part of the bridge of our ship. This was enough for the Germans. They decided to suspend operations, and at seven p.m. the *Wolf* sheered off, having coaled six hundred tons in twenty-five hours. The coaling process had severely damaged the *Wolf,* many of whose plates were badly dented. We had lost eighteen large fenders between the ships, and the *Wolf* was leaking to the extent of twelve tons an hour. The *Igotz Mendi* had come off better. None of her plates were dented, she was making no water, and the only visible signs of damage to her were many twisted and bent stanchions on the port side that met the *Wolf.*

We had been allowed to send letters for Christmas—censored, of course, by the Germans—to our *Hitachi* friends on the *Wolf,* and when the two ships were alongside we were allowed to speak to them, though conversation under such conditions was very difficult, as one minute our friends would be several feet above us, and the next below us with the rolling of the ship; and the noise of the coaling, shouting of orders, and roaring of the water between the ships was deafening.

There did not seem much point in censoring letters, as the prisoners on the *Igotz Mendi* and the *Wolf* were allowed to talk to each other a day or so after the letters were sent, and although a German sentry was on guard while those conversations were going on, it was possible for the prisoners to say what they liked to each other, as the sentry could only have caught an occasional word or two.

I have since been asked why the prisoners and Spaniards on the Spanish ship did not attack the prize crew and seize the ship when we were not in company with the *Wolf*. It sounds quite simple, but it must be remembered that although the prize crew was certainly a small one, they were well supplied with arms, bombs, and hand grenades, while the prisoners and Spaniards had no arms at all, as they had all been taken away by the Germans. Furthermore, an attack of this kind would have been far worse than useless unless its absolute success could have been definitely assured. There were very few young and able men among the prisoners, while the German prize crew were all picked men, young and powerful.

The working crew of the ship was composed of Spaniards and other neutrals, including a Greek and a Chilean. It would have been absolutely necessary to have secured the allegiance and support of every one of these. The plan of seizing the ship, which sounds simple, was discussed among us many a time, but it was in reality quite impracticable. What would our fate have been if we had tried—and failed? And what of the women and children on board?

Chapter 8

We had been encouraged by the Germans to think—they had in fact definitely told us—that the *Igotz Mendi* with us on board was to be sent to Spain when the Germans released her. This news greatly rejoiced the Spaniards, who had naturally become very depressed, more especially as they knew that if no news were received of them for six weeks after the date on which they were due at Colombo, a requiem mass would, according to Spanish custom, be said for them in their churches at home.

On December twenty-ninth, all of which and the previous day, together with many succeeding days, were spent in transferring our cargo coal to our bunkers, the Germans on our ship and on the *Wolf* ostentatiously bade each other goodbye, and letters from prisoners on the *Wolf* were brought to us to post in Spain when we landed. The idea of the *Wolf* remaining out till the war was over in six months was abandoned, and we were told she would now go home to Germany. Why we were told this, the first time we had been informed of the *Wolf's* plans, we never knew, except that it might have been an excuse to keep dragging us over the seas, for the *Wolf* would never have allowed us to get ashore before she reached Germany. Now that we knew the Germans always intended taking us to Germany, it is obvious that it was quite immaterial to them if they told us their plans. They wished to keep us, and having told us of their future plans, it is plain they could not afford to release us.

But at that time we really began to think we were going to be landed in Spain, and the news raised the spirits of all of us. Those who had been learning Spanish before now did so with redoubled energy, and some of us even marked out on a pocket atlas our railway route from Bilbao or Cadiz—for the Spanish captain thought it most likely we should be landed at one of those ports through Spain and France.

We even got information from the Spaniards as to hotels, railways, and sights to see in Spain. It seemed as if the end of our cruise, with our freedom, were really in sight, especially as the captain had told some of us on December sixteenth that in six weeks our captivity would be over. Some of us, however, still inclined to the belief that the Germans would release the ship and order her back to Java or Colombo or Calcutta; while others believed we should ultimately be landed in Dutch Guiana or Mexico, two of the few remaining neutral countries left.

On the last day of the year a rumour went round the ship that we should be taken far north—about 60° N.—to a point from which the *Wolf* would get to Germany before we could reach Spain. That, in the opinion of most of us, put an end to the prospect of landing in Spain. The Germans would run no risks of our giving information about the *Wolf*. But this scheme would have left uneliminated one very important risk. After the ships would have separated, there was still a chance of the prize being intercepted by an Allied cruiser before the *Wolf* got home, and if that had happened, the *Wolf's* goose would have been cooked indeed. So Spain looked very improbable.

I approached the captain on the last day of the year and spoke to him on the point. He confirmed the rumour, and said we should be sent back and landed at a Spanish island, most probably Las Palmas. I made a vigorous, though I knew it would be quite a useless protest against this scheme. I pointed out that the ship, which by then would be almost empty, was not a suitable one in which to carry women and children into the North Atlantic in mid-winter gales, and that people who had spent many years in the tropics would not be able to stand such weather, unprovided as they were with winter clothing (although the commander of the *Wolf* had certainly sent over some rolls of flannelette—stolen from the *Hitachi*—for the ladies to make themselves warm garments!) Also that in case of distress we could call for no help, as our wireless would only receive and not send messages. The captain brushed these complaints aside, saying the ship was in good trim and could stand any weather, that it would only be intensely cold on a very few days, that arrangements would be made that we should suffer as little from the cold as possible, and that there was very little likelihood of our being in distress.

I then pointed out to him that our own government prohibited our women from traveling through the submarine zone at all, but that he proposed to send them through it twice, and to give us a double dose of the North Atlantic at the very worst time of the year. He replied that going north we should go nowhere near the submarine zone, that he was just as anxious to avoid submarines as we were, and that when we parted far up in the North Atlantic, the *Igotz Mendi* would be given a "submarine pass" guaranteeing her safety from attack by the U-boats, and special lights to burn at nights.

I replied that I failed to see the use of a "submarine pass" as U-boats torpedoed at sight, and would not trouble to ask for a pass. He replied by asking me if I had ever heard of a neutral boat being torpedoed without warning. I answered that I had heard of such being done many times, and reminded him that the *Igotz Mendi* was painted the Allied grey colour and therefore would not be recognized as a neutral but regarded by the U-boats as an enemy ship. He ended the interview by saying that he was carrying out the orders of the *Wolf's* commander, and had no choice but to obey. This news of the *Wolf's* intentions angered us all, and we all felt that there was very little chance of ever seeing land again, unless an Allied cruiser came to our aid. We regarded this plan of the Germans as a deliberate one to sink us and the ship when they had got all they wanted out of her.

The two ships had parted on the evening of the thirtieth, both going north, and we did not see the *Wolf* again till the morning of January fourth. She was then seen to be overhauling a ship on the horizon. We followed at a short distance and before long saw a ship in full sail. The *Wolf* approached her, spoke her, and to our intense astonishment released her. It seemed too good to be true that the *Wolf* would leave any ship she met quite unmolested, but so it was—for a short time. It was between ten and eleven when the *Wolf* and her prize proceeded on their original course and the sailing ship crossed our course astern. About one-thirty p.m. however, we changed our course and turned about. We were all mystified as to what was going to happen, until we saw a sail on the horizon.

The *Wolf's* purpose was evident then. She was going back to destroy the ship whose existence she had forgiven in the morning. Imagine the feelings of the crew of her prey; seeing the *Wolf* bearing down on them in the morning, their suspense as to their fate and that of their ship, their joy at their release, and—here was the *Wolf* again! What would their fate be now? The *Wolf* did not leave them long in doubt. She came up to her prize about five p.m. She was a *Wolf's* shipping register that she was four-masted bark in full sail, in ballast from the Cape to South America, and made a beautiful picture as she lay bathed in floods of golden light from the setting sun. Before dark, however, preparations had begun to remove her officers, crew and provisions, and this was completed in a few hours.

We were invited by the Germans to stay up and see the end. We waited up till past eleven and saw lights flitting about the doomed ship, as the German sailors were removing some things, making fast others, and placing the bombs to blow her up. But none waited up for the end, which we heard took place after midnight. The ship first canted over, her sails resting on the water, righted herself and then slowly disappeared. It was a beautiful moonlight night for the commission of so dark a deed. The Germans afterwards told us that when the *Wolf* first spoke the bark, she gave her name and said she was a Norwegian ship, and so was released. The Germans had later discovered she was from the British owned before the war, and therefore to be destroyed.

The Germans told us that on the bark they had seen some English newspapers, and in them was some news of the two men who had escaped from the *Wolf* near Sunday Island. One of them had died while swimming ashore—the other, after some weeks alone on the island, had been picked up by a Japanese cruiser. The news this man was able to give was the first that the outside world had known about the *Wolf* for many months, and the Germans realised that their enemies would be looking out for them and trying to prevent their return to Germany. This man would also be able to give an exact description of the *Wolf*, the names of the ships she had captured before his escape, and the probable fate of other vessels since missing. This, we felt, would bring at least a little comfort to our relatives, who might conclude we were on the raider and not hopelessly lost, as they must have feared.

We had hoped our captors might have put us all on the sailing ship and sent us off on her to South America, as the *Wolf* would have been well away and out of danger before we could have got ashore. But they did not entertain any such idea. Some of us requested that the lifeboats of the sailing ship might be sent over to our ship, as we had only two lifeboats, a couple of small dinghies, and an improvised raft, not sufficient for sixty-five people; but the Germans would not send us these lifeboats, as they said they were leaky!

The question of baggage had to be again considered. It was evident we should be able to save very little, perhaps not even a handbag, if the ships were sunk by the Germans, and the prisoners put into the lifeboats. However, we ourselves packed in a handbag our most precious treasures we had brought from Siam. But in case it was impossible to save even so little, we collected the most valuable of our letters and papers and had them sewn up in sail cloth to put in our pockets. The King of Siam had conferred a decoration on me before I left—this was carefully packed and sewn up. I was determined to save this, if nothing else, though it seemed hopeless to expect to save many treasures, parting presents and addresses presented to me by my Siamese friends.

Earlier in my service, the King of Siam had conferred another decoration on me, and I was carrying with me His Majesty's Royal License for this, signed by him, and also King George V's Royal License with his sign manual, giving me permission to accept and wear the decoration. Both of these documents, together with others highly valued which I was also determined to save, were secured in watertight cases, ready to be put in my pockets at the last moment.

We remained in company of the *Wolf* for the next few days, and at seven p.m. on the tenth the *Wolf* again came alongside in the open sea and coaled from us till seven p.m. on the next day. Conditions were slightly better than on the previous occasion, but still quite sufficiently unpleasant. More fenders were lost and the *Wolf* was further damaged. The great uproar caused by the winches going all night, the periodic emptying of ashes dragged in iron buckets over the iron decks, the shifting of coal from the bunkers immediately underneath our cabins, and the constant bumping of the ships made sleep quite out of the question, and we were very glad indeed when the *Wolf* sheered off. On this occasion the way in which she came alongside and sheered off was a beautiful piece of seamanship. On the eleventh we again saw and spoke to our *Hitachi* friends on the *Wolf*— the last opportunity we had of doing so. On the next day we crossed the Equator and then for some days we saw the *Wolf* no more.

About this time, I experienced a little trouble with one of the German sailors. Most of them were courteous and kindly disposed, but one, a boorish, loutish bully who served us with drinks at table, was a painful exception to this. I complained to him once about not serving me properly. He waited outside the saloon and cursed me afterwards. "I, a German sailor," he said, "not your steward!" I told him that if he had any reason to complain of what I had said or done he should report me to his captain, and that if he had not done so by six that evening, I should report him for insolence. Needless to say, he said nothing to the captain, so I reported him. The captain at once thanked me for doing so, called him up at once, and gave him a good wigging. I had no more trouble from him afterwards.

On January fourteenth I approached the captain and asked him if the Germans on the *Wolf*, when they got to Germany, would have any means of finding out whether we on the *Igotz Mendi* had safely arrived in Spain. He replied that they would. I then asked him whether, if we were all lost on the *Igotz Mendi* on her return voyage to Spain, the German Government would inform the British Government of our fate. He replied that would certainly be done. I further asked him whether we might send letters to the *Wolf* to have posted in Germany in the event of our not arriving in Spain. Most of us had to settle up our affairs in some way in case we might be lost at sea, and wished to write farewell letters to our home people. We ourselves had to write a farewell letter to our daughter, born in Siam, from whom we had been separated, except for short periods of furlough spent in England, for twelve years. It seemed very hard that after this long separation, and just when we were looking forward to a joyful and fairly speedy reunion, we should perhaps never see her again.

The captain said we might write these letters, which would not be posted if the *Igotz Mendi* with us on board got back safely to Spain, he added:

> But, we have changed our plans, and now intend that you should be landed in Norway. It will be safer for you all, and you will not have to risk meeting our submarines in the Atlantic again. When we arrive in Norwegian waters, the German prize crew will be taken off the ship after the *Wolf* has got home, the ship will be handed over to the Spaniards, and you will all be landed in Norway, from where you can easily make your way to England.

Here was quite a new plan—how much truth there was in this declaration will be seen hereafter. From now onwards definite promises began to be made to us concerning the end of our captivity, "in a month you will be free," "the next full moon will be the last you will see at sea," etc., etc.

We were now of course proceeding north every day, keeping in mid-Atlantic—always well off the trade routes, though of course we crossed some on our way north. On the nineteenth the captain again thought he saw distant smoke on the horizon, and we careered about to avoid it as before. But on this occasion we were running away from a cloud! The next day we left the tropics, and with favourable weather were making an average of about 180 knots daily. On several days (about this time) we passed through, large masses of sea-wood, drifting from the Sargasso Sea. We did not meet the *Wolf* on the twenty-second as our captain evidently expected to do, and we waited about for her several hours.

But next day we did meet her, and we were then told that in eighteen days we should be ashore. We were then about 30° N. and we parted from the *Wolf* the same afternoon.

It was always a great relief to us all when we parted from her keeping our ship's company of prisoners intact. For the men amongst us feared we might all be put upon the *Wolf* to be taken to Germany, leaving our wives on the *Igotz Mendi*. This, so we had been told, had been the intention of the *Wolf's* commander when the prisoners were first put on the Spanish boat. He had ordered that only women, and prisoners above sixty and under sixteen should be put on the *Igotz Mendi*, but the German doctor, a humane and kindly man, would have nothing to do with this plan, and declared he would not be responsible for the health of the women if this were done. So that we owe it to him that wives were not separated from their husbands during this anxious time, as the commander of the *Wolf* had inhumanely suggested.

Chapter 9

A last effort was made to persuade the captain to ask the *Wolf's* commander to release the Spanish ship here, take all the prize crew off, and send us back to Cape Town, for a suspicion began to grow in our minds that Germany and nowhere else was the destination intended for us. But our captain would not listen to this suggestion, and said he was sure the Spanish captain would not go back to Cape Town even if he promised to do so.

On the next day, January twenty-fourth, relief seemed nearer than it had done since our capture four months before. I was sitting on the starboard deck, when suddenly I saw coming up out of the mist, close to our starboard bow, what looked like a cruiser with four funnels. The Spanish officer on the bridge had apparently not seen it, or did not want to! Neither apparently had the German sailor, if, indeed, he was even on the bridge at that moment. I rushed to inform the American sailing ship captain of my discovery, and he confirmed my opinion that it was a four-funnelled warship.

The Germans were by this time fully alarmed and the ship slowed down a little; the captain, evidently also thinking that the vessel was a cruiser, went to his cabin to dispose of the ship's papers, the crew got into their best uniforms to surrender, and it looked as if help were at hand at last. We were all out on deck, delighted beyond words, and saw the ship—it must be remembered that it was a very misty day—resolve itself into two two-funnelled ships, apparently transports, one seemingly in distress and very much camouflaged, and the other standing by. Soon, however, they proceeded on their course and crossed our bows fairly close. We were then all ordered to our cabins, and we saw the two ships steam off to the westward, without having spoken to us or given any evidence of having seen us at all.

It was a most bitter disappointment to us, comparable to that of shipwrecked sailors on a desert island watching a ship expected to deliver them pass out of sight. But it was a great relief to the Germans. We never discovered what ships they were, but the American said he believed them to be American transports and that each mounted a gun. If only we had seen them the day before, when we were in the company of the *Wolf*, they might have been suspicious, and probably have been of some help to us.

In the middle of the excitement the Spanish chief mate had rushed onto the bridge and into the wireless-room, and while the wireless operator was out of the room, or his attention had been diverted, he took from their places all the six or eight bombs on board and threw them overboard. It was a plucky act, for had he been discovered by the armed sentry while doing it, he would have undoubtedly been shot on the spot. On the next day, on the morning of which he saw two sailing ships far distant, an inquiry was held as to the disappearance of the bombs, which would of course have been used to sink the ship, and the chief mate owned up. He said that he did it for the sake of the women and children on board as the sea was rough their lives would have been in danger if they had been put in the lifeboats when the ship was bombed. He was confined to his cabin for the rest of the voyage, and later sentenced by the commander of the *Wolf* to three years' imprisonment in Germany and a fine of two thousand *marks*. From this time on all the Spanish officers were relieved of their duties.

The Germans had told us that, in the event of the prize being captured while the weather was rough, the ship would not be bombed or sunk, as they had no desire to endanger the lives of the women or children amongst us. In fact, so they said, the ship would not be bombed under any conditions when once the *Wolf* had got all the coal she wanted. It was indeed difficult to see what purpose would be served by the Germans in sinking the Spanish ship, if she were overhauled by an Allied cruiser. The Allies could not keep her, as she would have to be restored to Spain—the Germans said they would not keep her, but return her to her owners. To have deliberately sunk her would only have meant a gratuitous offense to Spain.

Nevertheless, the next time we met the *Wolf* a new supply of bombs and hand grenades was put on board our ship. At the same time an extra Lieutenant came on board, additional neutrals were sent over to help work the ship, and the prize crew was increased from nine to nineteen. All the prize crew now wore caps and the words "S. M. S. *Otter*" inscribed thereon.

The *Kaiser's* birthday, which fell on a Sunday, was marked by a most terrific storm. The wind was raging for hours at a hurricane force between eleven and twelve, the seas were between thirty and forty feet high and it seemed impossible that the ship could live in such a sea. But notwithstanding terrible rolling, she shipped very little water, but all of the prisoners were alarmed at the rough weather and the rolling of the ship.

From this day onwards we lived in a condition of great misery and death stared us in the face many times. It got colder and colder every day for a considerable time; the food got worse and worse and we were on short rations; the ship became more and more dirty, smokes ran short—only some ancient dusty shag brought from Germany by the *Wolf*, and some virulent native tobacco from New Guinea remained—and conditions generally became more and more beyond endurance. Darkness fell early in these far northern latitudes, and the long nights were very dreary and miserable. Sundays seemed to be the days on which the worst storms occurred, though on very few of the days from this time onwards did we have anything but extremely dirty weather.

On February fifth we again met the *Wolf*—we had sighted her on the evening of the fourth, but it was too rough then to communicate. With the *Wolf's* usual luck the weather moderated next day, and the ships stopped. Just as the Germans on land always seemed to get the weather they wanted, so they were equally favoured at sea. This was noticed over and over again.

Those who had written letters to be sent on the *Wolf* sent them over on this day, and the Spanish chief mate expected to be sent aboard the *Wolf*, as we might not meet her again. Luckily for him, however, he was not transferred, and neither he nor we ever saw the *Wolf* again, after the morning of February sixth.

We heard from the *Wolf* that she was getting very short of food, and that there was much sickness, including many cases of scurvy, on board. Some of the prisoners, we knew, had very little clothing, and positively none for cold weather, and our hearts were sore at the thought of so many of our fellow countrymen, many of whom we had known in good and ill fortune, being taken into captivity in Germany.

The next day we entered the Arctic circle. The cold was intense and the cabins were icy, the temperature falling as low as 14° F. in some of them. There was no heating apparatus on the ship, with the exception of a couple of small heating pipes in the saloon. The cabin curtains froze to the ports; all the cabin roofs leaked and it was impossible to keep the floors and bedding dry; and in our cabin, in addition, we had water constantly flowing and swishing backwards and forwards between the iron deck of the ship and the wooden floor of the cabin. This oozed up through the floor and accumulated under the settee, and on many nights we emptied five or six buckets full of icy water from under the settee which had also to be used as a bed.

At last I persuaded the captain to allow one of the sailors to drill a hole in the side of the cabin so that water could have an outlet on to the deck. Since the great storm on the *Kaiser's* birthday our feet had never been dry or warm, and were in this condition till some hours after we got ashore. The ports of the cabins had all long ago been painted black in order that no light might show through at night. We had to sit in these cold and dark cabins during the day.

The weather prevented us from being on the deck, which was often covered with frost and snow, and often there was nowhere else to sit. The electric light was on for only a limited time each day, so, as the ports could not be opened on the account of the cold, we asked and obtained permission to scratch a little of the paint off the ports in our cabin. This made things a little more bearable, but it can easily be imagined how people who had been living in tropical climates for many years fared under such conditions.

It was nothing short of cruel to expose women and children to this after they had been dragged in captivity over the seas for many months. The captain had ordered a part of the bunkers to be cleared, so that the prisoners might sit there in the cold weather. But the place was so dirty and uncomfortable and difficult of access, in addition to its being in darkness, and quite unprovided with seats, that most of the prisoners preferred the crowded little saloon.

On the morning of February seventh we for the first time encountered ice floes, when attempting the northern passage between Greenland and Iceland. About eleven a.m. we stopped and hooted for the *Wolf* as a fog had come on, the first time we had heard a steamer's siren since the day of our capture. We waited for some hours in the ice, but no answering signal came back, so the captain decided to turn back as he thought it impossible to force his way through the ice. We therefore went back again on our course, the captain hoping that the wind would change and cease blowing the ice floes from off the shores of Greenland.

After a day or two of slow steaming on this course we resumed our attempt to go to the north of Iceland, evidently to escape the attention of the British ships which the Germans expected to encounter between the south of Iceland and the Faroes.

But before long it became evident that ice was still about, and in the darkness of the early morning of February eleventh we bumped heavily against ice several times. This time the captain abandoned his attempt to go through the northern passage, and turned the ship round to try his luck in the passage he did not expect to be so free from British attentions.

We thought perhaps that as we were on short rations and water was running short and the case of us all really desperate, the captain would land us and give up the ship at Reykjavik, leaving us there to be rescued. Even a stay in Iceland would be better than one in Germany, for which country we now all suspected we were bound.

To add to our miseries, the captain told us on February eleventh *for the first time* that it was, and always had been the intention to take us on the *Igotz Mendi* to Germany, there to be interned in civilian prisoners' camps. He told us too, that the women and those of the men over military age would be released at once, but we all declined to believe anything else our captors told us, as they had deliberately and repeatedly deceived us by assuring us at various times that they were going to land us in Spain, or Norway, or some other neutral country.

At daybreak on the eleventh we were still among ice floes, but going away from instead of meeting them, and on that morning we saw in the distance the coast of Iceland, the first land that we had seen since the Maldive Islands, a week after our capture, *i.e.* more than four months before. We also saw a few fishing boats off the coast.

We now shaped a course for the coast of Norway, keeping to the north of the Faroes. On Sunday, the seventeenth, we again ran into a very heavy storm. Ever since the storm on January twenty-seventh the propeller had been constantly racing and sending shudders through the ship from stem to stern. On this day this feature, which was always disconcerting and to a certain extent alarming, became more marked, and the thud with which the ship met the seas more and more loud, so loud indeed that on one occasion the captain thought we had struck a mine and rushed from the saloon to the bridge to ascertain what damage had been done.

The captain and crew had by this time become very anxious as to the fate of the *Wolf*, as no news had been received concerning her.

213

Day after day on which the captain told us he expected news went by without any being received. But on the evening of the nineteenth the captain informed us that he had received a wireless message announcing the safe arrival of the *Wolf* at a German port. The Germans seemed singularly little elated at the news, and hardly ever mentioned the subject again after that evening. This was so different from what we had expected that most of the prisoners did not believe the *Wolf* had got home. We hoped that she had been intercepted and captured by a British cruiser, and that with any luck a similar fate might be in store for us.

The *Wolf* had certainly made a wonderful cruise and the Germans were naturally very proud of it. They had successfully evaded the enemy for fifteen months, and had kept their ship in good repair, for they had first-class mechanics and engineers on board. But she must have been very weather-worn and partly crippled before she arrived at a home port. She had touched at no port or no shore from the day she left Germany till the day she returned to the Fatherland. She had sunk seven steamers and seven sailing ships, and claimed many more ships sunk as a result of her minelaying.

Beside the prizes already named she had captured the *Tarantelle*, *Wordsworth*, *Jumna*, *Dee*, *Winslow*, and *Encore*, the last three of which were sailing vessels. Her first prize, the *Tarantelle*, taken in February, 1917, in the Indian Ocean, was originally a German ship captured by the British. On her recapture by the Germans, she was equipped as a raider and minelayer and sent off on an expedition by herself. But soon afterwards she came to grief near Aden "through enemy action."

Chapter 10

The Germans were now getting very anxious as they approached the blockade zone. They affected, however, to believe that there was no blockade, and that there was no need of one now that America was in the war. "No one will trade with us," they said, "accordingly there is no need for a blockade." Nevertheless, they were at great pains to keep as far as possible from any place in which British ships might appear. But unfortunately not one did appear, here or anywhere else, to rescue us, although we felt certain in our own minds that some of our ships would be present and save us in these parts of the seas which we believed were regularly patrolled. It was a bitter disappointment to us that we saw none.

But as some of the passengers remarked to the captain, "If there is no blockade, as the Germans say, why haven't you more raiders out, instead of only one, and why have so few been able to come out?"

There was of course no answer to this! The captain further remarked that even if there were a blockade it would always be possible to get through it at the weekend, as all the British blockading fleet returned to port for that time! "The *Wolf*," he said, "came out and got home through the blockade at the weekend." It was quite simple, we were to do the same, and we should be escorted by submarines as the *Wolf* had been on both occasions.

On the twentieth we were off Bergen and saw the coast in the distance. I suggested to the captain that it would save much trouble if he would land us there. He smilingly replied that he would very much like to, but was afraid it was quite impossible! The next day we were nearer the coast and saw a couple of suspicious-looking steam trawlers which gave the Germans a few anxious moments, and on that night we encountered the greatest storm we experienced on the cruise. The wind was terrific, huge seas broke over the ship, the alleyway outside the cabins was awash all the night, and the water even invaded the saloon to a small extent.

Articles and receptacles for water that had not been made absolutely fast in the cabins were tossed about; many cabins were drenched and running with water. The noise of the wind howling and the seas breaking on the deck was so alarming to those in the outside cabins that they left them and assembled in the saloon, though sleep that night was utterly impossible, there or anywhere else on the ship. The ship, though steaming full speed, made no progress that night, but went back, and in three days, the nineteenth, twentieth and twenty-first, made only a hundred knots.

After such stormy nights, and in such bitter cold weather, a breakfast of cold canned crab, or dry bread with sugar, or rice and hot water plus a very little gravy, or bread and much-watered condensed milk, was not very nourishing or satisfying, but very often that was all we had. This weather of course pleased the German captain, who said that no enemy ship would or could board him under such conditions. In fact, he said no enemy vessel would be out of port in such weather! The weather alone was sufficiently terrifying to the landsmen amongst us, and the prospect of having to take to the lifeboats at any moment if the Germans took it into their heads to sink the ship were she sighted by an enemy vessel, added to the fears of all of us.

There had been no boat drill, and the lifeboat accommodation was hopelessly inadequate for the more than eighty people now on board. It is certain that with the mixed crew there would have been a savage fight for the boats. The prospect was alarming from any point of view, and one of the greatest anxiety for us all. Physical distress and discomfort were not the only things we had to contend with—the nervous strain was also very great.

On February twenty-second we rounded the Naze. Here we thought we should certainly come across some British vessel. But that day and the next passed—it seemed as if we, too, were to get in during the weekend!—and hope of rescue disappeared. Many messages had been dropped overboard in bottles and attached to spars, etc., during the voyage, but all apparently in vain. The bearing of the Germans towards us became markedly changed. We were almost in their clutches now, the arrival at Kiel and transfer to Ruhleben were openly talked of, and our captors showed a decided inclination to jeer at us and our misfortunes. We were told that all diaries, if we kept them, must be destroyed, or we should be severely punished when we arrived in

Germany. Accordingly, those of us who had kept diaries made ready to destroy them, but fortunately did not do so. I had written mine in Siamese characters during the whole time, so the Germans could not have gained much information from it.

Sunday, February twenty-fourth dawned, a cold, cheerless day.

"I suppose this time next week we shall be going to church in Kiel," said one of the prisoners to the chief mate at breakfast.

"Or," the latter replied, "I might be going to church with my brother, who is already a prisoner on the Isle of Man!"

We were now in comparatively narrow waters of the Skagerrak, and we saw only one vessel here, a Dutch fishing boat. Our last chance had nearly gone. Most of us were now resigned to our fate and saw no hope—in fact, I had written in my diary the day before "There is no hope left, no boat of ours to save us"—but some said we still might see a British war vessel when we rounded the Skaw. At mid-day the sailor on the lookout came into the saloon and reported to the captain that a fog was coming on.

"Just the weather I want," he exclaimed. "With this lovely fog we shall round the Skaw and get into German waters unobserved." It looked, indeed, as if our arrival in Germany were now a dead certainty.

But the fog that the captain welcomed was just a little too much for him; it was to prove his undoing instead of his salvation. The good old German *Gott* about whom we had heard so much was not going to see them through this time. For once, *we* were to be favoured. The white fog thickened after the mid-day meal, and luckily for us, it was impossible to see far ahead. Soon after two we passed a floating mine, and we knew that before long we should be going through a mine field—not a very cheerful prospect with floating mines round us in a fog.

But we were all too far gone to care now; nothing could be much worse than imprisonment in Germany, and some of us gathered together in our cold and gloomy cabin were discussing the prospects and condition of this when, at three-thirty on that Sunday afternoon, we felt a slight bump, as if the ship had touched bottom. Then another bump, and then still one more! We were fast! Were we really to be saved at the very last minute? It began to look like it, like the beginning of the end, but it would not do to build too much on this slender foundation. The engines continued working, but no progress was made; they were reversed—still no movement. The fog was fairly thick but we could just make out through it the line of the shore and the waves breaking on it some distance away. Two sirens were going at full blast, one from a lightship and one from a lighthouse.

The German officers became agitated; with great difficulty a boat was got out, soundings made, and various means adopted to work the ship off, but all were of no avail. The captain admitted that his charts of this particular spot were not new and not good. It was impossible to tell the state of the tide at this moment; we all hoped it might be high tide, for then our rescue would be certain. The engines were set to work from time to time, but no movement could be made. Darkness fell, and found us still stuck fast. Our spirits had begun to rise, the prospect was distinctly brighter, and soon after six o'clock the assistant lieutenant went ashore in mufti to telephone to the nearest port, Frederikshavn, for help. What reply he received we never heard, but we *did* hear that he reported he was on a German ship bound from Bergen to Kiel and wanted help. Lourenco Marquez to Kiel, *via* Iceland, would have been nearer the truth!

About eight o'clock we heard from one of the neutrals among the crew that the captain of a salvage tug was shortly coming aboard to inquire into matters. The ladies among us decided to stay in the saloon while the captain of the tug interviewed the German captain in the chartroom above it. On the arrival of the tug the captain on the bridge, the ladies in the saloon created a veritable pandemonium, singing, shrieking and laughing at the top of their voices. It sounded more like a Christmas party than one of desperate prisoners in distress. The Danish captain departed; what had been the result of his visit we did not know, but at any rate he knew there were women on board. The German captain came down into the saloon, asked pleasantly enough what all the noise was about, and said:

> I have offered the salvage people £5,000 to tow the ship off; money is nothing to us Germans. This will be done at four tomorrow morning, and we shall then proceed on our way to Kiel.

Some of us had talked over a plan suggested by the second mate of a captured ship, by which one of the neutrals among the crew should contrive to go ashore in one of the tug's boats in the darkness and communicate with the nearest British Consul, informing him of the situation and the desperate case we were in. We promised him £500 to be raised among the "saloon passengers," if by so doing our rescue should be accomplished. We had remained in the saloon to talk over developments when we heard that a Danish gunboat had come nearly alongside, and that her commander was coming on board. He had presumably received a report from the captain of the tug.

We heard afterwards that he had his suspicions about the ship and had brought with him on board one of his own men to make inquiries of the crew, among whom were Norwegians, Swedes and Danes, while he kept the German commander busy in the saloon. The previous mistake of taking the Danish captain on to the bridge was not to be repeated. The commander of the gunboat was to come into the saloon, so the ladies could not remain there and make their presence known. But some of them contrived to leave some of their garments on the table and settee in the saloon—a muff, hats, gloves, etc.

These the Danish commander must have seen; and not only that, for he saw some ladies who had stood in one door of the saloon before they were sent to their cabins, when he entered at the other one. He also saw a passenger in khaki uniform, the Australian major of the A.M.C., and other passengers standing with the ladies in the alleyway. If he had entertained any suspicions as to the correct character of the ship, which the Germans were of course trying to conceal, they must have been strongly confirmed by now. It was now too late for us to be sent to our cabins, as a German sailor came and ordered. We had achieved our object.

It was a night of great unrest, but finally most of us lay down in our clothes. For very many nights we had been unable to rest properly owing to the violence of the weather, the possibility of having to leave the ship at any moment, and our general anxiety concerning our desperate condition.

We had not had our clothes off for many days. At four a.m. we heard the engines working, as the captain had told us they would, but still no movement could be heard. Soon the engines ceased; it was evident then that the attempt to get the ship off must for the present be given up. The wind was rising, and the sea getting rougher, and at six a.m. a German sailor came and knocked at the door of all the cabins, saying, "Get up, and pack your baggage and go ashore."

It was too good to be true—never was an order more willingly and gladly obeyed! But first we had to see how the ship stood with regard to the shore; we went out on deck to look—there was the blessed green shore less than half a mile away, the first really solid earth we had been close to since we left Colombo exactly five months before. Only those who have seen nothing but the sea for many months can imagine with what a thrill of joy we saw the shore, and realized that we were saved at last. We had seen the sea under nearly every aspect possible from the Equator to the Arctic regions, and we had appreciated more than ever before its vastness. Not many of us wished for sea travel again.

It did not take us long to dress and throw our things into our bags. When we had done so and were ready to go to the lifeboat, we were told that we might take no baggage whatever, as the lifeboat was from a shore station and could save lives only, not baggage.

The German captain took his bad luck in good part, but he was of course as sick as we were rejoiced at the turn events had taken. He had known the night before that he could get no help from the Danish authorities, as they refused towing assistance till all the passengers had been taken off the ship. But he had hoped to get off unaided at four in the morning. He professed great anger with the Danes, saying that if they had only helped as he requested, the ship could have been towed off in the night, and we with all our baggage could have been landed at a Danish port alongside a pier the next morning, instead of having to leave all our baggage behind on the ship.

I fancy not many of us believed this; if the ship had been got off we should have brought up at Kiel and not at any Danish port. And, as the tug captain said afterwards, if he had towed the ship off the Germans probably would have cut the hawser directly afterwards, he would have received no pay for his work, and we certainly should not have landed in Denmark.

Chapter 11

A fine lifeboat manned by sturdy Danish sailors was alongside the ship; the sea was very rough, but our ship steady, firmly embedded in the sandy bottom. The packages we had decided to save at any cost were put in our pockets, lifebelts and life-saving waistcoats once more put on, and once more we all climbed a ship's ladder, but as the lifeboat was rising and falling almost the height of the ship with the heavy seas, descent into it was not easy. But nothing mattered now; once over the side of the ship we were no longer in German hands, and were free! The waves dashed over and drenched us as we sat in the lifeboat; we were sitting in icy water, all of us more or less wet through.

At last the lifeboat crew pulled for the shore, the high seas sweeping over us all the way. We grounded on the beach, the sturdy sailors carried some, others jumped into the water and waded ashore, and we were all on *terra firma*, free at last, after weary months of waiting and captivity. Groups of villagers were waiting on the beach to welcome us even at this early hour. They plied us with questions as far as they could, and great was their wonder at what we had to tell.

We had been saved at the eleventh hour, almost the fifty-ninth minute of it; we were at the very gates of Germany, being due at Kiel the very next day. It was a miraculous escape if ever there was one, and came at a moment when all hope had gone. Would that the *Wolf* had gone ashore in the same place! All our fellow-countrymen on board her would then have been free and they could have given information and saved us as well.

What emotions surged within us as we trod the free earth once more! What had we not gone through since we were last on shore! Then it was on British soil; now it was on the soil of a friendly neutral country. We had escaped imprisonment with the enemy, escaped making acquaintance with the notorious Ruhleben of evil fame—the more we reflected on it, and we did so every minute, the more wonderful did our escape appear. But our thoughts also turned to our friends on the *Wolf* who were doomed to meet the cruel fate from which we had so mercifully been delivered.

Once on dry land, and escorted by the villagers, we walked over the sandhills to the lighthouse about half a mile away. There we were received with open arms. The kindly Danes could not do enough for us. We had only what we stood up in; we dried our clothes, other dry garments were offered us, hot drinks and food were supplied liberally, and we were generally made much of. We had come back to life and warmth once more. The lighthouse staff and villagers vied with each other in their effort to make us feel at home and comfortable, and after interviews with some Danish Government official, we were taken to hotels in Skagen, the name of the nearest town, a small summer bathing resort, just to the south of the Skaw. After lunch, the first square meal we had had for months, we set off to telegraph to our relatives and friends, and announce we were still in the world. It was one of our greatest anxieties on board that we could not communicate with our friends, who we knew would be grieving over our disappearance and, we feared, would have given us up for lost.

The same afternoon we walked back to the beach to see if we could go aboard the stranded ship to retrieve our luggage, but the sea was far too rough to allow of this, and the German and Spanish crew had not been taken off. While on the beach we saw two floating mines exploded by a Danish gunboat. We had not only had a narrow escape from the Germans but also from the dangers of a mine field. The next day was also rough for us to go aboard, in fact it was so rough that the lifeboat went out and took everybody off the ship, both Spanish and German. The Spanish first mate was thus saved and after all did not serve his sentence in Germany. It was reported that a German submarine appeared to take off the German officers on this day, but as it was too rough to lower the boats this could not be contrived.

The *Igotz Mendi* was now deserted, but as the Danish authorities had adjudged her, twenty-four hours after her stranding, to be a Spanish ship, she had reverted to her original owners. Accordingly, before leaving her the Spanish captain had hoisted the Spanish flag at her stern, the first time that or any other flag had appeared there since that November morning when the Germans had captured her far away in the Indian Ocean. She was no longer a German prize. She would have been the only one the *Wolf* had secured to take home—a neutral ship with only a few tons of coal on board, and a few married couples, and sick and elderly men as prisoners. Not much to show for a fifteen month's cruise, and even that was denied the Germans; though the *Wolf* had certainly carried home a valuable cargo, and some hundreds of prisoners, besides doing considerable damage to the shipping of the Allies.

The position of the stranded ship was a unique one. She was a neutral ship, a German prize, stranded in neutral waters, with a crew composed of Germans and neutral prisoners, and carrying passenger prisoners of many enemy nationalities—English, Australian, American, Japanese, Chinese and Indian.

Never was there a more dramatic turning of the tables; the Germans were now interned, and we were free. The German officers were sent off under guard to an inland town, and the sailors sent to a camp in another part of Denmark. The sailors did not attempt to disguise their joy at the turn events had taken. On their return to Germany they would have had a few weeks' leave, and then done duty in a submarine, or at the front. Now, they were interned in a land where there was at least much more to eat than they could have hoped for in Germany, and their dangers were at an end till the war was over. They were marched under an armed guard of Danes, up and down the village street several times on one of these days; they were all smiles, singing as they marched along.

The next day a hurricane was still blowing, and going aboard was still out of the question. The ship was blown further in shore and it began to look as if she would break up and we should see nothing of our personal belongings. The day after, however, was beautifully fine, and we left Skagen Harbour in two motor-barges and boarded the ship, which was in charge of the Danish authorities. After some difficulty, for the ship was in a state of great chaos, we secured all our baggage, which was landed that night at Skagen much to our relief, as up to that time we had only what we stood up in at the time we landed from the lifeboat. We had set foot on the *Igotz Mendi* for the last time.

During the week we had to give evidence to the Danish authorities concerning our capture and treatment on board. We were overwhelmed with kindness by the Danes who made no secret of their sympathies with the Allies; invitations to dinners and parties flowed in, and we could not have accepted them all if we had stayed as many weeks as we had days.

On Friday, March first, most of us left Skagen. The whole village turned out to give us a good send off, and snapshots galore were taken—this indeed had been going on ever since we landed. The ladies among us were presented with flowers and chocolates, the men with smokes, and we left with the heartiest good wishes of our warm-hearted hosts.

From Skagen our passage home was arranged by the British Consular authorities. We stayed a few days in Copenhagen and then travelled through Sweden and Norway, leaving a port somewhere in that country for another somewhere in this, and so to London, where we arrived in a characteristic pea-soup fog on the morning of March tenth, after incessant traveling by train and sea for a week. We had not relished another sea voyage—and one across the North Sea least of all—but there was no help for it. We feared that as we had escaped the Germans once, they might make a special effort to sink us crossing the North Sea. But fortunately the U-boats left us alone, though few, if any, of us, turned in during those last few nights.

No comment need be made on the German procedure of dragging their prisoners month after month over the oceans. Such a thing had never been done before. The Germans had had opportunities to release us, but had taken none to do so, as they had evidently determined not to allow any account of the *Wolf's* cruise to be made known. They might have landed the *Hitachi* prisoners on the Maldives and left them there to get to Colombo as best they could, the Germans taking the ship; they might have sent the prisoners on the *Igotz Mendi* to Colombo or Java after they had taken what coal they wanted. As the Spanish captain said, they had a right to take his contraband, but not his ship.

But a question of right did not bother the Germans. Many times they promised him to release his ship, never intending to do so. Whenever they were asked why they did not release us when we thought it possible they always advanced "military reasons" as the excuse. "That," as I said to the captain, "covers a multitude of sins." The commander of the *Wolf* had personally assured the married couples on the *Matunga* that they would be kept no longer than two months. But they were kept seven. Some men had been kept prisoners on the *Wolf* for nearly a year.

It was hard enough on the men, but infinitely worse for the women. One had been eight months, one seven, and others five months in captivity, often under the worst possible conditions. But they all kept cheerful throughout, even when it appeared that they were certain to be taken with their husbands into Germany.

Every man is likely to think under such conditions that he is in a worse case than his fellow-captives, and there were certainly examples of very hard luck amongst us. The American captain had abandoned his sea-calling for six years, and decided at his wife's request, to make one more trip and take her to see her relatives in Newcastle, N.S.W.

They never got there, but had eight months of captivity and landed in Denmark instead. Many sailors had left the Atlantic trade after encounters with the U-boats in that ocean, only to be caught by the *Wolf* in the Pacific. One of the members of the Spanish crew had been a *toreador*, but his mother considered that calling too dangerous and recommended the sea as safer. Her son now thinks otherwise, perhaps she does, too!

The captain of a small sailing ship from Mauritius to West Australia, in ballast to load timber, saw the *Wolf* when a day off his destination. Not knowing her, he foolishly ran up the red ensign—a red rag to a bull, indeed—and asked the *Wolf* to report him "all well" at the next port. The *Wolf* turned about and sunk his little ship. Although the captain was at one time on the *Wolf* almost in sight of his home in Mauritius, his next port was Kiel, where it is to be feared that he, an old man of seventy, is the reverse of "all well."

One of our fellow prisoners had been on the P. & O. liner *Mongolia* when she was sunk by one of the *Wolf's* mines off Bombay. Later, on the *Hitachi*, he was caught by the mine-layer herself! But he defeated the enemy after all, as he escaped on the *Igotz Mendi*. One of the seafaring men with us had already been torpedoed by the Huns in the Channel. Within a fortnight he was at sea again. The next time he was caught and his ship sunk by the *Wolf* off New Zealand. He also escaped on the *Igotz Mendi*, and when last seen ashore was dying to get to sea again, in a warm corner, he said, so that he could "*strafe* the Huns" once more. They had held him prisoner for eight months and he had some leeway to make up.

I thought until our timely rescue came, that our own case was a fairly hard one. I had retired after spending twenty years in government service in Siam, and we had decided to spend some months at least, possibly "the duration," in South Africa before proceeding home. It seemed hard lines that after twenty years in the Far East we were to come to Europe only to be imprisoned in Germany! We have escaped that, but our plans have gone hopelessly astray, our health has not been improved by the treatment on our long voyage, and although we took

225

six months to get from Siam to London, the Germans have succeeded in getting us home much earlier than we, or they, anticipated.

I had been shipwrecked on my first voyage out to Siam in 1897, and taken prisoner on my last voyage home twenty years after. Fortunately, one usually forgets the miseries of sea travel soon after one gets ashore. But never, I think, will one of us ever forget our captivity at sea with our enemies, or the canned crab, the bully beef, the beans, and the roll of the *Igotz Mendi*.

Ten Months in a German Raider

Contents

Introduction

Captain John Stanley Cameron, master of the American bark *Beluga*, who tells the story of his great adventure on board the German raider *Wolf*, and subsequently on the prize ship *Igotz Mendi*, in this volume, is of Scotch parentage, thirty-four years old; a smooth-shaven, canny graduate of the "before the mast" school, and prematurely grey. His father is a well-known figure on the Pacific Coast, being the oldest sailing master living in his part of the world.

Captain Cameron went to sea at the age of three. At thirteen he was earning his living as an able-bodied seaman, and he has been a master of sailing vessels since he was twenty-one. He figured in the news some few years ago by taking a sailing yacht of seventy-four tons from New York to San Francisco; the smallest vessel of her class to beat through the Straits of Magellan. Since then, Captain Cameron has retired from sea—until his last trip as master of the *Beluga*.

In setting down Captain Cameron's story much as it came from his own lips, I have treated it as a simple record of human experience, avoiding any chance of spoiling this bully sea yarn by attempting to give it a literary finish.

Cyril Brown.

CAPTAIN CAMERON AND HIS DAUGHTER NITA

Part One

Captured by Pirates

Little did I dream when I sailed away from San Francisco in the little bark *Beluga* that I should finish my voyage, not in Australia after a two months' trip, but in Denmark, on the other side of the world, after a ten months' experience that has never before been equalled in the annals of sea-going history.

My story could well be called *An Escape from the Jaws of Hell*—for a prisoner's life in Germany under the present conditions is surely a hell on earth. During my six weeks' stay in Denmark I have interviewed neutral sailors who have been sent out of Germany, and old men who have been passported out on account of extreme old age; also prisoners who have escaped over the border into Denmark *via* the coal-train route, and these men one and all paint a picture of a prisoner's life in Germany as being a veritable hell on earth.

We sailed from San Francisco on the 15th day of May, 1917, with a cargo of 15,000 cases of benzine, for Sydney, Australia. After letting go the tug boat and getting sail on the ship, we all settled down for a quiet and uneventful passage. Seldom have I gone to sea under more favourable circumstances. A tight little vessel, a good deep water crew of Scandinavian sailor men, plenty of good wholesome provisions and a cook who knew his business. Both the first and second mates were officers of the old school, with years of experience, so it seemed that I was fortunate in getting so evenly balanced a crew, as owing to the frenzied state of shipping along the Pacific Coast at that time the master was indeed fortunate who found on getting to sea that half of this crew could box the compass, much less hand, reef and steer.

Even under these favourable circumstances there was a "*fly in the ointment.*" On counting noses I made the discovery that the entire ship's company amounted to thirteen (an unlucky number, as every "salt" will testify). A ship's crew of eleven, counting myself, and two passengers, my wife and little daughter. When I called this fact to my wife's attention she laughed at me, saying that was "old sailor's tommyrot" and that we were living in the twentieth century and should have outgrown such silly superstitions. Nevertheless, owing to a strain of Scotch blood in my veins, the superstition remained in my mind for many days until, owing to the humdrum uneventfulness of our progress, this thought died a natural death.

I crossed the equator well to the westward, passing the Fiji Islands and hoping that when I ran out of the southeast trade winds I would get a favourable wind and cut close by the southern ends of New Caledonia. I had a hunch, and if I had been lucky and had two days favourable wind this story would never have happened. But unfortunately, unfavourable winds were encountered, forcing me to the southward and into the regular sailing vessel route.

My wife, an Australian girl by birth, had not been home to see her family since she left them something over ten years ago, and naturally was very anxious to get home and see her many brothers and sisters who had grown up and married since she left. In fact, she had talked of nothing else for the past several years. Each year I promised that we would make the visit "next year," but something or other would show up and spoil my plans. I had given up the sea about six years ago for a "shore job," and was so well pleased with the change that I did not care to go back to the sea again, fearing that I would not be able to change from the sea to the shore life again, as there is something about the sea that gets into the blood and makes it difficult to stay away from it. It was only then an unusual chain of circumstances that left me foot loose at this particular time to take charge of the *Beluga* on this trip. The fact is, it was what my wife called the "Scotch Jew" in me that finally decided me to take this means of making money out of visiting the mother-in-law.

Each day at noon when I placed the vessel's position on the chart, my wife was a very interested spectator and used to measure the distances that remained for us to go. Then she would figure out just how long it would take, under various weather conditions, before she would be able to see her beloved Australia again. Some days when we had a favourable wind and had made a good day's run in the right direction, she would be as happy as could be and singing all the time, but other days when we had made but little progress she would be away down in the dumps, and it would be extremely difficult to get a smile.

On July 9th I was having some work done aloft on one of the masts, when about two o'clock in the afternoon Fritz, a Norwegian sailor working aloft, shouted down, "Smoke, oh, on the port beam." I had a look through my binoculars, and, sure enough, on the horizon to the southwest I could make out the smoke of a steamer. The weather at this time was fine and clear, with a light breeze from the south and we were making only about four knots per hour. In a short time, it became evident that the steamer was coming in our direction, as she was gradually getting larger and more plainly seen. I shouted down the cabin skylight to my wife to come on deck and see the steamer, as she was the only vessel of any description we had seen since leaving San Francisco, almost two months before. She and Juanita, my six-year-old daughter, scampered on deck and were very much interested in watching her. It soon became evident that the steamer was going to pass close to us, and thinking it just possible that she would speak us, my wife and Nita went below to change their frocks.

The steamer was getting closer by this time and her hull was plainly visible. The old superstition regarding the unlucky number "thirteen" flashed through my mind but was instantly dismissed. To all appearances she was the ordinary black-painted, dingy-looking ocean tramp. I studied her intently through the glass, trying to discover some detail that would show her nationality, and had just about concluded that she must be a Jap when Mr. Buckert, my chief officer, came along to where I was standing and asked if I could make her out. I told him she appeared to be either a British or Jap tramp, and handed him the binoculars so that he could have a look.

After studying her for a while he said, "By God, Captain, I don't know her nationality, but she carries the largest crew I have ever seen." I snatched the glasses out of his hand and had a look. Sure enough, by this time the rails both forward and aft were black with men in the regulation man-of-war jumpers. Even at this time I did not think she was a German, but possibly a British armed merchantman, or a British converted auxiliary cruiser, sent from Australia to some of the South Sea islands for patrol duties. However, she soon showed her true colours.

Suddenly she changed her course, heading to pass directly under my stern. At this moment she broke out the German Imperial Navy Ensign at her jackstaff aft and at her signal yard amidships she showed the letters G. T. E., which interpreted from the International Signal Code means "Heave to and I will send a boat on board." After giving me time to read this signal, possibly two minutes, the steamer dropped her bulwarks forward, uncovering her guns, and fired a shot across the *Beluga's* bow. This dispelled any lingering doubt I had in my mind as to what was wanted, and it didn't take us long to clew up our light sails and throw the main yard about.

It was only then that I actually realised that my little vessel had been stopped by a German raider in the South Pacific Ocean almost fifteen thousand miles from the war zone. I stepped to the forward end of the quarterdeck and looked down at the crew on the main deck to see how they seemed to be taking it. These Scandinavian sailor men were standing on the waist, smoking their pipes and discussing the appearance of the steamer, just as if to be captured by an enemy's raider were an every-day occurrence. For myself, I knew that this day marked a crisis in the lives of any of us that were American or British born, and as for my wife and child—God, the thought was like a stab in the heart and seemed to leave me numb and cold. In a moment there flashed through my mind all the accounts I had read in the papers of the German atrocities towards women and children in Belgium and barbarisms practised along the Russian front, and the thought of my wife and child being at the mercy of these people nearly drove me crazy.

On walking aft I saw my wife leaning up against the wheelhouse, her face absolutely bloodless and a look of horror in her eyes that fairly chilled my blood. God! For months after I could see this expression in her eyes every time I closed my eyes. Even now, when I think of it, it makes me feel cold all over. When she saw me she came over and took my hand in hers, looking all the time into my eyes and not saying a word. We stood there for what seemed a century. Presently I called Juanita to us and the three of us went down below to the cabin. We sat on the settee, never saying a word, and poor little Nita started to sob, feeling something sinister in the air, which she did not understand.

In a minute the mate came to the cabin skylight and sang out that the launch would be alongside in a minute. I answered "All right." My wife got up and walked over to the bed and took one of my revolvers (I had two) from under the mattress and handed it to me. Suddenly she threw both her arms around my neck and drew my head into such a position that she could look into my eyes, and said, "Stanley, I want you to promise me that they will never get Juanita." I threw both my arms round her, hugging her tight to myself, and said, "Mamie, I promise; but you must leave it to me." And with a sob I left her and started on deck.

When passing through the wheelhouse, I stopped for a moment to pull myself together. On going on deck I saw a small motor launch just arriving alongside, crowded with German bluejackets, armed to the teeth. A moment more, and a young lieutenant sprang onto the deck and came aft to the quarterdeck where I was standing. Coming to a stand in front of me he saluted and asked in excellent English, with an American accent, "Are you the captain of this vessel?"

I answered, "Yes."

"Where are you from?" was his next question.

I told him San Francisco to Sydney, Australia, fifty-two days out.

"Captain," he said, "I take charge of your vessel in the name of the German Imperial Navy."

He gave an order in German and two German sailors sprang to the flag halyards and hauled down the Stars and Stripes and ran up the German Ensign. They carefully saved the American flag and the Company's burgee and took them aboard the *Wolf* afterwards as trophies. Our crew meantime had been lined up and searched for weapons. Among the things the boarding crew brought on board was a black case containing twenty pairs of handcuffs and three large bombs to blow the vessel to pieces with. They didn't need the handcuffs, however.

After the lieutenant had gone through the ship's papers and found out all particulars regarding the *Beluga's* cargo, he had his signal men wigwag the information to the commander of the *Wolf*, which was standing by. The commander, on finding out that I had a cargo of benzine, decided not to sink the vessel immediately, but to take on board some three hundred cases for use in their hydroplane, as their supply was getting low.

In a short while we received instructions from the *Wolf* to proceed due east for sixty miles and wait there for them. The *Wolf* then left us, going off at right angles. I learned from some of the German sailors that there was a large steamer approaching and that the *Wolf* would probably run along parallel with her during the night and capture her in the morning. About nine-thirty that night this steamer passed us about a mile and a half off, heading to the southward and westward.

She was apparently a large steamer of about seven or eight thousand tons, heavily loaded. She resembled in appearance the type of vessel used on the Pacific Coast as an oil tanker, having the high forecastle head, long bunk deck amidships, and her engines and stack

THE GERMAN AUXILIARY CRUISER, RAIDER AND MINE LAYER
WOLF LEAVING KIEL ON HER FIFTEEN-MONTH CRUISE,
NOVEMBER 21ST, 1916

away aft; she was probably a freighter of this description belonging to New Zealand, bound from San Francisco to Australia. When she came abreast of us she signalled by Morse Code, asking what vessel we were; but the German prize crew took good care that none of us could answer or make any signals of any kind. I can use both Continental and Morse and had a signal lamp on board, so that if I had had an opportunity I could have warned this steamer that there was a raider about.

One of the first official acts by Lieutenant Zelasko after taking charge of my vessel was to call the cook up on the quarterdeck where he was standing and give him instructions to cook a good large meal for his men, and not to forget to have plenty of white bread. To assist him in preparing this meal for the unwelcome addition to our family, he assigned one of his men as an assistant in the kitchen.

In the meantime, the balance of his crew were searching the vessel and making an itemized list of everything that they thought would be worth transferring to the *Wolf*. I had a chance to look over this list later on and was surprised to find how complete and businesslike it was. It gave the name of the article, the amount, where located, and a remark as to how best to remove it, whether in the original package, to be repacked, or carried in bulk in large canvas sacks, furnished by the *Wolf* for that purpose. This is only one incident showing the method and thoroughness with which even the minor details of their business were carried out.

During the evening I had a chance to get acquainted with Lieutenant Zelasko, the prize officer, and found him a very decent chap indeed. He, and all the rest of the *Wolf's* officers, excepting the commander and the artillery lieutenant, were members of the Imperial Marine, or Naval Reserve, men that in peace time commanded and served as officers in the merchant service, like myself. In fact, I found that Lieutenant Zelasko had served part of his time as able-bodied seaman on the American ship *Roanoke*, a vessel that I had been in some years before. He had the second class Iron Cross which he had won at Antwerp.

Lieutenant Zelasko assured me on his word of honour that my family would receive nothing but the best of care possible under the circumstances on board the *Wolf*. In fact, after finding out that the *Wolf* was manned by ex-merchant marine officers and men, my fears for the safety of my wife and little girl subsided greatly. My wife herself cheered up a great deal after hearing this, thinking that people from our own walk of life could not be as barbarous as we had been led to believe.

Early in the morning of the tenth we arrived at the position where we were to wait for the *Wolf*. Here we hove to, and the prize crew, assisted by my sailors, who were forced to do all the work pertaining to the handling of the ship, took off the hatches and took on deck three hundred cases of benzine, ready to be transported to the *Wolf* when she showed up. During all this time there were always five or six guards or sentries posted at various positions around the ship, and also the balance of the prize crew always wore their side arms, whether they were working or not.

The navigating officer of Zelasko's prize crew and the bo'swain were both American navigators, one having been, prior to the war, master of a sailing vessel plying on the Atlantic Coast, and the other a chief mate, also in sail, on the Atlantic. At the outbreak of the war both resigned their positions and went home to lend Kaiser Bill a hand. These fellows received eighteen *marks* per month and have a rating of only "*over matrosa*," or just one step higher than that of common sailor. Several months later, after we had got better acquainted, I asked this ex-American skipper if he did not think it rather a scurvy trick to sail as Master on American ships during peace times and as soon as war was declared to leave America and help sink the very class of ships that he had hitherto made his living on. He replied by saying that at the time he resigned and went home to enlist America was not in the war, but even had she been, he would have gone just the same.

From conversations I had with other ex-American seamen, I am led to believe that at the outbreak of hostilities the German Consuls at the port where their vessels hailed from ordered these men to resign and go home to the Fatherland. I also believe that their fare and expenses were paid. There are many, many cases similar to this, and I believe it would be a good thing for the American shipowners to remember when employing officers and captains to man their vessels after the war is over.

The German prize crew made a great fuss over Juanita, she being quite a novelty to them, and I am sure that she had the time of her life. Nobody on board the *Wolf* had seen a woman or a child for nearly nine months. My wife and little girl were the first woman and child they had taken prisoner.

On July 11th, early in the morning, the *Wolf* picked us up again. It seems that the steamer we saw got away from them. The *Wolf* put four large lifeboats on the water and took off some three hundred cases of benzine and all the provisions and ship's stores we had on board the *Beluga*.

When the vessel was taken charge of by the German prize officer, he told me that I would be allowed to take only a few absolute necessities aboard the *Wolf* when I was transferred; but later, on the 11th, when the *Wolf* picked us up, Commander Nerger sent over word that I was to be allowed to take everything I wanted. Unfortunately, the permission came almost too late, because by this time the German crew had ransacked my quarters very thoroughly and many articles that I would have taken with me for the comfort of my family were gone. Weeks later some of these were recovered. For instance, I had a pair of rubber-soled, leather-topped yachting shoes. Some weeks after joining the *Wolf* I noticed a man with these shoes on his feet. I called the attention of one of the officers to it and told him that they were formerly my property. The following morning those shoes were just outside my stateroom door, nicely polished.

Among the things I took on the *Wolf* was the wife's sewing machine, which proved of great value later on, as she had to make under and over garments for both herself and Nita. My nautical instruments, books and charts were taken from me, but I was told that they would be returned to me on my arrival in Germany.

At 1:20 we got into the boats and said a last farewell to the poor little *Beluga*, and she did look little in comparison with this big black brute of a raider. As we were being rowed over, the *Wolf's* rails were lined with grinning faces, and not one of them that I could see had the least trace of sympathy. Not that I wanted sympathy for myself, but it seemed strange to me, at the time, that out of over three hundred German sailors and officers there was not one whose face showed any sympathy for the position a woman and little child were in.

We climbed on board by means of a Jacob's ladder, myself first with Nita on my back, and my wife next. Many offered to lend her a hand, but she managed to make it without any help. There was a certain satisfaction in this, as afterwards I found out that the Germans anticipated a lot of trouble in getting her aboard, as there was quite a bit of sea running.

On arriving on deck we were met by the chief officer, Captain Schmell, whose first words were, "Tell your wife and little girl that they have nothing to fear, that we are not the Huns you probably think we are." He took us aft under the poop and showed us an ex-storeroom which some men were cleaning out for our use. This room was in the centre of the prisoners' quarters and had absolutely no ventilation, and there were Negroes, Indians and various other nationalities passing up and down to the hell hole, before the door, in various stages of *décolleté*, to say the least. The chief told me that we three could have this room together, or my wife and child could have a more comfortable room on the berth deck amidships, but that I would have to remain down below and that I would be allowed to visit my family two hours daily.

My wife would not hear of this latter arrangement, saying that we would live in a pig-sty together rather than be separated. Just then Commander Nerger came along and spoke to us, saying that he was very sorry to find that the *Beluga* had a woman and child on board, and had he known that such was the case he would have passed right on; but that once he had shown himself to be a raider, to protect himself he would have to keep us prisoners until such time when he could land us at a place where it would not jeopardise the safety of his vessel or crew; and that in the meantime he would make us as comfortable as possible under the circumstances. He then gave orders that we three should be given one of the deck officers' staterooms on the berth deck and that we were to be given the freedom on the side our room was on, and that as long as I paid attention to my own business only and did not talk to any of the sailors, I was to continue to enjoy this privilege; but just as soon as I gave them cause to believe that I was trying to gather information, I was to be sent down into the hell-hole aft—as the prisoners called their well-named quarters.

Needless to say, I gladly agreed to his proposition, knowing myself to be lucky not to be separated from my family. At 4:30 p.m. a man (who was afterwards my orderly) came to our room with cotton batting to put in our ears, as they were going to sink the *Beluga* by gun fire. I was granted permission to go onto the boat deck and watch. They fired nineteen shots at her with the six-inch gun forward, and the nineteenth shell hit her amidships. The other eighteen were clean misses—rotten shooting, as the target was only two and a half miles off. *Beluga* burst into flames and immediately when she caught fire the benzine exploded, making one of the most wonderful sights I have ever seen. The sea for miles around us was covered with burning petrol, the weather was almost calm, and occasionally a "cat's-paw" of wind would come along and cause this flaming field of oil to run in various directions, opening a path of black water through a sea of flames.

As soon as this "cat's-paw" of wind was over the flames would run together again. When the spars fell out of the ship the splash was not of water but a veritable cataract of flames. Even the Germans were impressed by the picture of three square miles of burning sea, flames leaping thirty feet high and raging for hours. God! It was a wonderful thing. In fact, the sight was so great that I did not realise for some minutes that it was my own little home that was going up in flames. My wife could not, of course, stand this sight, and had remained in her room.

On account of there being no place ready for us to sleep, we were given temporary quarters in the forward end of the deckhouse, immediately over the pump room on the main deck. There was only one very narrow bunk here, possibly eighteen inches wide, which my wife and Nita occupied. For myself I picked out a nice soft iron plate on the floor and slept on that. The only means of ventilation here was a square hole in the roof or ceiling, probably eight inches' square. There was, I believe, some kind of ventilator attached to this opening outside. There was an ironbound rule enforced at all times on the *Wolf* that no light from any source should be visible on the deck. All doors were fitted with a patent mechanism so that when the door was opened the electric light current was broken and consequently the light went out.

Immediately on closing the door the light would come on again. This made it necessary to sit in the dark if we wanted to have either the port hole or door open for fresh air, and if the door was closed, in a very short time the air became actually suffocating.

On several occasions the temperature, with the door and port hole open, was 104 F. at night, so it can be imagined just how hot it was when the door had been closed for ten or twenty minutes. The first night none of us slept a wink, owing to the excitement of the day and the incessant hammering and knocking of the air pumps and ice-making machines immediately under our feet. This made the fourth night since we had been captured that my wife did not get a wink of sleep. Fearing complications from this loss of sleep, I called on the German doctor and finally made him understand the situation. He gave me a powder for her and asked if he should visit her.

Thinking possibly that under the circumstances the near approach of a German, even a doctor, would do more harm than good, I told him I did not think it necessary.

Doctor Hausfelt, the senior surgeon of the *Wolf*, prior to the outbreak of the war, was a specialist in women's nervous diseases and was the head of a clinic at the Hanover University. The doctor spoke French and Italian fluently but could not speak the English language, although he read it very well. He insisted that we be moved the following morning further down the deck, to a room similar to the one we were in, but much quieter. In reality, although quieter, this room was hotter than the one forward. The bunks, of which there were two, one for the wife and one for Nita, were fastened to the iron engine room bulkhead, and the mattresses that lay up against this wall absorbed a great deal of this heat, making them very uncomfortable. I slept on the floor, which was concrete laid over the iron deck, and although very hard was really cooler, by a good deal, than the bunks.

Early in the morning after making this change I had to go down to the Antiseptic Department and have my trunks very minutely searched and my clothes disinfected. In fact, I had to appeal to the second doctor to escape being run through the dis-lousing plant. Here anything that proved of interest to the prisoner officer was taken away from me, with the promise that it would be returned later. My books, letters and paper clippings were religiously read and returned. I had a 3A Eastman Kodak which they seized, and imagine my surprise some days later when a roll of films—half of which had been exposed by me—was handed to me by the officer in charge of the photographic department. They had taken this roll of films out of my camera and developed them, just for curiosity, I suppose.

From here I was taken to the Recording Lieutenant's office and put through a rigid examination, being asked questions regarding my movements in the past five years, also questions regarding my parents' origin, occupation and present standing. All this fuss because one of the prize crew had found in my quarters a pamphlet giving information regarding the United States Naval Reserve requirements. I thought I had got rid of all this junk, but evidently I must have overlooked something.

My officers and sailors were taken to the regular prisoners' quarters aft, and I was not allowed to see or speak to them.

Now comes what I consider the most awful period of my experience. My wife, who is naturally of a highly strung and courageous disposition, broke down under the preceding five days' strain and loss of sleep. Luckily Doctor Hausfelt, the *Wolf's* senior surgeon, had been in private life a woman's specialist, and owing to his skill and untiring services my wife pulled through. She lay in her berth, packed in ice, for three weeks, absolutely delirious. Owing to the experience I had undergone during the past few days my own nerves were all ragged and upset; and the continual raving and shrieking of my wife, who imagined herself undergoing the most awful torture, drove me nearly crazy. Some days and nights seemed never to come to an end. During this time, on July 17th, to be exact, *Wolf* captured and set on fire the American Schooner *Encore*, Captain Oleson, bound from Columbia River to Australia with a cargo of lumber, but owing to my state of mind I remember it only as an incident; it seemed trivial to me at the time.

During all this time my wife had been gradually sinking until she had come to the place where she either had to make a turn for the better or pass into the Great Beyond.

Commander Nerger, at the doctor's request, during this crisis, gave orders that all traffic on our side of the berth deck should stop, and guards were placed at each end to see that his orders were carried out. On the night of August and Doctor Hausfelt told me that, barring accident, my wife would recover. I have often wondered whether a physician realises just what it means to an anxious husband when he tells him, "The crisis is past and your wife will recover."

I know they were the most welcome words I had ever heard! During all this time I never gave a thought as to where we were going or how we were going to get there. I didn't give a damn what happened, only that my wife pulled through. However, after my wife had passed the critical point and commenced to get better, a load seemed to be lifted off my shoulders, and the mere fact of being a prisoner on board a German raider seemed of no consequence. I then commenced to take an interest in things around me. My continual silence, with nobody to talk to, and the long periods of darkness, from 7:10 p.m. to 6:30 a.m., it being winter in the South Pacific, grew very irksome.

On account of the extreme heat in the cabin when the door was closed and the light on, I was unable to sit inside and read, so the only thing left was to sit outside my door on the deck and think, and God knows I didn't have many very agreeable things to think about. At this time my wife was still too weak to talk, and anyway I didn't want to get her asking questions, thinking it would only make her worry, which I knew was not good for her. My days were usually taken up in washing clothes and nursing the wife. I never knew there were so many clothes in the world, and to think that they came from one sick wife and a perfectly healthy six-year old kiddie! I, like a darn fool, kept putting on clean white frocks and all the other white fixings that go with it.

When the Missis got on the job again, Miss Juanita got a pair of overalls on week days and a dress on Sundays, all this going to prove that as a nurse maid I was a fizzle. I came a Steve Brodie on the wife's hair also, letting it get into such a mess that I couldn't comb the rats' nests out of it and had to cut the whole business off short. However, this didn't make much difference, as it all came out itself anyway. At all times on the *Wolf* the fresh water situation was of great importance, as we were on a strict allowance of drinking water, which they condensed and purified themselves. We were also allowed a minute quantity of semi-condensed water for washing purposes. I used to save up for several days and get enough for a bath, all of us using the same water.

After bathing, this water was used to wash clothes in. On other mornings we had to be content with a salt water bath, which is very refreshing but has little cleansing quality. Every effort was made to catch all the rain water possible, and then everybody had the big wash. During a heavy rain it was customary for all hands to strip and stand out in the rain and have a good rain water bath. It was quite odd to see from one hundred and fifty to three hundred men taking their bath in this manner. It makes one think of the Garden of Eden before Eve showed on the job.

I used to look forward to the evening when the prize officer, Lieutenant Zelasko, used to come to my quarters and talk for half an hour. His talk usually was of the war, and it was interesting to get the German view of it. Of course, from their viewpoint "poor Germany" was the defendant, and they figure they are fighting to protect their homes and not in a war of conquest.

Many of the crew of the *Wolf* had seen service on the various fronts and in Belgium and had some very interesting experiences to tell. These stories were always from the German viewpoint. One chap in particular had a unique and unenviable experience, having been wounded in six places at six different times. He was shot once through the shoulder on the Russian front. On two occasions, while on service in France, he was shot, once through the arm and on another occasion through the leg. At the storming of Antwerp, he was wounded on the head by a flying piece of shell, and later on, while trying to storm a bridge, he was bayoneted. While serving as a member of the prize crew on the S.S. *Melunga*, after her capture by the *Wolf*, he lost an eye, while knocking off the head of a beer bottle, a piece of the glass striking him in the eye. The bottle of beer was "*Gambe Carlsburger*," a Danish beer, and as this accident happened on an Australian steamer in the Indian Ocean, I don't know just exactly who should get the credit for this, although I think that Denmark should be credited with an asset.

One of the officers, a lieutenant, was in the sailors' foot regiment the first time the Germans entered Antwerp, and told of the civil populace throwing large rocks, flat irons and cooking utensils down on the soldiers' heads while they were marching into the town, and spoke as if this was a grave breach of the Marquis of Queensbury's rules as to how to conduct a war. After many of the brave Teuton soldiers had been wounded in this undignified and unwarlike manner, they withdrew and the artillery bombardment followed. From other, sources I have heard that this regiment marched up the street taking pot shots at anybody, male or female, who happened to look out of a window or door. I judged from this man's conversation that this sailor regiment shipped to stop bullets and not flat irons and other nameless weapons.

One afternoon I asked Commander Nerger for permission to talk to some of the men, saying it was not healthy for a man to sit around all day and not say a word to anybody. This he granted, so after that I could hold short conversations with a good many members of the crew, and in a short time had practically the run of the ship. It was absolutely forbidden, however, for me to talk to any of the other prisoners who had been on board the *Wolf* for a long time and knew of its various mine-laying activities.

Our meals were served in our cabin, on dishes taken from the *Beluga*; in fact, for the first month a good deal of our food was *Beluga's* food. Little delicacies that I had bought for our own use, such as potted meats, jellies, crackers and a case of wine, were reserved for our own use by the purser of the *Wolf* at Commander Nerger's suggestion. One of the most valuable foods to us, taken from the *Beluga* and reserved for our use, was four cases of canned milk of the liquid variety, which proved very beneficial to the wife during her sickness, and also was greatly appreciated by Nita. The doctor, thinking probably that the black bread would prove too strong for Nita's stomach, endeavoured to have the ship's baker make a small quantity of white bread for her, but unfortunately the baker could not make a success of the wheat bread and the effort was given up. As far as I could see, this black bread, while being far from palatable, was very wholesome and nourishing.

I should like to state here that my family and myself were treated with the utmost courtesy and consideration by the commander himself and his officers while we were prisoners. I am not speaking for the poor devils down below aft, nor of our treatment while under the charge of Lieutenant Rose on the Jap prize ship *Hitachi Maru*, or later on the Spanish prize *Igotz Mendi*, which was decidedly different.

On the *Wolf* our meals were regular and methodically worked out, so that at the end of each day a person had received just so much rationed nourishment. Myself and family received the same food as that served in the officers' mess. Our breakfast usually consisted of "near" coffee, syrup or treacle and three slices of black bread. I have seen the cook's department roasting this alleged "coffee," and believe it to be nothing more nor less than wheat roasted until it is scorched or burnt, the larger kernels being saved for this purpose. Some years ago I was on a sailing vessel and the supply of coffee gave out. The cook used to take burnt bread and make a substitute for coffee from it that was identical in taste with this coffee on the *Wolf*.

Dinner at mid-day consisted of a soup, a meat-ball composed of canned beef ground fine and mixed with bread crumbs, plenty of preserved peas and carrots. Monday, Wednesday and Friday we had a dessert, usually stewed prunes or a corn-starch mixture. For supper we had tea, bread, and sardine paste, or pickled, cold corned beef. Quite often rice in various disguises was given instead of the "bully beef" at noon. But on Sunday—oh, joy!! A regular, honest-to-Grandma dinner, consisting of asparagus soup, real fresh meat from the refrigerator, evaporated potatoes, a vegetable, prunes and a sweet. This for a regular menu, day in and day out, doesn't look very good, but considering that we were prisoners I don't believe we had any cause to complain. The food we received was the same as that which the commander and deck officers had, and superior to that of the warrant officers and seamen.

The German auxiliary cruiser and minelayer *Wolf* was formerly a freighter belonging to the Hansa Line, a subsidiary of the Hamburg-American Line; of 6,728 gross tons; single screw, one funnel; two well decks, two telescoping masts, equipped with wireless, double bridge; two Sampson posts on poop and four sets of cargo booms. On the poop rigged from the Sampson posts were two faked cargo booms whose real purpose was to disguise a six-inch gun mounted there. On her boat deck she showed three life-boats, working boats from each side. The vessel was painted all black and had no particular distinguishing marks.

Wolf carried two six-inch ordinary guns, one mounted forward

SHOWING "MANLICHER" TYPE TORPEDO TUBE, PORTSIDE FORWARD
ON *WOLF*

FINAL DIVE OF JAPANESE STEAMER *HITACHI MARU*. 6558 GROSS
TONS. CAPT. KOKMOA. CAPTURED SEPTEMBER 26TH OFF MALDIVA
ISLANDS, INDIAN OCEAN. SUNK BY BOMBS NOVEMBER 7TH.

under the forecastle head and the other on top of the poop; four 4.7 ordinaries, two forward and two aft mounted on the well deck. The bulwark or rails at these guns, as at the six-inch forward gun, were fitted with hinges and spring catches, so that by one blow of a hammer they dropped down, giving the guns ample room for action. Under ordinary circumstances nothing of these guns could be seen above the rail. She was further armed with four torpedo tubes, two forward and two aft, on the well decks. The torpedoes forward were "Red Heads" and especially effective for short distances, while those aft were "Mannlichers" and used for long distance work. She also had four machine guns mounted, two on each end of the boat deck in such a manner that they could control the decks and the prisoners' quarters aft.

On leaving Kiel *Wolf* had a crew of three hundred and seventy-five men, including one commander and corvette captain, one lieutenant commander, three senior and six junior lieutenants, two surgeons and twelve warrant officers, including gun mechanics, torpedo mechanics, mine experts, navigating sub-lieutenants and boatswains. She had a wireless crew of seven men, including one wireless expert. The signal corps consisted of six signal men in charge of a code expert, who had had several years of training at a school in deciphering various codes. I am led to believe from what I saw that this man was able to decipher naval and private codes used in the South Pacific, but was unable to handle codes used in the North Atlantic.

On leaving Kiel *Wolf* had on board five hundred mines, seventy-five hundred tons of Westphalian coal, three thousand tons of water, and twenty-five hundred tons of food and ammunition. This heavy cargo overloaded the *Wolf*. I understand she was drawing over two feet more than her normal loaded draft when she left Kiel, and on getting safely through the blockade she encountered a very heavy series of gales in the North Atlantic, causing the vessel to labour heavily. This labouring strained her hull and topside and she dropped a good many rivets. As soon as she ran out of this bad weather repairs were made and all her topsides double riveted. Something like nine thousand rivets were driven, this work being done by her crew as the *Wolf* proceeded down the Atlantic. Among her mechanics she seemed to have representatives from almost every trade, and apparently an inexhaustible supply of materials for making repairs or new additions to her equipment.

Wolf was equipped with a triple expansion engine and three boilers and one auxiliary donkey boiler. Her power plant was unique in that she could steam seven knots per hour on a consumption of eighteen tons of coal *per diem*, and eleven and a half knots per hour, her maximum, on twenty-eight tons of coal *per diem*. I have heard it said that she had one of the most efficient power plants out of Europe, having a fuel consumption of 1.2 per I.H.P. *Wolf* was further equipped with a powerful searchlight, situated abaft the bridge, on a tower that could be raised or lowered at will. When not in use this light could not be seen above the top of the house. *Wolf* sailed from Kiel on November 21, 1916.

The commander of the *Wolf*, Corvette Captain Nerger, of the Imperial German Navy, was a man of probably thirty-five years of age, of moderate height and slim build. He was immaculate in all things pertaining to his person, and was a strict disciplinarian. I was in Commander Nerger's quarters one day. I had visited him to thank him for the courtesy he had extended to my family and to myself, and found him a very agreeable man to talk to; a thorough gentleman and apparently anxious to do anything he could to make our lot bearable. In talking with him I found nothing to denote the arrogant Prussianism which is said to predominate in the higher branches of the German Navy.

And yet Commander Nerger was a man "all alone." He kept absolutely to himself; took no man into his confidence. No man ever knew an hour ahead what his plans or the vessel's plans were. He was the only one who knew when we started for home. On the fifteen months' cruise of the *Wolf* Nerger was in full charge and ran his vessel as a "one-man ship." He lived in comfortable quarters on the boat deck, just under the bridge, and had his meals served in his private dining room. In the five months I was on the *Wolf* I do not think I saw him on the berth deck more than a dozen times, and then only on an inspection trip of some kind. He always had the appearance of having just stepped out of a bandbox, he was so immaculate in his dress.

I was told by his officers that Nerger never gets excited; always remains cool under all circumstances. They tell a story of his being in command of a light cruiser in the battle off the Dogger Banks, and throughout this engagement he calmly passed back and forth on the bridge, with a cigar in his mouth, giving his orders as calmly as if at some gun practice or manoeuvres. His officers and men all respected him, which to my mind is a good enough recommendation.

One of the peculiarities of the *Wolf's* cruise was that nobody, excepting the commander, knew where she was going, when she was going, and how long she was to be away. The majority of the officers, thinking she would probably try to duplicate the raider *Moewe's* operations, took only enough clothes to last them about three months, and only augmented their supply from the various vessels captured. From one of the captured steamers they got several rolls or bolts of heavy dress goods, but unfortunately for them, they didn't have enough cotton thread to make them up into wearing apparel, although some of them, in more need than the rest, sewed their new suits with ordinary sail twine, similar to that which the grocer uses to tie up his parcels. The cloth was all dark goods, and it looked odd to see the coarse white string stitches against the dark background. Many of the suits were very well cut and fitted in the regular naval style.

The *Wolf's* method of getting away from Kiel was unique. Each day about eleven o'clock in the forenoon, she would up anchor and steam out of Kiel harbour, manoeuvring outside and having gun practice, returning each night to anchor in the harbour. This procedure was kept up for over three weeks, until finally one night the *Wolf* failed to return. During these three weeks nobody was allowed ashore or to hold any communication with the shore. Even the German naval authorities did not know the date she was to sail, until she had gone. All this goes to prove that the German Naval Department had considerable respect for the Allied Intelligence Department.

On leaving Kiel the *Wolf* went through what is known as the "Big Belt," a passage through Denmark into the Kattegat, from there along the Danish coast across the Norwegian coast, and out to the Atlantic between the Farrows and Iceland. On returning to Germany she merely retraced her course, the only difference being that she passed through the "Little Belt," a very narrow piece of water, one-half of which is German territorial water and the other half Danish.

From where I used to sit on deck outside my quarters I could see the other prisoners aft on the poop, at that time some two hundred of them. Over half of them had no shoes, socks or over-shirts, and fully one-fifth of them wore no undershirt. I asked a couple of them why they did not wear a shirt in that blazing tropical sun. They told me that they had only one shirt apiece and that the sweat rotted them so fast, that they were going without shirts at present and saving them till the weather got cold. Three times a day each squad flunkey (a squad consisted of fourteen prisoners) would troop up to the galley amidships and get their rations for the meal—a kettle of alleged tea or coffee, black bread, and at noon a kettle of goulash, resembling a soft stew. I had been on board the *Wolf* for some time before I finally got the chance to sneak down below aft and see what the prisoners' quarters were like and have a talk with some of the men.

The prisoners' quarters on the *Wolf* were located aft in the cargo hold, and had their only entrance under the poop, on the main deck. The quarters themselves were reached by means of a narrow ladder only, and this ladder was built in such a manner that not more than two persons could pass up or down at the same time, or one person up and one down simultaneously, thereby guarding against a concerted rush in event of an escape being planned.

Over the entrance or hole in the deck leading to these stairs was slung a heavy iron hatch or cover, in such a manner that it could be dropped into place instantaneously by one of the guards. This hatch would effectually close the only exit from the quarters where there were over two hundred prisoners confined. Also the closing of this hatch would cut off nearly one-half the air supply; during the times when this hatch was closed, when the *Wolf* was passing through some danger, the suffering in the hold from lack of air was often intense. Even under normal conditions the air supply was inadequate.

It was probably 8:30 p. m. when I was there, and I would judge the temperature to have been between 118 and 120 degrees Fahrenheit, and the reek of feet, breath and bodies was something awful. On this particular night, I should judge from one-quarter to three-eighths of an inch of sweat was on the floor, and when the vessel rolled there would be a thin scum of liquid running from side to side. The walls and ceiling were literally running water, which was caused by moisture drawn from the bodies of the men by the hot iron sides of the ship and the deck overhead. Combine stale tobacco smoke with this atmosphere, and it was a wonder to me that a human being could exist in it.

At this time everybody was herded into the one compartment—captains, mates, engineers, firemen, sailors, cooks and flunkies, all together—white men, niggers, Turks, Greeks and Japanese. At night everybody slept in hammocks and during the day these hammocks were "made up" and piled away in one corner, thus leaving enough room for several rough plank tables and benches to be set up. There were no lockers or any compartments where a man could put his spare clothing or shaving gear, therefore no man's gear was safe from theft. A man who didn't have a shirt would steal one from a man who had two;

253

this made it impossible for a man to have any more clothes than just what he stood in. Later on many of the men were given empty cases or boxes and fixed them up to keep their spare gear in.

The sanitary arrangements at this time were very poor, there being only three toilets for all hands. Certain squads of men would take turns in keeping these quarters clean, the whole place being thoroughly scrubbed out three times a week. I mean thoroughly in the full sense of the word. Everything moveable, excepting the clothing boxes, was taken on deck, then the room scrubbed with heavy brushes and sand. Next the tables and benches were scoured with sand and canvas, the hammocks scrubbed and the various tin dishes used for food were scoured bright. After everything was dry it was put back in place and the prisoner officer made an inspection. It was very seldom that he found anything to complain of, as the men seemed to welcome this house-cleaning as it gave them something to do to occupy their time. Reading material was very scarce, so the time passed very slowly.

There was supposed to be a regular daily routine; but owing to the many interruptions, such as gun practice, fire drill, boarding drill and drills with small arms, this routine was not always carried out. At 5:30 a.m. all the prisoners were waked up and by six o'clock all the hammocks were made up and stowed away. Then the tables were set up in place and the table laid for breakfast. At seven o'clock the squad flunkies would get their gear ready, and promptly at 7:20 breakfast would be ready. Immediately after breakfast the dishes were cleaned and the quarters given their regular daily clean up. Usually during the forenoon, after their work was done, the prisoners were allowed to go up on deck and enjoy the fresh air. Dinner at 12:30 noon, coffee at 3:30 p.m., and supper at 6:30. Very seldom was anybody allowed on deck after coffee. At 8:00 p.m. all lights were extinguished excepting three, one over the steps at the exit and two at the back of the quarters.

The distribution of the fresh water was also very poor. Each prisoner was allowed half a gallon per day for washing, drinking and bathing purposes. This amount, properly conserved, will answer the purpose, but unfortunately the method of distribution was so poor that not all got their regular allowance; and the loss of this water caused the unfortunate ones great inconvenience, especially during the time that the *Wolf* was in the tropics. Many of the men used tea to brush their teeth in; and I have heard of cases where tea had been used for shaving purposes, but imagine these cases to be rare.

While there, a captain of a big British oil tank steamer that had been captured and sunk told me the following piece of history. I afterwards verified this and can vouch for its truth. While the *Wolf* was lying at Sunday Island undergoing repairs to her boilers, the prisoners were furnished with fish hooks and line and a couple of jolly boats and allowed to row into the rocks and catch fish. Each boat, of course, was in charge of an armed sentry. After fishing they would return to the *Wolf* each night. On the night before the *Wolf* was to sail two men, the chief mate and first assistant engineer of the S.S. *Turitella*, dropped overboard and swam for the shore. Before leaving the vessel these men had secreted on their persons a supply of fish hooks and lines, a small hunter's hatchet, two large sheath knives each, matches and a good supply of tobacco. The matches and tobacco were securely wrapped in waterproof oilcloth.

Just at dusk, as the prisoners were being ordered below, these two men slipped over the side, sliding down a rope into the water. They then swam under the stern and climbed up on the rudder and sat there in such a manner that they could not be seen from on deck. A confederate in the meantime had taken care of the line hanging over the side. About nine o'clock, when it was good and dark, they again slipped into the water and swam for the shore some half a mile distant. There is a strong current setting parallel with the shore in this particular locality and, as the water is infested with sharks, the betting among the men was two to one that neither of them would make it.

Later on, from some of the officers that had been on shore at Sunday Island, I found out there had formerly been a family living there, but at this particular time they were away on a visit, probably to New Zealand, as they had left their house fully furnished and with quite a supply of provisions on hand. Everything indicated that they intended returning at a later date. A calendar hanging on the wall indicated that this family had left there between April 17th and 23rd. When the loss of the prisoners was finally discovered there was a great rumpus, and as a punishment all the prisoners were kept below for twenty-eight days, being allowed on deck for only one hour each day, weather permitting, for exercise.

The British captain said that those were the most awful days he ever experienced in his life and that each day he and the rest were getting perceptibly thinner. Just about this time I got the sign from the sentry that the prisoner officer was coming and I had to beat a retreat. Afterwards I found out that it was not the prisoner officer but the mine officer, Lieutenant Dedrick, who proved to be a humane officer and a champion of the prisoners. Dedrick came down below into the hell hole and got one good lungful of the rotten atmosphere and went immediately to the commander and reported conditions. Commander Nerger at once called both doctors and accompanied them aft on a tour of inspection.

The next day everybody was chased on deck and the "Hell Hole" below was cleaned out and better ventilation arranged for; it was also painted; also the captured captains and ships' officers were given quarters to themselves, while the whites and blacks were separated. On the whole the conditions for these two hundred men were improved one hundred *per cent*. The prisoner officer was confined to his room for five days for allowing such conditions to exist. Nerger had inspected these quarters before, but only when the men were on deck and the place freshly cleaned out. Personally I do not think he knew how bad conditions were.

Along in the first part of January I learned by wireless that of the two men who swam for shore at Sunday Island the first assistant engineer was drowned, while the other reached shore in an exhausted condition. He and his companion while swimming ashore became separated in the dark and the mate did not know for a certainty whether his chum was taken by a shark or drowned from exhaustion. He stayed on the island for somewhat over two months, living on the provisions that were left in the house and on fruit, of which there was a great abundance. He was finally taken off by a Japanese cruiser whose attention was attracted by his signal fire, which he kept burning day and night. The cruiser finally landed him in New Zealand.

All this time we were steaming in a northerly and westerly direction. When we arrived at the southernmost end of New Guinea we stopped and lay to for a couple of days. I soon learned that we were waiting for a steamer and expected her any minute. During these days the *Wolf's* hydroplane would go up to reconnoitre three times a day. It would travel fifty or sixty miles on clear days, and from a height of three thousand metres it had a vision of ninety miles, so the Germans claimed. One of the German sailors told me that in another day or so we should have plenty of beer—that they had picked up a wireless message stating that the Australian steamer *Matunga* would soon arrive in Kabul with five hundred tons of coal and three hundred tons of foodstuffs, so many hundred cases of beer, etc., for the government.

Sure enough, on the morning of August 4th I was awakened by my orderly with the usual supply of cotton batting for our ears.

Shortly thereafter there was a bang from one of the cannons and the *Matunga* stopped. Lieut. Rose and the prize crew went on board and took charge. In about an hour the launch came back with the *Matunga's* captain, Donaldson, and his officers and crew, also sixteen Australian soldiers who were *en route* to the Islands. Both steamers then proceeded north, arriving on August 10th at a place in northern New Guinea that we named Pirate Cove.

On the way to Pirate Cove Commander Nerger practised all kinds of naval manoeuvres with the *Wolf* and the *Matunga*. At one time he would engage her in battle and finally after a fierce encounter, by superior manoeuvring he would destroy her. The next time the *Matunga* would be an enemy's merchant vessel and the *Wolf* would sneak up to her, suddenly dropping her ports, and make the capture. This manoeuvre was carried out quite realistically, the boarding crew supposedly meeting resistance and finally taking charge of her after a fight on deck, in which the boarding crew's bayonet drill would come in handy. At another time the *Matunga* would be a German cruiser and Nerger would direct her attack against the enemy. At this time, he was probably anticipating being made an admiral on his return to Germany and was getting what practice he could.

At Pirate Cove naked New Guineans, men, women and children, came out to the *Wolf* in thirty feet long canoes for tobacco, which was the only understandable word they could say. They offered to swap parrots, pigs, cocoanuts, sugar cane, bits of coral, woven mats of garish colours and queer pattern, showing whales, birds and primitive human figures. The *Wolf's* officers got first whack at the bargains and went in strong for the fancy mattings, but when they got them aboard found them full of native vermin. These souvenirs for their wives and sweethearts were promptly turned over to the antiseptic department and cleaned, for the *Wolf* had on board a complete dis-lousing plant through which all new prisoners were put, whether they needed it or not.

The German sailors had second choice after their officers and went in strong for parrots and cocoanuts. The prisoners, who could buy tobacco at the *Wolf's* canteen, if they had any money, had last choice of the New Guinea merchandise. I had no money on the *Beluga*, having sent mine by draft to Sydney, but I had stacks of clothes, and to get a little ready "canteen" money I sold some of them, the *Wolf's* officers paying me $25.00 for second-hand suits and $3.00 for second-hand shoes. The natives were cleaned out by the *Wolf*. Among the purchases

SHOWING 4.7 "ORDINARY" PORTSIDE GUN FORWARD ON *WOLF*.
LIEUT. ROSE WITH BINOCULARS

was an alleged New Guinea pig, which had the legs and body of a deer and the head of a porker and it had fur, too—God! I never saw anything like it. It didn't have an orthodox corkscrew tail but a compromise between a pig's and a deer's tail. The pig mascot was given the freedom of the *Wolf* and dashed if it didn't lick every dog on the ship. We had seven dogs on board, taken from sunken ships—dachshunds, fox terriers, all sorts—and the pugnacious deerpig cleaned them all up. But the Germans were too much for it. After two months in German company the pig couldn't stand it any longer and, after the slaughter of the *Hitachi Maru*, of which it was an eyewitness, it committed suicide by leaping down an open hatch to its death fifty feet below. The Germans buried the pig at sea with military honours.

While we were lying in Pirate Cove the cargo and coal of the *Matunga* were transferred to the *Wolf*; also nine of the *Matunga's* passengers and the balance of her crew. Quarters were provided for these prisoners on the same deck where I was. There was a colonel and a major with his wife, belonging to the Australian medical corps; three Australian military captains; three civilian planters, who were *en route* for the plantations on the Island, and the stewardess of the *Matunga*. This addition of prisoners to the top side was a welcome change to myself and family, as it gave us somebody else to talk to, and I was also able to get news of the war from another source than the German.

I was anxious to learn what steps America had taken or contemplated taking. To hear those Australian chaps talk you would have thought that the war was a high lark, and that just as soon as Great Britain got around to it she, ably assisted by the Australian forces, would chase Fritzy off the map.

The addition of these passengers to the top deck squad made it necessary for Commander Nerger to make certain rules and regulations to be observed regarding the distance we could go from our rooms. We were allowed a seventy-foot run-way. Also when anything was going on, such as gun practice, boarding drill, fire and boat drill, we were chased into our rooms. This caused a lot of grumbling but no doubt it was justified. I may add that there was nearly always something doing on the *Wolf*. They drilled and practised almost continually—practised sinking imaginary ships, indulged in "battle practice," and even practised abandoning the *Wolf* in boats and sinking their own ship.

While lying at Pirate Cove we had an exciting experience. It seems that some of the Germans had a suspicion that some of the prisoners were going to try to escape by swimming ashore. They doubled the guards both below and on deck and in addition had twenty-four marines sleep on the afterdeck with their muskets alongside of them. On this particular night the German sailors had stolen a couple of cases of whiskey from the cargo of the *Matunga* and many of them were pretty badly intoxicated. At 11:30 p.m. one of the guards down below aft imagined that he saw someone making a sneak for the stairs leading on deck. Next moment he shouted "Help! Help!" and blazed away with his revolver in the general direction of the stairway.

Naturally the prisoners sleeping on the far side of the stairs made a rush to get out of the line of fire. The guard saw this crowd rushing his way and ran on deck immediately. A general alarm was sounded and men and officers poured on deck from all directions. Just then a shoal of fish some little distance away in the water made a disturbance and the German crew, thinking that somebody was attempting to swim ashore, opened fire on the fish with two machine guns. Also everybody who had a rifle or a revolver opened fire at something. One officer, who stood in front of my room, emptied his revolver into the air, just shooting because everybody else was doing it.

Meanwhile, Chief Officer Schmell and three sailors had jumped into the launch and also mistaking the shoal of fish for prisoners trying to swim ashore, made for the spot—and were enthusiastically fired upon by the German machine guns in the dark. It sure was bum team work and a miracle that Schmell and his men were not killed. The launch was punctured in several places. As soon as the big searchlight was put into commission, it became apparent that there was nobody in the water. All the prisoners were then mustered out and counted, and as there were none missing, the Germans decided that it must have been a false alarm and everybody blamed everybody else. When Schmell got back on the *Wolf* he was raving mad at having been fired at by the machine guns. He wasn't red, but green with anger, and he talked so fast that I couldn't make out what he said, but I heard afterwards that he wanted to court-martial everybody, including the cook.

It always will remain a miracle to me that some of our own fellows weren't shot as the frenzied guard emptied his gun before running on deck. On account of the high hills surrounding our anchorage the *Wolf*'s wireless was not of much account, so the members of the wireless squad erected a station on the top of one of the highest hills. Here they would pick up any news that was flying around and transfer it to the *Wolf* by means of an ordinary flash light. This was easily readable with a pair of glasses, but unfortunately there was nothing of interest excepting the "press"; however, it gave me an insight of just how much reliance to put into the press reports that the Germans would let us see from time to time. This, of course, was all British press and reports were given as to advances and repulses on the various fronts and also the weekly sinkings. Should the Allied forces advance or the Germans lose a position, their press did not note it, but on the other hand, if the Germans had a victory or there were any political reports in their favour, the news was given us in full detail.

From one of the officers who had been ashore I learned that the native settlement, which at one time evidently had been quite large, must have been visited by some dreadful plague, as the houses in the village were deserted, not a single native living on that side of the bay. He also said that in many of the houses the skeletons of the dead still lay, some inside and some outside of the huts, leading a person to believe that this sickness struck them down suddenly and that they died nearly instantly, as on the porch of one of these huts there was a skeleton with some kind of a dish alongside of it, making it appear that death had come suddenly.

Here at Pirate Cove the doctors were greatly worried on account of fever and malaria and dosed us vigorously with quinine. Lord! I ate enough quinine to last me the rest of my life. There were no capsules on board and we had to eat the raw article, and there was no way of dodging it. Each morning and evening all hands, officers, crew and prisoners, were marched past the hospital steward's office and each was handed his little bit on a spoon, with a glass of water to wash it down. The only satisfaction I had was that it tasted just as rotten to the Germans as it did to me. Strangely my little girl did not dislike it a great deal and I was greatly pleased as I anticipated a riot when she got a taste of the first dose. My wife's share, she being still confined to her room, I used to throw overboard, giving her only an occasional small dose. The quinine used to cause a drumming in my ear and make me halfway deaf.

Undoubtedly it had the same effect on the German sailors yet they were forced to work transferring coal from one vessel to the other. They usually worked three shifts in the twenty-four hours. They would go down in the hold with nothing but a breech cloth on and when they came up they would resemble negroes and their bare bodies would be just running in sweat. At these times I used to feel sorry for them; then they would sink one of our vessels and I would wish them doomed to eternal labour of this kind.

Among the *Matunga's* heterogeneous cargo were two large horses and one small pony. These were taken care of by the butcher department and I suppose I ate my share. I afterwards told my wife about her eating horse flesh and nearly lost a handful of hair for my information.

On August 26th both *Wolf* and *Matunga* proceeded to sea and at 1:20 p.m. the *Matunga* was sunk by three bombs. From the time of the first explosion until she disappeared beneath the waves was just six and a half minutes. She sank stern first, and as she made the final dive the rush of air below decks blew out the forecastle bulkhead, making it appear as if there had been a fourth bomb concealed there.

Here I am convinced was the only time during the eight months that I was a prisoner on the *Wolf* that there was ever any serious thought on Nerger's part regarding landing the women, children and medical officers. Before taking the *Matunga* to sea to sink her, they transferred one of her large life-boats to the *Wolf*, also a small gasoline launch. These were hoisted on deck and placed in such a manner that they could be put overboard again easily, also they were in such a position that it interfered with the movements of the gun crew, thus proving that they were there only temporarily.

One of the officers asked me if I had ever had any experience with gas engines and was familiar with this particular make. I told him I was, having owned at one time an engine of this make. After giving the officer this information he was overheard by one of the women-folk repeating it to the chief officer. We top side prisoners were some worked up, believe me. We had it all "doped out" that after sinking the *Matunga* we should proceed off some island that was inhabited but had no wireless or cable connections, there the women, children and *medicos* would be put in the life-boat and I would tow them with the launch to some nearby harbour.

This would have been the logical thing to do if Commander Nerger wanted to conform to the articles of the Geneva Convention, which specifically states that medical officers in event of capture shall be set free at the first available opportunity. Nerger also told me and my wife that he would land us in some safe place at the first opportunity, provided he could do so without jeopardising his own safety. He also told the medical officers and the rest of the women the same thing. I maintain that at this time Nerger could have landed us with perfect safety to himself and his ship as the *Wolf* was about to leave the Pacific Ocean, having finished her activities in that locality.

At that time nobody had information regarding the *Wolf's* previous movements nor any knowledge of her mine-laying operations. However, at the last minute he must have concluded that this was too "humane" a procedure and ordered the boats over the side; they were fastened to the *Matunga* and went down with her. I claim this to have been the acme of inhumanity. He might just as well have condemned the women and children to death right there, because at that time there were ninety-nine and a half chances to a hundred that they would be either killed in action or drowned. I don't believe that there were five men in all the crew of the *Wolf*, officers included, who ever expected the *Wolf* to win safely into Germany.

There is another point to consider: why did Nerger and his officers continually assure us that the womenfolk should be landed shortly? If he had told the truth like an officer and a man and said he had no intention to land us, then we would have had more respect for him and would not have suffered the bitter disappointment that we did.

PART TWO

A Prisoner on a Passenger Steamer

From New Guinea the *Wolf* steamed southwest through the Malay Archipelago, then between Borneo and Java and Sumatra, thence through the Java sea; and on the night of September 6th the *Wolf* laid over one hundred mines across the Northwest approach to the entrance of the Singapore harbour.

Going up the Java sea, we were continually sighting vessels, and it was only the barefaced gall of the *Wolf* that saved her from destruction. Less than a month previous to this the Australian Government had sent wireless messages broadcast stating that there was a raider somewhere in the South Pacific or Indian Oceans, and giving a complete description of the *Wolf*. Yet here we were, steaming calmly along as if bound for Singapore, meeting many merchantmen, and at one time one of the officers said he could see the smoke from five torpedo boats steaming along in squadron section. When the *Wolf* would pass another vessel close to, she would usually have only a couple of men about the decks doing odd jobs of painting and repairing. I believe that it was the innocent appearance of the *Wolf* which led to her safety. She ignored all signals (which is characteristic of the merchantman).

The night before the *Wolf* mined Singapore harbour we had a narrow escape from being discovered. At 11:30 p.m., just as I was dozing off to sleep on my bed on the floor, I heard the call to stations and sprang up to see what it was all about. I looked out-of-doors and saw the two ship's surgeons passing aft, both with their first aid kits strapped to their waists. Slipping to the rail I saw that all four cannon were swung into position, clear for battle, and I could also see that both of the *Wolf's* torpedo tubes were protruding over the side. Just on the port bow was a small cruiser or battleship. From where I stood I could see her funnels and two masts, also the outline of her hull. She was travelling without lights, the same as we were.

I slipped back into my room, closed the door and switched on the light. I dressed my little girl while my wife got into her clothes. This did not take long as we always slept with our clothes in such a position that we could get into our "emergency outfit" in short order. Every moment while dressing I expected to hear and feel the crash of the *Wolf's* guns, but fortunately the other fellow didn't see us, and in a few minutes the signal was given to swing the guns in. The danger was past, but there was a mighty nervous crew of men on board the *Wolf* that night. On the other hand, it was perhaps just as well for the Japanese cruiser that he did not spot us, because the minute he had made any signal and given us any indication that he had seen us, the *Wolf* would have launched both torpedoes and given him a broadside, and at that short range they could not have missed very well.

Personally I was satisfied the way things turned out, as I did not like my chances of getting the family into a boat under the circumstances, neither did I have any wish to be present when the actual firing began. While counting my chances of getting the family safely into the boats, should an engagement ensue, I thought of just how much chance the poor devils down in the hell hole had of being saved. They would have been battened down and probably would have gone down with the vessel, should she have been sunk, without a fighting chance for their lives. Even if the German crew had released them at the last moment, what chance did they have of being saved?

Under the most favourable circumstances the *Wolf's* equipment of life-boats and rafts was probably sufficient for only three hundred and fifty at the outside, and there was a total of about seven hundred on board. It would be only natural for the German crew to have the life-saving equipment themselves and our poor chaps would have been left to drown, there being no articles of an inflammable or floating description around her decks.

On the wall of my room was a typewritten notice over Commander Nerger's signature, stating that in event of the *Wolf's* engaging an enemy a boat would be lowered and the women, children and medicos would be placed in same, under my charge. This provided that there was sufficient time and the weather conditions favourable. I could imagine just about how many chances we had that there would be sufficient time to execute this manoeuvre. However, this sign served the very good purpose of alleviating the women's anxieties to a certain extent. It is quite possible that this was the only reason this notice was given us. However, I am grateful for the part it played. The preceding was the tensest crisis in the *Wolf's* fifteen months' history. Commander Nerger sent down word to me afterwards that it was a Japanese man-of-war, and to keep the news from my wife if possible.

The next night, September 6th, the *Wolf*, which was primarily a mine-layer and not a raider, laid ninety-eight mines at a distance of from seven and a half to ten miles off shore. The lights of Singapore were plainly visible from the port-hole. On this occasion I was locked in the room for about two hours, but it was not difficult to count the "eggs" as they were being laid, for the mines came up out of No. 3 hatch on an elevator and were conveyed aft to the "chute" on a small rail car which had a flat wheel, and I could hear it going along the deck "*humpety-hump, humpety-hump.*" I estimated that it took about one hour and forty minutes to lay these ninety-eight mines.

From off Singapore we practically retraced our steps back through the Java sea and entered the Indian Ocean on October 9th, passing between the islands of Java and Canor. We then proceeded to the northward and westward until we arrived on the trade route running from Colombo to Delagoa Bay. Here *Wolf* cruised around slowly for a day or so, crossing and recrossing the route at regular intervals. While lying here waiting for the prey, the wireless man told me he could hear several cruisers working their wireless and that there was one British cruiser patrolling the Straits of Malacca, one at Bombay, two lying in the harbour of Colombo—the *Venus* and the *Vulcan*, I believe and another at a naval station in the Mauritius Islands. All this time the bird, *i.e.,* the *Wolf's* hydroplane, had been down below in the hole undergoing general repairs from an accident she had had, which nearly ended her activities and drowned both of the operators.

Some two weeks previous, while she was rising from the water and at a height of about sixty metres, something suddenly went wrong with the balancing mechanism and the plane made a dive for the sea, which she hit at a terrific speed; the back wings and the pontoons or boats were completely demolished. The mechanic and the observing lieutenant were catapulted into the sea and had much difficulty in swimming back to the wreck, which had the appearance of a gigantic bird sitting on its nose with its tail standing up in the air. It reminded me of an ostrich with its head buried in the sand. The bonnet around the engine and mechanic's seat, in all seaplanes of this description, is watertight, so that in case of an accident of this kind the weight of the engine will not cause it to sink.

However, in this case, one of the struts supporting the pontoons had caused this watertight bonnet to leak and, although both operators baled for dear life, the water gained on them steadily. When the rescuing launch finally arrived alongside the machine it was just on the verge of sinking. The crew of the launch tied the machine to the launch with ropes in such a manner that it could not sink and the whole outfit was hoisted on board the *Wolf*. All six cylinders of the engine were cracked and the "bird" appeared a total wreck. However, the "aeroplane" squad set to work and repaired the planes and put spare cylinders on the engine; and in a few days she was ready for duty again. The crew of the plane apparently were none the worse for their mishap.

One day one of the officers told me that probably in a few days they would pick up a nice fat steamer with plenty of food on board. On the morning of October 26th, immediately after breakfast, I noticed that they were getting the "bird" on deck and assembling it. I asked one of the officers whether there was "something doing" and he said: "If we have any luck after lunch we shall have fresh meat for supper." About 11 a.m. the "bird" was finished and the engine warmed up. Suddenly somebody shouted, and everybody got his binoculars and looked astern of us, and, sure enough, a faint outline of smoke could be seen on the horizon.

The hydroplane went up and in half an hour came back and reported a large steamer approaching. Commander Nerger shaped his course so as to meet this steamer but still give him the impression that we were *en route* from the Cape to Colombo. At 3:05 p. m. the steamer was right abreast, She was a fine big Class A Japanese passenger steamer, deeply loaded, and I could see passengers on her saloon deck. At 3:07 p. m. the *Wolf* broke out the Imperial Navy flag and signalled for the *Hitachi Maru* to stop and not use her wireless, also dropped a shot across the *Hitachi's* bow. When the *Hitachi* failed to stop, the *Wolf* fired another shot closer to her bow.

The Jap concluded to run for it and started in to work his wireless, also swung his ship into such a position as to bring his gun for submarine defence, 4.7 quick firer, into action. Meantime the *Wolf* had opened fire on her in deadly earnest. One six-inch shell from the after gun struck the *Hitachi* and exploded just under her gun where the gun crew was working, killing six Japs and blowing the balance into the water. I saw one Jap in particular hoisted high into the air above the smoke of the explosion, and he was spinning around like a pinwheel. Another shot from the after gun put the gun on the *Hitachi* out of commission altogether, and killed another man. In the meantime, from forward the *Wolf* had succeeded in putting a 4.5 shell through the wireless room, where the operator was working.

This shell came through one side of the room, passed between the operator and his "set," cutting one of his aerial leads in two, and passed out through the opposite side of the room, decapitating a man standing outside. This shell eventually hit a ventilator shaft, ripped it to pieces and knocked a man down in the engine room so hard that he afterwards died of internal injuries. There were several more hits, one on the water line in No. 4 hatch, two more in the stern, and one in the wheel-house on the bridge. About this time the flying machine came along and tried to drop a bomb on deck forward but missed, the bomb exploding when it hit the water just ahead.

The cannonading, while it lasted, was very severe, there being something over forty shots fired in as short a time as possible. Of these shots only nine were direct hits. I must add that the first possible twenty of these shots were directed in such a manner as to hit (if they did) the vessel in such a position as not to sink or permanently disable her; but towards the last, when it became evident that the Jap was trying to make her getaway, the shooting was in deadly earnest. Several broadsides were fired, which I think did more damage to the *Wolf* than to the *Hitachi Maru*, as the air concussion stove in the doors and glass ports on all the staterooms on the berth deck. In several of the rooms the wash basins and plumbing were broken.

I was standing in my open doorway with one foot on the threshold in such a manner that half of my foot protruded outside the line of the wall. When the first broadside was fired the concussion or rush of air passing my doorway, hit the part of my foot outside the door, feeling just exactly as if somebody had kicked it away or hit it with a baseball bat. Something went wrong with the six-inch gun mounted on the stern of the *Wolf* and a shell exploded a few yards away from the muzzle, putting the gun crew and gun out of commission for the balance of the voyage.

The prisoners who were confined directly below this gun said that the shock and concussion down below was dreadful during the firing, and that when the shell exploded they thought the *Wolf* had been hit. At this time, they did not know but that the *Wolf* had met a cruiser and many thought they were about to be drowned, especially when suddenly all firing ceased; they thought that the *Wolf* had been vitally hit and that the Germans had scuttled her and were abandoning her. Many of these men will remember this experience for the balance of their lives.

By this time the Japanese captain had decided that he did not have a chance, and stopped his vessel, while the *Wolf* sent the prize crew on board. In the meantime, the passengers and crew had managed to get clear in the lifeboats, which were picked up. The people were taken on board the *Wolf.* There were some 70 odd passengers, 1st and 2nd class, among them 6 women and one little black girl. They were a sorry looking sight as they climbed on board the *Wolf*; many of them were only half dressed, being just awakened from their afternoon nap by the cannonading. Over a hundred of the Japanese crew came along with the passengers. The *Wolf* could not accommodate such a large addition of prisoners without making new quarters for them, so they had to live and sleep on deck for the first three days, when they were transferred back to the *Hitachi.* The *Hitachi* had altogether 16 killed or mortally wounded. The *Wolf* incidentally lost its fresh meat for supper, because one shell had wrecked the refrigerator plant and spoiled all the fowl and fresh meat.

One of the passengers on the *Hitachi Maru*, an American chap hailing from Chicago, told me his experience.

When the *Wolf* was first sighted he was in bed reading; someone told him that they were going to pass a steamer, and he got up and dressed and went on deck to watch her. There was speculation regarding her nationality among those watching although none of them imagined her anything but what she seemed—an ordinary tramp. When she dropped her ports and fired across their bow, everybody for a moment was dumbfounded.

He ran into the cabin giving the alarm to those sleeping and secured some valuable papers he had in his cabin. The Jap crew were in a panic after seeing their gun crew killed, and many of them rushed the boats. The first boat to be lowered was filled with members of the Japanese crew, only one second class passenger being among them. On landing in the water this boat was capsized; but the occupants were shortly picked up by a boat, also manned by Japs.

The first boat to be launched with passengers in it was handled entirely by the white passengers. In this boat were four women and twenty-eight men; on being lowered the davit fall on one end fouled; and it looked very much as if everybody were going to slide out, as the boat was nearly perpendicular. Fortunately for all concerned, the fouled davit fall broke, and the boat dropped into the water. A lot of water was shipped but the boat floated right side up. The men immediately pulled away from the vicinity of the vessel. It was the firm belief of the occupants of this boat that they were to be shelled later on by the Raider.

One of the lady passengers during the excitement lost a lot of jewels. Some days later a German sailor clearing out one of the life-boats found these jewels. He came down the deck to where there were several of the passengers standing and asked: "Does anybody belong to these things?" He held out for their inspection a handful of diamonds, rubies, pearls and other valuable articles. Needless to say, he had no difficulty in finding an owner. This sailor earned 18 *marks* per month and the value of the find was in the neighbourhood of ten thousand dollars. I wonder how many men, under the circumstances, would have returned these jewels.

The *Wolf* and the *Hitachi* now steamed to the southernmost group of the Maldive Islands, arriving there on September 27th. The vessels tied up alongside of each other and coal and cargo were transferred from the *Hitachi* to the *Wolf*. The cargo of the *Hitachi Maru* was valued at over a million and a half pounds sterling, chiefly copper, tin, rubber, thousands of tons of silk, tea and hides. It always seemed uncanny to me that these "deep-sea vultures" seemed to be able to capture a vessel loaded with any particular kind of cargo they wanted. About a month before this capture, I heard the officers talking among themselves and one of them remarked, "Now the next ship we get should be loaded with copper and rubber and tin." Sure enough the *Hitachi* had what they wanted.

It seemed a pity to me to see the thousands of bales of silk goods, ladies' blouses and silk *kimonos* being dumped from one hold to another and trampled on. When the *Hitachi* was finally sunk there were a couple of thousand tons of expensive Japanese lingerie and other ladies' wear and miscellaneous department store merchandise sunk with her. The mermaids must have had "some" bargain sale.

It was the intention of Nerger to pick up, if possible, a vessel that could furnish him with enough coal to take both the *Hitachi* and *Wolf* back to Germany. At this time there was a lot of talk about landing us on one of the islands where there were missionaries. However, none of us took any stock in this "landing talk," as it was too apparent what their intentions were.

It was here that the married folks with their wives along, sent a written petition to the commander of the *Wolf*, begging to be given one of the *Hitachi* life-boats and a supply of provisions, so that on the eve of the *Wolf's* departure for parts unknown, we could make our way to one of these islands and there await the arrival of some trading schooner to take us to civilisation again. Nerger sent word back that he could not do that, and repeated the same old "bull" about landing us in some safe place, some time. Lord, he must have thought we were a bunch of "gillies" to believe that guff.

On October 1st we were transferred from the *Wolf* to the *Hitachi* along with all the rest of the "top side" prisoners. Our quarters on the *Hitachi* were splendid. We fell heir to the bridal suite. It seemed mighty good to sit down at a regular table with a white cloth and napkins again. I shall never forget my feelings as we sat there for the first meal, waiting for the white-coated Jap waiter to bring on the food. I could feel myself getting up from the table with that satisfied, contented feeling amidships. Soon the waiter came and set before us each a plate containing two ordinary soda crackers or ships' biscuits, with a poor lonely god-forsaken sardine stranded on the top.

This, and a cup of the regulation "near" coffee comprised our first evening meal on the *Hitachi Maru*. For the following morning's breakfast, we had porridge with kerosene spilt on it. Absolutely uneatable. For dinner, rotten meat with good potatoes, water—or soda water, if you had money to buy it with—and in the evening canned crab and crackers. In the meantime, our commander, Lieutenant Rose, was having a banquet in his room with his brother officers on the *Wolf*.

On the *Hitachi* it was noticed that Rose very seldom made his appearance in the dining room at mealtimes. Quite frequently at meals one of the Australian passengers who belonged to Lieut. Rose's bridge-playing clique, would send a card up to his room asking if it were not possible to have an extra slice of bread or a cracker. The answer would come back: "Sure, boys, just ask the steward." But on asking the Jap steward he would only smile and say: "Velly sorry, but captain write his name each day on paper that speaks how much you eat." This was the fact, as I have seen the paper.

The German chief engineer and chief mate used to eat at the same table as we did, and used to complain of the food as being inadequate; and one night the chief engineer took the matter up with Rose and told him a few truths. Rose said that it was "too bad," that he did not know anything about it before but now he would straighten it up. The engineer told Rose that if he cut out a lot of his private champagne

271

suppers and looked into what the rest of us were getting it would not be necessary to make these complaints.

This is a condition that could not exist on the *Wolf* because there we were under the charge of a gentleman and an officer and we got square treatment, but on the *Hitachi* and later on the *Igotz Mendi* we were under a sub-lieutenant, a snob and a man who did not know the meaning of the word gentleman. In my opinion it is this class of "under officer" that gives the Germans the unenviable reputation that they have.

My wife at this time was convalescing rapidly and regaining her strength; and it was of the utmost importance that she be provided with sufficient food. Luckily I was able to purchase from one of the stewards a couple of large cans of biscuits, some preserved ginger and an occasional piece of cheese. This helped out a whole lot, although even at that she was under-nourished. Little Juanita did not fare so badly as she was given as much as her elders, and being only a child did not require so much as they.

At this time, it was possible to purchase stout on the *Hitachi*, which was a Godsend to us. A few days after coming on board, when ordering stout, I was told that it had all gone. On making inquiries afterwards I found out that Lieut. Rose had stopped its sale and was reserving it along with all the beer and wine for his own use, and for the use of his particular friends, who were all able-bodied persons. There were three women, in addition to my wife, who actually needed something of this description.

The Jap stewards on board were being paid their regular wages by the German Government, but as their captain was a prisoner on board the *Wolf*, and they were away from his authority, they paid absolutely no heed to any of the prisoners' needs, merely contenting themselves with keeping the lieutenant well supplied with booze and anything else he wanted. Afterwards Rose told me that the service of the Japs on the *Hitachi* was splendid. I told him that it was rotten and told him why; Rose merely pulled that Prussian smile of his and said: "What do you expect? You're not first class passengers, you know." To this I agreed and told him all I wanted was an even break with the rest of the prisoners, or "ex-passengers," as he used to call us.

There were some sixty of us occupying the first class cabins, among whom were many of the original passengers of the *Hitachi*. We were, with one or two exceptions, all young people, and despite the short rations we had and the rough experience we'd undergone, we managed to have some very enjoyable times, playing deck billiards, quoits, cricket and various card games. In the dining saloon was a piano. Some of the Australian chaps were great mimics and had good voices, so we had some very enjoyable evenings. The last night we were on the *Hitachi*, in particular, the Japs came to life and were almost human. One of them unlocked a large closet that was filled with masks, costumes, false beards, hair, etc., which were used for amateur theatricals. We all dressed up as various characters, and we had a regular variety show.

Among the offerings were clog dancing, sword dancing, highland fling, the good old cake walk, and the Texas Tommy. The last number was what we called the *"Hitachi Rag"* and was danced by everybody. It consisted of the regulation "rag" varied by every conceivable step, including high and lofty tumbling. All during the performance the German sailors on the *Hitachi* were peering in through the portholes and lining the alley ways and steps, enjoying the show almost as much as the rest of us. But this *"Hitachi Rag"* was more than the disciplined Teutons could stand. First two of them tried it, and in a few minutes all the Germans were dancing. The news spread to the *Wolf* and there was a general stampede of Teuton guards and sailors in our direction. For a few minutes we had full charge of the ship, as the Teutons wouldn't stop when their petty officers called them. Shortly afterwards the chief officer appeared and made us all stop, saying that it was the commander's orders, and that we were "stopping the work of the ship"—to say nothing of undermining German discipline.

On the *Hitachi*, many of us lost things out of our rooms, such as razors, a camera, combs and various toilet articles and articles of clothing. One day, one of the British chaps caught a Jap steward in his room using his safety razor. As this particular Jap had pimples and sores all over his face, the British ally and owner of the razor was very hostile. I asked him what he was going to do about it. "I shall report the bally rotter to the management," the Briton replied. Not being used to such violent outbursts of emotion I beat it.

All the time that we were lying here among the Maldive Islands, 12 days in all, transferring cargo, the flying machine made regular observation trips twice a day, once in the morning and once in the evening. On three different occasions it reported seeing steamers passing not more than 50 or 60 miles off, and once it reported seeing a fast cruiser, probably British, travelling along at full speed. This island where we were lying was only 50 or 60 miles off the regular trade route and I had hopes that some patrolling vessel would blunder on to us, but no such luck; although one night our hopes were raised to a great height.

Just shortly after sunset, my wife imagined that she saw something on the Western horizon. I got my glasses and concealing myself so that I could not be discovered I had a look. I, too, could see something, but at that time could not make it out; although in another ten minutes I had another look and sure enough it was bigger and plainer. Shortly after, it was discovered by the Germans, and an alarm sounded. Everybody was thrown into great excitement, and the lines tying the *Wolf* and the *Hitachi* together were let go. All of us prisoners ran to our rooms and got our "emergency kits" ready.

Just across the hall from our "Bridal Suite" there was tremendous confusion. A corpulent British technical mining expert was rushing about his room in a perfect frenzy, looking for a heavy blue sweater he had carefully hung on a peg against just such an emergency as this;— of course, manlike, he blamed his wife for having mislaid it (my wife contributes this *slam gratis*.) However, after a few minutes' search, one of them discovered that the sweater was just where it belonged—on the man's back.

I met "Father" Cross—a veritable giant of a man and the greatest authority on Chinese dialects in the country—shouting in a great, roaring voice: "Bar steward! Bar steward! bring me a bottle of whiskey, quick!" I could hear him mumbling: "You don't get *me* into a life-boat without a bottle of something to keep me warm." This same man lost his trousers while climbing out of the life-boat onto the *Wolf* when the *Hitachi* was first captured. Somebody sent him a package a few days afterwards containing an old pair of suspenders, and I think that "Father" would have murdered the sender if he could have found out who it was. I have often regretted that the sender did not enclose Lieut. Rose's calling card.

Just about the time I reached the deck there was an order given from the bridge of the *Wolf* in a very disgusted voice, which was shortly followed by a very choice assortment of cuss words, some of which were in English. I looked to the Westward and saw that our rescuing cruiser was only a cloud, and at that time was about five degrees up from the horizon. Later on I kidded some of the German officers about it, and they each passed the blame on to somebody else; but just as this cloud had fooled me it had fooled them as well. "Father" Cross, however, averred that he knew what it was all the time, and that it was only a "sandy" on his part to get an extra bottle of whiskey.

On October 7th both ships sailed from the Maldive Islands, the *Wolf* going in search of a vessel loaded with coal, so that both *Wolf* and *Hitachi* could fill their bunkers with coal which would enable them to get "home" to Germany. We on the *Hitachi* loafed along at a slow speed in a south-westerly direction, meeting the *Wolf* again on the 19th, when we both steamed to the Chagos Archipelago, arriving there on October 20th, when we both tied up together and dropped anchor. During this time the *Wolf* had not been able to pick up a vessel, but the "bird" came back one day from an observation trip and reported a large steamer some 180 miles distant; later in the day she again went up and reported this steamer to be a big B. B. Liner of about 16,000 tons, and that she was equipped with 4 or 5 big guns. Needless to say, the *Wolf* wasn't looking for anything that could bite back, so the Commander decided to pass her up, and, returning to the Chagos group, take the balance of the *Hitachi's* coal and provisions on board the *Wolf* and sink the *Hitachi*, relying on getting another steamer in the Atlantic to furnish him with enough coal to complete his voyage.

It was during this cruise that Mr. Johnson, second officer on my vessel, died on board the *Wolf* from heart trouble (so they reported to me). The Germans gave him a burial at sea with full naval honours, Capt. Oleson, of the American Schooner *Encore*, reading the burial service, the commander and his officers standing by in full dress uniforms. The corpse was covered with an American flag and launched overboard from under the muzzle of one of the cannon.

Before shifting all the prisoners 'from the *Hitachi* to the *Wolf*, some arrangement for accommodation had to be made. The Germans cleaned out and fitted up No. 3 hold between decks for the ex-passengers of the *Hitachi* and also for the Japanese crew, a total of 170 odd persons. Iron berths were taken from the *Hitachi* along with wash-stands and other furnishings; and one corner of this "Glory Hole" was set aside for the whites and the fittings installed there. The Japs had wooden bunks built in the opposite corner for them, and rough wooden tables were knocked together for all hands to eat from and to play cards on. Also one of the pianos from the *Hitachi* was installed there to the best of my knowledge this piano was never played, and my chief mate, Mr. Bucker, who was quartered there, used the top of the piano to keep his clothes in, while the cover of the keyboard was used as a kind of mantelpiece or shelf by all hands.

The whole place below was lighted by three clusters of electric

THE BURIAL OF A. JOHNSON, SECOND OFFICER OF THE AMERICAN
BARK *BELUGA*, WHO DIED ON THE *WOLF*.

light, at night, and three fans were installed and the whole given a coating of white paint. The ventilation down below was very poor, and it was tough on the white men being forced to breathe this air as it was full of all kinds of oriental odours, and no doubt also oriental germs. A couple of armed sentinels were on guard below, continually, and also four on deck in the immediate vicinity of the hatch, at such times when the German crew were not at their almost continual gun drill and practice; at which times all hands were chased below, as also on the appearance of any vessel. The greatest hardship these men had to contend with was the lack of drinking water, as there seemed to be an unequal division of it between the Japs and the whites, with the latter getting the worst of it.

Immense quantities of iron piping and pipe fittings were taken from the *Hitachi* to be used later in fitting the prisoners' quarters under the poop and in No. 3 hatch, with heaters against the cold weather that was to be encountered before they finally reached Germany.

Auction bridge, poker and a German game called "*Mussel*" were the favourite card games and the stakes were very small; one *pfennig* ante and five *pf.* limit. Considering that it takes 100 *pfennigs* to make 25 cents, nobody won or lost a fortune, although on several occasions diplomatic relations were temporarily severed between some of the players. It was laughable, for instance, to hear an Australian chap named McEnally, who is very well off, owning plantations and big manufacturing concerns, squabbling over who would shy a penny in the pot. Taking it all in all, these men, amongst whom were some splendid fellows, adapted themselves to conditions as only the Britisher and the American can.

PART THREE

Bound for Germany the Rescue

On November 7th, the transfer of cargo being complete, and everything movable or floatable on the *Hitachi* being secured so that it would not float off when she sunk and leave any trace to make a passing steamer suspicious, we steamed out well clear of the Chagos Islands and at 1:30 p. m. the *Hitachi Maru* was bombed. She sank in 29 minutes.

We on the *Wolf* were quite close to the *Hitachi Maru* and could see everything very clearly. First the "bombing squad" were very busy placing their bombs: two amidships and one each in No. 1 hatch forward and No. 2 hatch, aft. The fuses from these bombs were all led on to the deck and brought to one centre. After everything was in readiness and all of the men, excepting the mine lieutenant, were in the launch, the lieutenant lighted the fuse and ran for the boat. Usually the fuses are set for 12 minutes, which gives the launch ample time to get away. We all stood there gazing intently at the steamer, expecting every minute to see the explosion.

The twelve minutes' wait in a case of this kind seems nearer half an hour. Suddenly there was a dull boom sound, and the water was convulsed, and smoke from the burnt powder appeared. And that was all, as the explosions all take place below the water line. The vessel sinks very rapidly at first, and in the case of the *Hitachi Maru*, the vessel settled evenly; that is, she went by neither head nor stern. Soon the water was nearly even with the rail, and the *Hitachi's* bow sank a little faster by the head. Pretty soon the waves were breaking on deck, and every moment might be the last; but still she hung on as if fighting for her very life. Suddenly a shudder seemed to pass over her, caused by the bursting of a bulkhead; her head disappeared below the wave, she hung there an instant and then her stern rose high out of the water;

she made her final dive . . . and the *Hitachi Maru*, 1st class Japanese passenger steamer, ceased to be.

There were a great many satisfied *Ah, Ahs* from the German crew as she disappeared, and a general feeling of satisfaction among them. For myself, I am afraid there was a tear in my eye, and all that I can wish these destroyers of good honest ships is that may they sometime think of how they smiled as they sank these ships, when they are standing around with empty bellies waiting for a chance to earn a living as sailors. I can understand a landsman sinking a ship and thinking it a joke, but a sailor, to my mind, should feel sad at seeing the end of an honest vessel, may she belong to friend or enemy.

I know one German officer who told me that, when the *Wolf* returned to Germany, he would never go in a raider again; that he made his living going to sea and could not stand seeing ships sunk.

From the Chagos Islands we steamed toward the Cape of Good Hope, and on November 10th, at 6:30 a.m., *Wolf* captured the Spanish steamer *Igotz Mendi* with a cargo of coal from Delagoa Bay to Colombo for the British Government. This was a very tame capture, the captain stopping as soon as he was signalled, thinking possibly that he was immune because he was neutral. No such luck. Lieutenant Rose and his prize crew went on board and took command, all the Spaniards staying on board. The first official act of Rose was to order Captain Uralda to vacate his room so that he, Rose, could use it. Captain Uralda answered temperamentally by throwing an inkstand at Rose. Unfortunately, Capt. Uralda is no Christie Mathewson and the first one was a ball. However, the Spanish Captain gave up his room. Both vessels now returned to the Chagos group and tied up together.

There was weeping and wailing on the *Wolf* that they did not hang on to the *Hitachi Maru* for a few more days. If they had, and the *Wolf* had captured *Igotz Mendi*, all three of us would have gone to Germany and the Imperial Government would very probably have been richer by many thousands of *marks* worth of valuable cargo that was sunk with the *Hitachi*.

The Germans transferred some two thousand tons of coal from the *Igotz Mendi* to the *Wolf* at this time. On November 12th, the two Australian medical officers and the major's wife, a British professor from Siam and his wife, "Father" Cross—an eminent British barrister from Singapore—and his wife, the technical mining man and his wife, one Chinese woman and husband, one Mauritian woman and a little black girl, and two male invalids were suddenly ordered on board the *Igotz* just as they stood. There was lots of excitement, as the *Wolf* had picked up a wireless message from a cruiser which was within 30 miles of us, but which unfortunately kept right on going. A couple of German sailors dumped everything in our room on the *Wolf* into a couple of bed sheets and dumped them down on the deck of the *Igotz Mendi* for us.

Our quarters here on the *Igotz Mendi* were fairly good, especially in warm weather, but later on in the cold regions they were far from liveable. "Father" Cross, the colonel and the two sick men were quartered aft under the poop in a room that had formerly been a boatswain locker; the rest of us were housed amidships in what was before the Spanish officers' quarters. The Spanish deck officers doubled up with the engine room squad, thereby leaving their rooms vacant for us to occupy.

I wish to add here that at the time of the transfer of the prisoners from the S.S. *Metunga* to the *Wolf*, Mrs. X, steward of the *Metunga*, was quartered on the top deck with the rest of the womenfolk. Mrs. X was an Australian woman of middle age and the widow of a chief engineer in the same company that owned the *Metunga*. After her transfer to the *Wolf*, she was ordered by the German officers to take care of the ladies' quarters. On account of the overbearing and insolent manners of some of her fellow shipmates, she refused duty, stating that she was a British subject and a prisoner of war and entitled to the same treatment as the rest of the women prisoners.

In this she was perfectly justified and I am certain it was through Lieut. Rose's influence that this demand of her services was made, as Rose was very partial to one of these ex-passengers. Later on when transferred to the *Hitachi Maru* Mrs. X was quartered aft in the second class, she being the only white woman there; and things were made generally disagreeable for her. This no doubt was because she was brave enough to show her independence and stand up for her right.

When we were transferred from the *Wolf* to the *Igotz Mendi* she asked to be kept on the *Wolf*, rather than go on the *Igotz Mendi* under the charge of Rose, stating that she would rather take the chances with the rest of them on the *Wolf* than be treated as she felt she would be on the *Igotz Mendi*.

This permission was granted her; but, a few days later on, she was transferred to the *Igotz Mendi* against her will, and quartered in the same room as the coloured people, among whom was one male.

Many of us were highly incensed because of this treatment of a white woman, but were powerless to do anything with Rose in the matter although we tried to make her lot as bearable as possible. Later on this woman took sick owing to the dampness of her quarters and my wife nursed her for three weeks until she finally recovered.

The *Igotz Mendi* was a product of wartimes, being built in 1916, and built in the cheapest possible manner, both in hull, equipment and accommodations. In her saloon, ten of us could sit down fairly comfortably in good weather, but when the vessel was rolling as nearly always was the case, only eight could sit down at the table, as the chairs at the ends were not stationary. We were waited upon by a steward named "Manuel." Manuel was quite a character and had his own ideas about how much a man should have a day for two *pesetas*. One day we were talking together, and he said that he shipped to take care of three men only and now he had twenty-two, among whom were four women, any one of whom (the women) were more trouble than the original three men he had shipped to serve.

I think Manuel had the largest thumb I have ever seen. When he brought in my plate of alleged soup the plate would be brimming full; on setting it down and withdrawing his thumb the plate would be only half full. This thumb would have been a valuable asset to some Yankee boarding house mistress in the States. Later on Manuel took a violent dislike to some of our party and used to spill the "coffee" or soup on them. This he did with malice aforethought and I don't know that I blamed him much, as some of our party imagined they were first class passengers on a modern liner with servants to supply their every whim.

On November 15th both steamers left the Chagos Islands, the *Igotz Mendi* going at slow speed to a point 300 miles south of the Cape of Good Hope, and the *Wolf* followed the regular sailing vessel route, where on November 18th she captured and sank the American bark *William Kirby* of New York, Captain Blum commanding. The *Kirby* was *en route* from New York to Port Elizabeth with a general cargo, the major part of which was automobiles destined for the African Christmas market. After transferring the crew, provisions, and what food stuffs were handily got at, the bomb gang got in their work and at 5:30 p. m. on November 18th the *Kirby* made her final bow.

On December 6th we met the *Wolf* again for a short time, exchanged signals, and received a further supply of canned crab? the *Wolf* having an inexhaustible supply which she had got from the *Hitachi*. We had so much crab that the very sight of a can of it was nauseat-

Last of the American bark *William Kirby*. 1200 gross tons. Captain Blum. Captured November 15th, Three hundred and twenty miles S. E. of Port Elizabeth

ing. I feel sure that should a waiter in a restaurant ever suggest crab to any of the ex-prisoners on the *Wolf* he would have a very unpleasant time of it. During the night of the 6th, the *Wolf* left us, taking a more northerly route than we.

At this time, Lieutenant Rose had told the Spanish ex-captain that we were *en route* to Trinidad Island, Brazil, where *Wolf* would get what additional coal she required, and then we, the *Igotz Mendi*, should, after waiting 10 days at the island, proceed to Spain. This, of course, made us feel very happy and I know that the Cameron family were over-joyed with the prospects of getting safely landed after such a long time. Many of us took up the study of the Spanish language, and some very queer conversations were carried on. When I tried to talk Spanish, I would usually get stuck for a Spanish word and put in a German one; then if I couldn't think of the German word, would use English, the result was that neither a Spaniard nor a German could understand me. Sometimes I couldn't figure it out myself.

We enjoyed fine weather and managed to keep alive on the food, which was some task. When we got up from the table hungry, we would think of Spain and freedom in a few short weeks, and forget all about how empty we were. On December 18th the *Wolf* again picked us up; it seemed that she could appear at will like some gigantic evil spirit. The *Wolf* wigwagged the information that on December 14th she met and sank the French bark *Marechal Davoust,* bound from Australia to France with a cargo of grain. This bark was equipped with wireless and had two guns mounted on her, but offered no resistance to the *Wolf*. *Wolf* took the crew, provisions, ships stores, the wireless, and also his two cannon, off the Frenchman, later in the day sinking her by bombs.

Both the *Wolf* and *Igotz Mendi* now proceeded together toward the Island of Trinidad and expected to get there early on the morning of December 20th. I had made arrangements with Lieutenant Rose so that I could have a jolly boat in the morning and the wife and I go fishing off the rocks on the lee side of the island, as this island is celebrated for its good sea bass fishing. At 9:30 p.m. on the 19th, while pacing the deck with the wife before retiring, I noticed that the *Wolf* suddenly changed her course to the Northward and signalled us with her flash light. We immediately changed also, and put on all available speed to the northward after the *Wolf*. Soon the explanation came: there were two cruisers of the Brazilian Navy anchored at Trinidad and the *Wolf* had picked up a wireless message from one of them to the Brazilian authorities.

Needless to say, it didn't take Commander Nerger long to decide that he had business elsewhere. If these confounded gossipy cruisers had not used their wireless, in another few hours we should have run right into their arms. On the other hand, if they had been lying in the harbour of some big sea port as seems to be the custom with battle ships, and not off Trinidad Island, we should probably have carried out the regular schedule of freedom *via* Spain. Of the two, I should much have preferred the Brazilian Navy to rescue us, as then I should have been sure of freedom, while on the other hand, I had only Rose's word that we would proceed to Spain.

There was a bitter gloom on our ship for a good while after this; in fact, the spirits of the prisoners never regained their previous buoyancy. The great question now was "What next?" We could see only Germany ahead of us, and that was not very encouraging. For myself, I felt quite confident that we should never get through the blockade and the mine fields. Captain Rose had often told us that in the event of our meeting a cruiser, we would go into the boats and the ship would be bombed and sunk.

This was a very alluring proposition for a family man to look forward to but was better than the conditions on the *Wolf*, as there now were nearly 800 crew and prisoners on the *Wolf*, while its lifeboats and rafts under the most favourable conditions could hold only 400, so it can easily be figured out just how much chance our poor chaps had of getting into the boats, in the event of the *Wolf's* meeting a superior enemy. Probably they would be battened down below in the hold, and would be sent down to "Davey Jones' Locker" with the *Wolf*. In our case on the *Igotz Mendi* we were about thirty souls to a boat, and if the weather conditions were favourable and we had a little luck, we should have been all right. The women naturally lived in a continual dread of having to go into the boats.

We had all been looking forward to eating our Christmas dinner at the island of Trinidad and were going to have a royal feed, as our German "hosts" were going to kill a pig and a cow that were on board the *Igotz Mendi* when captured. However, the Brazilian Navy changed our plans as to where our dinner was to be eaten; though we had "Sir Pig" just the same. Owing to the sudden change of our plans (gaining freedom *via* Spain) we all felt very blue on Christmas day, which was not the enjoyable affair it would have been if everything had worked out as expected. I know I had the blues all Christmas as I got thinking about other Christmases spent under more enjoyable circumstances, which thoughts naturally didn't make me feel any more cheerful. Lieutenant Rose was around bright and early, wishing us all a merry Christmas and "many happy returns" of the day. I intend next Christmas, if Rose is still interned in Denmark, to write him a letter returning the compliment, and then he can possibly appreciate the subtleties of a joke of this nature. My wife wanted to stick a hat pin into him when he came around with his "many happy returns of the day." The German crew, too, appeared to be blue on Christmas.

New Year's Eve we all sat up to see the New Year in, and one or two of us worked up enthusiasm enough to make a little noise, but the situation was so depressing that we soon subsided. Not so our German crew, however. They held high festival in the Engineer's mess, having a bowl full of punch, whose chief recommendation was that its foundation was "*Aguadenti*" and it had an awful kick. The Spanish engineer, who had a splendid voice, sang several songs, and the German sailors sang patriotic songs. At about two o'clock on New Year's morning, someone woke me up by shoving a bottle of wine through the porthole for me, and later on around three a.m. another bottle made its appearance.

Some of the German sailor boys had imagined we were not happy because we had no wine. The gifts were received in the spirit in which they were sent. This was by no means the only act of kindness shown my family and myself by the members of the crew. In fact, throughout the trip, officers and crew, with the single exception of Lieutenant Rose, were very friendly toward us. The American contingent was decidedly popular, though they had no use for the rest. As an illustration, on my birthday on January 25th several members of the crew came and presented me with presents in the form of bottles of wine, and even Rose came across with a box of cigars. Several of the German crew had lived in America for many years; two had even taken out their first papers. And all of these talked enthusiastically of going back to America as soon as the war was over.

I was very much interested in trying to find out just what the German opinion was of America coming into the war. Lieut. Rose used to stick his chest up in the air and say that the United States coming in wouldn't make any difference in the ultimate outcome of the war, and that the only difference it would make was that the States would lose a lot of men and money. Just the same, I am of the opinion that Rose knew that America's coming in spelled the finish of Germania, though of course he wouldn't admit it. One day at the table he said that the "Star Spangled Banana," as he loved to call our flag, was only a joke and that it looked like a gridiron to him. I made the remark that possibly the stars and stripes would not prove the joke he imagined.

My retorts to sallies of this kind were very moderate, as I considered I was in no position to argue the point with him, and didn't want to lose any of my liberties. I was always afraid to start an argument with him, as I am very hot-headed and knew that in the event of a row I was sure to get the worst of it eventually. Rose used to laugh at the American soldier, saying we were crazy to imagine that we could take a man and make a soldier out of him in a year, that at best these men would only be cannon fodder, that Germany had proved it takes three years to make a soldier, also that our submarines were mere toys, and that as for submarine defence, just as soon as we figured out some Yankee patent to protect our ships, they (Germany) would invent some other way to destroy them. Rose believed that the submarine would eventually decide the war. It was pretty hard to sit at the same table and hear an enemy slam the American government and not to be able to "hit back" or even "argue" the point.

On January 20th, in latitude 33 degrees north and longitude 40 degrees west, we again met the *Wolf*, and, the weather being exceptionally fine and the sea very smooth, the *Wolf* came alongside and we transferred some 800 tons of coal to her. Each vessel's side was well supplied with large fenders or bumpers made of large coils of rope, so that when the vessels would bump together they would do as little damage as possible. Even under these favourable circumstances, however, the vessels rolled and tossed around a great deal, and occasionally some very severe crashes were experienced; but Commander Nerger, realizing how great was his need for coal, and knowing it might be months before he would get as smooth sea again, held on and worked every man available despite the heavy bumping that was damaging both vessels.

The gang of men on the *Wolf* trimming the coal in the bunkers could not handle the coal as fast as the other gang brought it to them, so, rather than delay the coaling, to save every minute, they dumped the coal on deck; and when the vessels were forced to part owing to the increasing swells, both guns and both torpedo tubes on the after deck were covered with coal. If a cruiser had happened along at that particular moment, the *Wolf's* after battery would have been out of commission. However, these conditions did not continue long, as all hands worked feverishly at the job until all the coal was under decks.

After the two vessels had parted, we took stock of damages and found that several frames or ribs in the side of *Igotz Mendi* were broken, that some plates on her side were badly stove in. These flattened or stove-in places varied in size from six feet to forty feet in length. Luckily all our damage was above water line, and the vessel leaked only when rolling heavily, or when a big sea was running. The *Wolf* was also damaged, having several frames broken and four plates cracked. She was leaking eleven tons of water per hour, while we averaged about one and one-half tons per hour.

From this point the two vessels separated after arranging another and final rendezvous at latitude 61 degrees north and longitude 33 degrees west, a point some little distance southwest of Iceland. The weather from now commenced to get colder and we with our impoverished blood and scanty clothing commenced to feel the cold keenly.

Then came another heart-breaking disappointment. Be it remembered that our daily prayer and hope was that we would meet a cruiser before we got into the extremely cold weather, where the suffering in the life-boats would be intense.

On January 24th the weather was very overcast, and drizzly, and inclined to be squally—regular Channel weather. I was lying in my bunk reading a four months' old newspaper printed in Africa, when at about five bells (2:30 p.m.) my wife came to my door and said: "Stan, there is a cruiser with four funnels just ahead of us."

I thought she was kidding, and said: "All right, Mamie, tell them to reserve an outside room for me." I then looked at her and saw she was white as a sheet. I jumped up, knowing immediately there was "something doing."

Just as I hit the floor, the professor stuck his head in at the door and said: "My God, Captain, a cruiser at last."

I ran out on deck and there just on the edge of a rain squall was what appeared to be a four-funnelled cruiser. Just about this time the Spanish second mate, who was on the bridge, discovered her, and a sailor ran into Lieutenant Rose's room calling him to come to the deck. As soon as I looked at the cruiser through my glasses, I saw that instead of being one four-funnelled cruiser, it was two American Army transports, both of them heavily armed with what appeared to be big guns. There was great confusion amongst the Germans, and in a few seconds two of them (armed) chased us into our cabins in no uncertain manner. We altered our course in such a manner as to pass under the stern of the two transports, and they were less than a mile from us when they crossed our bow. They paid absolutely no attention to us, and in a few minutes were swallowed up in the fog and lost to sight.

My God, you can't imagine how I felt after hoping and praying and building on running across a cruiser, not for days but for months, and when we at last did meet two of them, they passed calmly on, not even signalling, nor asking who we were. It was certainly disappointing. And then to have to sit at the same table and see Rose sitting with that "Chessy" cat smile of smug complacency on his ugly Prussian mug. Previous to this episode, he frequently made remarks about the Stars and Stripes, and after this incident, he never lost an opportunity to refer to it.

Just the same the Germans were a badly frightened bunch. The first thing they did on seeing the supposed cruisers was to run to their quarters and put on their good clothes, fully expecting to be the guests of the American Government. The next thing they thought of was their bombs, and the bomb man going to get them, found that they were gone. Somebody had stolen them. Holy Poker, wasn't there hell to pay! If words, looks or wishes could have killed we would all have been crucified where we stood.

This bomb episode, at this time, was as much a mystery to us prisoners as it was to Lieutenant Rose. For some reason or other my fellow prisoners must have thought that I was the guilty party, because every time I would meet one of them on deck and start talking, he would excuse himself, having pressing business elsewhere. They seemed to be afraid that if they were seen talking to me that they would be "accessories after the act" and liable to punishment. I was greatly flattered to think that these people thought I was "hero" enough for a job of this description, but nevertheless I could not help thinking of how much assistance or co-operation I could have got from this crowd in case I had undertaken something along these lines.

The following day Lieutenant Rose held an investigation to find out "who stole the bombs." We were all chased out of the dining room on to the cold iron deck in a drizzling rain while this investigation was being held behind closed doors. However, I had not been on board the *Igotz Mendi* for this length of time without knowing my way about and managed to get an "ear full." When the Spanish chief officer was called, Rose asked him if he knew anything about the bombs. He answered: "Yes, I threw them overboard. I'll tell why. It was not for me,

Captain Rose, but for the women and little children. I am not afraid of you. You can shoot me if you want to, but you can't drown the little children."

Rose confined him to his room and the next time we met the *Wolf* Commander Nerger sentenced him to three years' imprisonment in a German military prison. I consider this a very brave act of the Spaniard's and wish that I were in a position to show some substantial appreciation of his humane heroism. After this incident our guards were doubled and we were chased off the deck if anything appeared on the horizon.

One day the Spanish Chief Officer, Mr. ——, told me the details of this episode.

At the time of the cruiser alarm he was asleep in his bunk and was wakened by the unusual amount of noise. As soon as he saw the supposed cruisers he ran to the wireless room, under the bridge, where the bombs were kept. This room had two doors, one on each side. Luckily the side he entered on was the side towards which the wireless operator, who was intently "listening in" for signals from the other vessels, had his back turned to. —— reached under the table, secured the bombs and went outside again, where he threw them into the sea. The wireless operator never turned around, thinking that it was the "bomb man" who had come after his bombs. —— reached the deck and back to his room without being observed by any of the Germans. He said he owned up to the stealing of the bombs so that nobody else would get into trouble.

A peculiarity of this case was that some time previous to this, shortly after the *Igotz Mendi* was taken charge of by the Germans, I had approached on the subject of trying, should a favourable opportunity occur, to take charge of the vessel. I did not receive any encouragement along these lines and was afraid to go into the matter any further with him. I put it down as a case of cold feet.

Mr. ——, an ex-second officer of a captured British steamer, who was an invalid who had just come through three months' siege in the hospital on the *Wolf*, and I, had gone into the details of an enterprise of this kind, but unfortunately while this Britisher had the heart of a lion, he was physically unfit for anything as strenuous as this undertaking, and the matter was dropped, against his will, although he would admit that he might keel over any time. If the British Army has many chaps like this in it, Kaiser Bill is surely going to catch hell. It is my belief that at this particular time, owing to certain conditions that ex-

AMERICAN SCHOONER *WINSLOW* BEING TAKEN INTO SUNDAY ISLAND
AFTER CAPTURE BY THE SEAPLANE ON JUNE 7TH.
IN THE BACKGROUND IS THE NEW ZEALAND STEAMER *WIARUMA*
GOING OUT TO SEA TO BE SUNK BY THE *WOLF*.

THE BLOWING UP OF THE AMERICAN SCHOONER *WINSLOW*, 566
GROSS TONS. CAPT. TRUDGETT. SUNK JUNE 21ST OFF SUNDAY
ISLAND BY FOUR BOMBS AND THIRTY-NINE SHELLS

isted, four good two handed men could have taken charge of the *Igotz Mendi* and probably would not have met with much resistance, except possibly from Lieutenant Rose, and I am sure it would have been a pleasure to tap him on the head.

The co-operation of the Spanish crew could not be depended on at this time, as they believed that in a couple of weeks they were to be free again, after coaling the *Wolf* at Trinidad Island.

After the Trinidad Island disappointment, conditions were such that the taking of the ship by any of us, even with the unreliable co-operation of the Spanish crew, was not feasible.

The weather now was intensely cold and we all suffered intensely, as there was no heat of any kind in the cabins. Our bedding was continually wet and garments taken off on going to bed would be sopping wet in the morning from the "sweat" that gathered on the walls and ceilings. Personally I beat this part of the game by taking my clothes to bed with me. The food question, too, was getting serious, as owing to the cold weather we required more food to keep our bodies warm. The statement has been repeatedly made in the papers in Europe that on the *Igotz Mendi* the prisoners had the same food as the German commander and crew.

Let me show you how it was in reality. Eleven of us sat down at the first table with Rose at the head. The one platter started with him. He helped the party (a friend of his) on his right first, himself next, and passed the plate to the party on his left. This man was a glutton, and was without shame. These three people got very nearly and sometimes fully half of the contents of the platter; what was left was divided amongst the remaining eight, including five males, two women, and a little six-year-old child. If we asked for more, we were reminded that we were short of provisions and had to make them last. If the platter of food had been equally divided, and we had all shared alike, it would not have been so bad, but under this heads-I-win-tails-you-lose division I have got up from the table actually hungry. It is an awful sensation suddenly to realise that you actually covet the food another person is eating.

We continued in a northerly direction until February 5th, when we again met the *Wolf*, and owing to the bomb incident, sixteen additional Germans were sent on board with their side arms and clothing but no additional food was sent with them. We now had eighty-two souls on board the *Igotz Mendi* all told. Lieutenant Wolffe, division lieutenant of the *Wolf*, was also sent on board to assist Rose. Lieutenant Wolffe took over the control of the food and the cook's department, and made an honest effort to better things, which did improve somewhat, at least to the extent that on bean meals we frequently got all we wanted; but he was also the inventor of a weird concoction known as "Billposter's paste" and for this last crime I will never forgive him. Otherwise he was a decent and fair-minded officer. After his arrival, favouritism was abolished and we all got a square deal.

On February 6th the *Wolf* left us and was never seen again by any of us. We then started to go around the northern end of Iceland, but met ice and were forced back. We ran south for a couple of days and waited around to see if the *Wolf* made it or not, and as she did not return, we concluded she had either got through or passed to the southward of Iceland, chancing the blockade. The cold here was very intense and caused a lot of suffering amongst us. Helped by some of the German sailors, I fixed a place in an empty bunker, where my wife, Nita and myself practically lived, only going in the cabin for meals and to sleep. Lieutenant Rose had canvas put up here for us and lights put in so that I could lie there and read, and the wife could sit and sew. Nita of course enjoyed the comparative warmth. The only drawback was that the air was full of fine coal dust and gas from the fire room, and we used to get frightfully dirty.

On February 6th we again tried to get to the northward of Iceland, but again met ice and had to return. Rose was forced to go to the southward of Iceland, as he could not waste any more time, since the supply of drinking water was getting very low.

Now that we were about to actually enter the blockade zone, our hopes commenced to rise. I heard nothing from my fellow prisoners for the past six months but: "Just wait until they try to run the British blockade." I heard this so often that I got to believe it and used to figure the only chance the Germans had to get through was if it was foggy weather, and then if he was lucky he might slip through.

We ran the blockade between the Faroes and Iceland in fine clear weather, and did not even see any smoke. So I commenced to think that it was quite possible, it being winter, that the British weren't paying much attention to this particular spot and were keeping cases on the Norwegian Coast, especially in that district around the Naze at the southern extremity of Norway. On the night of February 18th we received a wireless from Berlin that the *Wolf* had arrived safely and on February 19th we picked up the Norwegian Coast, some sixty miles north of Bergen. From here we proceeded down the coast, bucking a heavy head wind and sea, at about five knots per hour, passing inside the light on the island outside Stavanger, and thence down the coast and around the Naze.

During this time, it was fine and clear weather, and a cruiser could have seen us at twenty miles distance easily; but the only vessels we saw were a Stavanger pilot boat and a Danish passenger vessel bound northward. We were a disgusted bunch and no mistake. For myself, I was sore; I was afraid to speak to anybody. Here I had been kidding myself and letting others kid me that when I got this far, somebody would surely pick me up. And then to come down this coast in beautiful clear weather and not even see anything resembling a patrol boat was very disappointing to say the least.

From here on all I could see ahead of me was the Gates of Germany and the certainty of spending from one to five years a hungry prisoner in a Teuton detention camp. I would have sold out cheap at this time, believe me. By this time, I had given up all hopes of getting free and had reconciled myself to going to Germany. ... If it had not been for the family I would have jumped overboard and had a swim for neutral land at some place when we passed fairly close.

The following day while crossing from Norway to the northern end of Denmark, Jutland, it set in foggy and Lieutenant Rose was strutting around with a smile on his mug, saying: "Just the weather I want; made to order; I am all right now." I didn't argue the point with him, as I thought he was right. About 3.30 in the afternoon we picked up a fog whistle ahead, of the character we call a "blatter" on the Pacific Coast. I was standing on deck just under the bridge, talking to Rose. I nodded my head toward the signal and asked him what it was, and he said: "Oh, that is the lightship." I thought at the time it was a peculiar character for a lightship, but dismissed the thought, thinking, "different ships, different fashions."

Rose had told the British colonel that this signal was a German torpedo boat with which he had arranged a meeting, and that the colonel had gone inside to tell the rest of the prisoner passengers, which would give them all a scare. He also suggested that I should go inside and tell them it was a U-boat, and that I recognised the sound of her signal. I laughed, and told him I had made so many remarks regarding the blockade that I was afraid to speak to them. Shortly after this I went into my cabin and was standing looking out of the porthole and talking to my wife, when I noticed that we had altered our course, by the bearing of the fog signal, and knew that Rose wanted to pass the lightship close aboard. Suddenly I felt the vessel smell the bottom. I looked at the wife and said: "Holy Poker! I thought I felt her smell the bottom." No sooner had I said this than the *Igotz Mendi* ran slap bang on the beach, about 350 yards off shore and less than half mile away from the lighthouse.

Rose's mistaking the lighthouse signal for the lightship's signal was a lucky piece of business for us because I knew for an absolute certainty when I felt the *Igotz Mendi* had taken the beach that it would require the assistance of a powerful tug to get her off again. I guess we all realised just how much this stranding meant to us, and the very nearness of freedom kept everybody quiet and busy with his own thoughts and plans. I know that for one I had decided to get over the side and swim for it, provided the vessel should give any indications of getting off the beach.

Right after the stranding, the weather being foggy, we were allowed on deck. One of the neutral sailors, a Dane named Jensen, identified the spot where we were ashore and gave me the good news that the little town of Skagen was only about two miles distant, and that one of the best lifesaving crews in Europe was stationed there. Sure enough, in about an hour a life-boat drew up alongside. We were all chased inside again. Rose invited the captain of the lifeboat on board, and took him into the chart room just above the saloon for a drink and talk. Our lady prisoners immediately commenced playing a game of "button, button, who's got the button?" laughing and talking at the top of their voices, so that this man on top of the saloon would know that there were women on board. Also little Nita did a crying act that could be heard, I am sure. Shortly Rose came down with a blank scowl on his face and said: "You people can cut out the noise now, as the stranger has gone ashore."

Somebody asked Rose why he didn't introduce us to his friend, and Rose answered: "What do you think I am—a fool?" Nobody went on record with an opinion, so the matter was dropped. In the meantime, Lieutenant Wolffe had gone ashore and had 'phoned from the lighthouse at Scow Point, where we were ashore, to a salvage company in Skagen, saying that we were a German merchant ship bound from Bergen, Norway, to Kiel, and that we had run ashore in the fog; and that if a tug was sent immediately we could be pulled off easily, but if we were allowed to lie any length of time, the ship would bed herself in the sand and it would mean a long delay in getting off.

I understand he offered 25,000 *kroner* for the job; at any rate, the manager of the salvage company ordered his largest tug, the *Viking*, around, but instructed his captain not to put a line on board until the manager had gone down overland and investigated a little. Lieutenant Wolffe in the meantime returned on board and reported to Rose, who was immensely tickled and told us that about midnight a tug would arrive from "a nearby town" and pull us into deep water, and that by four o'clock in the morning at the latest we would be on our way to Germany once more.

This news led to great consternation among us, and some great arguments regarding neutrality laws were carried on. On all the trip the colonel had been quoting the Geneva Convention, until we had all concluded that this particular convention was held for the express benefit of the medical officers of the army. I asked the colonel if he remembered anything in the Geneva Convention regarding the grounding of a belligerent's prize on neutral ground. He answered by saying that clause so and so, paragraph so and so, expressly stated that all medical officers should be exempt from . . . at this point I butted in and told him to "go to hell"; that there were women and children and other prisoners on board as well as medical officers.

All throughout the trip this man had behaved like a dog in a manger, being the quintessence of egotistical selfishness, and despised by us, one and all. The conclusion of all our argument was that might was right in this war, and that the Germans would do just what they liked, provided they could hoodwink the Danish officials.

The manager of the Danish salvaging company, on arriving at the lighthouse and talking with the various people there, concluded that perhaps things were not just right with the *Igotz Mendi* and that he had better get in touch with the Danish naval authorities before doing anything. He called up the commander of the Danish cruiser *Diana* and stated the case, saying that things didn't appear to be just right. The commander, a Lieutenant Lagoni, getting in touch with the authorities, 'phoned the manager of the salvage company that he would come right down to investigate.

At about midnight the *Diana* arrived and Lieutenant Lagoni, being a gentleman and also a shrewd, wide-awake officer, took his chief officer on board the *Igotz Mendi*, telling him that he, the commander, would keep the captain of the *Igotz Mendi* busy answering questions in the saloon while the chief officer should have a good look around and gather what information he could. As soon as the Danish commander arrived on board we were all pushed and shoved into our rooms and the doors closed. When Rose started to take Lieutenant Lagoni into the chart room above the lieutenant said: "Oh, no, captain, let's go into the saloon; it is not customary to entertain the commander of a cruiser in the chart room."

So they came into the saloon. Just as he came through the door he saw some of us being hustled out of sight—but said nothing. Shortly one of the ladies would shout down the alleyway: "Oh, Mrs. So and So, won't you come to my room for a minute? Don't be frightened." All this for the benefit of the Danish officer in the saloon. In the meantime, the Danish chief officer was wandering around the *Igotz Mendi*, taking notice of all he saw. While strolling through the bunkers, where our "temporary" warm place was, he noticed Nita's "kewpie" doll lying where she had dropped it. There were men standing around all through these quarters.

Suddenly the officer turned on a man standing there and said: "You're not a German."

The man answered saying: "No, sir; I am a Dane."

"Well, what are you doing here?" was the next question.

The Dane, Jensen, told him he was from the *Wolf* and was working here on the *Igotz Mendi*, and that there were American and British prisoners on board, including some women and children. After completing his rounds, the Danish officer went on deck and told Lieutenant Lagoni that he was ready, and calling him aside, told him what he had found out. Lieutenant Lagoni then gave orders to disable the wireless plant and told Rose that the tug could not assist him off the beach, and that at the end of twenty-four hours the vessel would be interned providing she was still under German flag, and advised him to land any prisoners he had.

Of course during all this talk we prisoners knew nothing at all of what was going on, and when we saw the Danish officers leaving we came to the conclusion that our case was lost, and as there was an armed sentry pacing back and forth in front of the two doors leading from the cabin to the deck, it looked black indeed, and I for one felt very, very disappointed. The strain was beginning to tell on my wife again; so we both lay down on the bunk with our clothes on and listened to Rose on the bridge, ringing the telegraph and working his engines in a vain attempt to get his vessel off the beach. As I lay there thinking, I could not but pity Rose, realising how he must have felt.

Just imagine what his feelings must have been on realising that after spending fifteen months on a raiding and mine laying cruise, and

IGOTZ MENDI ASHORE ON THE DANISH COAST. TAKEN THE
MORNING WE LANDED, FEBRUARY 26TH, 1918.

LIFEBOAT LEAVING THE BEACH FOR THE STRANDED *IGOTZ MENDI.*

always evading his enemies, he had run his vessel aground almost at the gates of Germany, and in place of receiving the Iron Cross first class, there was the possibility of his facing court martial on his arrival home, provided of course he was lucky enough to escape internment Thinking this I fell asleep and at 6.30 a.m. of February 25th (shall I ever forget the date?) I was awakened by one of the German seamen named "Hans" knocking at my door and saying: "*Kapitaine, Kapitaine*, wake up and get ready to go ashore in the boats."

I'll bet we broke all speed records getting on deck. Rose asked me to get into the lifesaving boat first, as the Danish crew could not speak English, and then I could help the balance as they came down the ladder. I got Juanita firmly on my back and climbed down into the boat. There was a large sea running and as the *Igotz Mendi* was stationary on the bottom and the lifeboat was riding on the seas, one moment it would be even with my feet and in another would be fifteen feet below. The idea was to jump at that instant the boat was even with me. This was easy enough with myself and wife, who understood such things and had had previous experience, but to the balance of the passengers it was hard to make them let go at the right time; they all having a tendency to hang on until the boat had started to go down again. Then, if they should let go, the drop was so great that the men in the lifeboat could not hold them when they tried to catch them.

In some cases, it was necessary absolutely to tear the passengers off the ladder by main force. However, we finally got all the women, children and men into the boat and we started for the beach. When we got into the breakers and the seas washed clean over us, many thought it would be a case of swim or drown, not reckoning on the kind of life-boat we were in or on the class of men that manned it.

I have seen various life-crews at drill and I spent a season on the beach at Cape Nome, where everything is surf work, but these old Danes, averaging fifty years of age and the living caricatures of that great soap advertisement, "Life Buoy Soap," familiar to all the reading public, were in a class by themselves. On entering the breakers, they dropped a kedge anchor with a long line on it, and literally slacked the boat through. A gigantic comber, one of those curling ones, just commencing to break, would rush upon us; up would go the stern of the boat and just at the instant that I would expect her to go end for end, the old "Sinbad" tending the anchor line would check her and in another instant we would rush for the beach, just as the Kanakas ride the surf on a board at Honolulu.

When we finally grounded the men from the beach ran out and seized the women, the balance then ran the boat higher up the beach. The natives must have thought that we were a bunch of raving maniacs, the way we carried on, getting our feet on good *"terra firma"* again. We danced, we shouted, and cheered, and made damn fools of ourselves generally; but to my mind the situation warranted it. What a fitting climax to an adventure of this kind . . . eight months a prisoner on a Teuton raider, and set free at the very gates of Germany, at the eleventh hour and fifty-ninth minute. It is hard to realise just what this meant to us all—possibly the very lives of my wife and kiddie, as I feel sure that they could not have stood much more, and at the best, there was from one to a possible five years' being buried alive in a German internment camp, and living under the conditions that I know to exist in that country.

We were taken to the nearby lighthouse, where the keepers and their families did everything possible for us, drying our clothes and giving us hot coffee to warm ourselves. About midday we went into Skagen, two miles distant, and separated, going to various hotels. My family and I put up at the Sailors' Home and were excellently taken care of by our host, Mr. Borg Hansen. I wish to go on record here as saying that at no place that I have ever been in have I met a more whole-souled, more hospitable or more likable class of people in my life than these Danish people of the little town of Skagen. I met people there who were the quintessence of courtesy and hospitality; in fact, they were "regular Danish ladies and gentlemen." Here at Skagen our various consuls took us in charge and sent us to Copenhagen, where we separated, going our several ways.

Appendix

During her fifteen months' cruise the *Wolf* laid approximately five hundred mines and captured fourteen vessels, as follows:

1. British tank s/s. *Turitella*, 7300 gross tons, Captain S. G. Meadows, captured on February 27, 1917, in the Indian Ocean, bound from Rangoon to Europe with a cargo of oil. The captain and officers were taken off this vessel and transferred to the *Wolf*. A crew of German officers and mine-men were put on board of her, under charge of Lieutenant-Commander Brandes, ex-chief officer of the *Wolf*, and she was sent away as a mine layer, laying mines at Bombay and at Calcutta, and was afterwards captured at Aden, while laying mines, by a British gun-boat; and her crew of Chinamen were sent back to China, while her German officers were taken prisoners.

2. British s/s. *Jumma*, 6050 gross tons, Captain Shaw Wickerman, bound from Torreirja, Spain, to Calcutta with a cargo of salt. Captured in the Indian Ocean, March 1st. After what coal and stores she had on board had been removed, she was bombed on the morning of March 3rd in latitude 8 degrees 9 minutes north and longitude 62 degrees 1 minute east.

3. British s/s. *Wadsworth*, of London, 3509 gross tons, built in 1915, Captain John Shields, captured on March 11th, in latitude 54 degrees 30 minutes north and longitude 67 degrees east. After taking off about fifteen tons of rice and ship's stores the vessel was bombed on the i8th. Wadsworth was bound from Bassinia, India, to London with a cargo of rice, and was six days out from Colombo.

4. Mauritius bark *Dee*, 1200 tons, Captain Ruug, bound from Mauritius to Bundbury, Australia, in ballast, thirty-nine days out. Captured May 21st, 300 miles off the west coast of Australia. Crew of blacks and stores taken on board the *Wolf* and the vessel immediately bombed.

5. New Zealand s/s. *Wairuna* of the Union S/S. Co. Line, of New Zealand, Captain John Saunders, with general cargo from Auckland to San Francisco. Captured May 21st off Sunday Island by seaplane. The *Wolf* was lying behind Sunday Island cleaning and repairing boilers at the time of capture. The flying machine flew over the *Wairuna* and dropped a message attached to a sandbag, saying to steer towards the *Wolf* or the flying machine would drop bombs on her. Thus she was taken by the raider. After taking off some forty live sheep and ship's stores and about 900 tons of coal, she was sunk by one bomb and fifteen shells. While towing the *Wairuna* to sea, *Wolf* discovered the schooner *Winslow*.

6. American schooner *Winslow*, 566 gross tons, Captain Trudgett, bound from Sydney to Samoa, with general cargo. Captured off Sunday Island on June 7th by the seaplane while *Wolf* was sinking the *Wairuna*. After removing ship's stores and some 450 tons of coal the *Winslow* was sunk on June 21st by four bombs and thirty-nine shells, the old wooden box simply refusing to sink.

7. American bark *Beluga*, of San Francisco, 590 gross tons, Captain Cameron, bound from San Francisco to Sydney, Australia, with a cargo of benzine. Captured latitude south 26 degrees, on July 9th. After removing 300 cases of oil, the stores and boatswain's supplies, the *Beluga* was set on fire on July 11th by gun fire, by the nineteenth shot.

8. American schooner *Encore*, 651 gross tons, Captain Oleson, bound from Columbia River to Sydney, Australia, with a load of lumber. Captured July 6th in latitude south 21 degrees and longitude east 169 degrees. After removing stores she was set on fire and left.

9. Australian s/s. *Matunga*, of the Burns & Phillips Line, Captain Donaldson, *en route* from Sydney to Kabul, New Guinea. Captured August 4th, about 122 miles southwest of Kabul. Both vessels proceeded from this point to Pirate's Cove, at the northernmost end of New Guinea, arriving there on August 10th. Transferred cargo to the *Wolf*, amounting to some 850 tons of coal and 350 tons of supplies; also prisoners (passengers), including two army medical corps officers and three military captains. On August 26th *Wolf* proceeded to sea and sunk the *Matunga* by three bombs, vessel sinking in six and one-half minutes. Full particulars of the *Matunga's* cargo was picked up by the *Wolf* in a wireless message to her consignees, giving a copy of her outward manifest, also all sailing dates from time to time by Burns & Phillips themselves.

10. Japanese s/s. *Hatachi Maru*, of the N.Y. K. Co., 6558 gross tons, Captain Kokmoa, en route from Colombo to England, *via* African ports. Captured on September 26th off the Maldive Islands and proceeded to southernmost group of the Maldives, where 800 tons of bunker coal were transferred to the *Wolf*, also 250 tons of copper and tin, silk, tea, approximately 400 tons of rubber, further cocoanuts and hides. On October 7th both vessels proceeded in different directions, the *Wolf* seeking for another vessel with coal while the *Hitachi* loafed along in a general south-easterly direction. *Wolf* picked up *Hitachi* again on October 19th, forty-two miles west of the Chagos group. On October 20th both vessels arrived at the Chagos Islands and tied up together. Additional rubber and silk and remaining coal were transferred to the *Wolf*. On the morning of November 7th both vessels left Chagos and the *Hitachi* was bombed.

11. Spanish steamer *Igotz Mendi*, of Bilboa, 4648 tons. Captured in the Indian Ocean November 10th, *en route* from Delagoa Bay to Colombo with a cargo of coal. This vessel was sent to Germany, but grounded off Denmark.

12. American bark *William Kirby*, 1 200 tons, of New York, Captain Blum, from New York to Port Elizabeth, Africa, with a general cargo; captured on November 15th. Crew, provisions and stores were taken off and the vessel bombed on November 16th. She was captured 320 miles southeast of Port Elizabeth.

13. French bark *Marechal Davoust*, 1200 tons, from Delagoa Bay to France with a cargo of wheat. Captured on December 14th. This vessel was armed and equipped with wireless. Guns and provisions were transferred to the *Wolf* and the vessel sunk on the 15th by bombs. Captured 130 miles southeast of the Cape of Good Hope.

14. Norwegian bark *Storebror*, 2000 tons, Captain Moller, bound for Europe from Montevideo in ballast. Captured on January 5th in latitude 18 degrees south and 27 degrees west. Crew, provisions and stores transferred to the *Wolf* and vessel bombed.

Printed in the USA
CPSIA information can be obtained
at www.ICGtesting.com
LVHW090725141223
766228LV00001B/153